PROPHET MUHAMMAD ﷺ SAID,

"There is a kind of tree whose leaves do not wither and fall—it is like the Muslim," explaining later, "It is the palm tree."

Commenting on this, Imam al-Nawawi, the great thirteenth century scholar, wrote: "The entire palm tree is beneficial, good, and beautiful. And so is the believer entirely good, owing to his abundant devotions and noble character."

BEING MUSLIM

A PRACTICAL GUIDE

BEING MUSLIM

A PRACTICAL GUIDE

ASAD TARSIN

Foreword by Shaykh Hamza Yusuf

Printed in the United States of America

First Printing, 2015

ISBN-13: 978-0-9855659-2-3
ISBN-10: 0-9855659-2-6

10 9 8 7 6 5 4 3 2

Library of Congress Control Number: 2015910485

Published by
Sandala Inc.
www.sandala.org

Cover design, layout, and typesetting: Umar Shahzad RGD.
Illustrations: Jessica Gallon.
Typeset in Linux Libertine, Brill, and Source Sans Pro.
Printed on Mohawk Carnival 100# vellum white cover
and Glatfelter Offset 60# natural.

To my grandfather, the late Shaykh Muhammad Bariun,
who was always teaching and only rarely speaking.
You showed us love of God and His messenger ﷺ.
We still reap what you had sown.

CONTENTS

CHAPTER 5: THE PROPHET ﷺ

CHAPTER 6: THE QURAN

CHAPTER 7: ISLAMIC HOLY DAYS

CHAPTER 8: LIFESTYLE

TRANSLITERATION & PRONUNCIATION KEY

ARABIC LETTER	TRANSLITERATION	SOUND
ء	'	A slight catch in the breath, cutting slightly short the preceding syllable.
ا	*ā*	An elongated *a* as in *cat.*
ب	*b*	As in *best.*
ت	*t*	As in *ten.*
ث	*th*	As in *thin.*
ج	*j*	As in *jewel.*
ح	*ḥ*	Tensely breathed *h* sound made by dropping tongue into back of throat, forcing the air out.
خ	*kh*	Pronounced like the *ch* in Scottish *loch*, made by touching back of tongue to roof of mouth and forcing air out.
د	*d*	As in *depth.*
ذ	*dh*	A thicker *th* sound as in *the.*
ر	*r*	A rolled *r*, similar to Spanish.
ز	*z*	As in *zest.*
س	*s*	As in *seen.*
ش	*sh*	As in *sheer.*
ص	*ṣ*	A heavy *s* pronounced far back in the mouth with mouth hollowed to produce full sound.
ض	*ḍ*	A heavy *d/dh* pronounced far back in the mouth with the mouth hollowed to produce a full sound.
ط	*ṭ*	A heavy *t* pronounced far back in the mouth with the mouth hollowed to produce a full sound.
ظ	*ẓ*	A heavy *dh* pronounced far back in the mouth with the mouth hollowed to produce a full sound.
ع	ʿ	A guttural sound pronounced narrowing the throat.
غ	*gh*	Pronounced like a throaty French *r* with the mouth hollowed.
ف	*f*	As in *feel.*
ق	*q*	A guttural *q* sound made from the back of the throat with the mouth hollowed.
ك	*k*	As in *kit.*
ل	*l*	As in *lip.*
م	*m*	As in *melt.*
ن	*n*	As in *nest.*

TRANSLITERATION & PRONUNCIATION KEY

ARABIC LETTER	TRANSLITERATION	SOUND
ه	*h*	As in *hen.*
و	*w* (at beg. of syllable)	As in *west.*
	ū (in middle of syllable)	An elongated *oo* sound, as in *boo.*
ي	*y* (at beg. of syllable)	As in *yes.*
	ī (in middle of syllable)	An elongated *ee* sound, as in *seen.*

ﷺ Used following the mention of the Prophet Muhammad, translated as, "May Allah bless him and grant him peace."

عليه السلام Used following the mention of any other prophet, translated as, "May peace be upon him."

عليهم السلام Used following the mention of three or more prophets, translated as, "May peace be upon them."

رضي الله عنه Used following the mention of a male companion of the Prophet, translated as, "May God be pleased with him."

رضي الله عنها Used following the mention of a female companion of the Prophet, translated as, "May God be pleased with her."

رضي الله عنهما Used following the mention of two companions of the Prophet, translated as, "May God be pleased with them."

رضي الله عنهم Used following the mention of more than two companions of the Prophet, translated as, "May God be pleased with them."

سبحانه وتعالى Used following the mention of Allah, translated as "the Sublime and the Exalted."

FOREWORD

Of all creatures in the world, the human is unique in that no other animal has the ability to acquire knowledge, preserve it, and transmit it. Animals have instinctual knowledge and display remarkable talents, from the highly developed dams of beavers to the majestic subterranean cities of ants, but as far as we know, no animals are discussing the purpose of life or teaching their offspring the rites of prayer. Because it is knowledge and the ability to reason that distinguishes us from other animals, it should be no surprise that the One who created us did so with that end in mind:

"Know that there is no god but God, and seek forgiveness for your wrongs."
QURAN 47:19

The ability to truly know God is a uniquely human ability. For this reason, the Islamic religion and the civilizations it produced put knowledge and its acquisition at the center of their existence. Muslims pursued knowledge to the edges of the earth. Al-Birūnī, the central Asian polymath, is arguably the world's first anthropologist. The great linguists of Iraq and Persia laid the foundations a thousand years ago for subjects only now coming to the forefront in language studies. Ibn Khaldūn, who is considered the first true scientific historian, argued hundreds of years ago that history should be based upon facts and not myths or superstitions. The great psychologists of Islam known as the Sufis wrote treatise after treatise that rival the most advanced texts today on human psychology. The great ethicists and exegetes of Islam's past left tomes that fill countless shelves in the great libraries of the world, and many more of their texts remain in manuscript form.

But all of the great learning that Muslims displayed throughout their history was always predicated on a foundational, core knowledge that the great *uṣūlī* scholars of Islamic jurisprudence called *farḍ ʿayn*, or "the individual obligations." *Farḍ ʿayn* knowledge is the bare minimum that every Muslim has to know, without which, upon reaching sexual maturity, he or she is considered to be in a state of sinfulness. It does not take a long time to acquire and is best done with a qualified teacher, but it can be learned, though this is discouraged, from books. Mālik bin Dinār, a great early scholar and saint, said, "Whoever seeks knowledge for himself (*farḍ ʿayn*) ends up with little knowledge, but whoever seeks knowledge for others should know that the needs of humanity are vast." In other words, while the knowledge each person is required to learn is important, it is also relatively little; there is a much larger body of knowledge which is a *farḍ kifāyah*, or collective responsibility for some of the community to take on.

This short book has that little amount of individually responsible knowledge necessary for a new Muslim or an unlearned Muslim rediscovering his or her religion. Dr. Asad Tarsin has rendered our community an important service by designing and writing a concise, useful, and accurate manual of core knowledge that every Muslim should know. It is a basic manual, and much needed in our time of great ignorance from within and without the Muslim community. Islam is a gentle faith, one based upon mercy and ease: "God wants for you ease" (Quran 2:185). Islam is a faith that rests on four solid pillars: mercy, wisdom, benefit, and justice. On this, Ibn Qayyim says:

> "Should any ruling go from mercy to cruelty, it is not Islam; should it go from wisdom to folly, it is not Islam; should it go from benefit to harm, it is not Islam; and should it go from justice to injustice, it is not Islam."

The foundational principles of our religion are not hard to understand or to practice, but the religion itself is vast like the ocean. Within this wondrous ocean, some must become master swimmers; however, all people must begin by simply learning to tread water. This manual is intended to keep beginners afloat and prevent them from drowning in the vast ocean that is Islam.

Hamza Yusuf
Ramadan 1436
June 2015

PREFACE

This book was written to help Muslims live and practice their faith—to learn what Muslims believe, how we pray and fast, and how to live life in a manner pleasing to our Lord. It highlights both our spiritual struggles and aspirations; how we can, on a daily basis, develop a healthy relationship with God, through both devotions and in ordinary daily life. This book is not meant to expound on abstract theoretical aspects of Islam, but to give readers practical and useful knowledge that can help them understand what it means to be Muslim.

In the winter of 2006 I met a young new convert who, unlike most converts I had met before, had almost no real exposure to Islam or Muslims before embracing the faith. I was caught off guard when he began to ask me for a list of do's and don't's. After affirming some things he already knew, I told him that first he needed to learn the basics, such as how to pray. Still, he continued to press me for guidelines.

While I admired his earnestness, I realized that this was not the best way for him to learn the religion; he needed context and prioritization for this new information. So I resolved to help him get started in a more systematic manner. I began to think of the books on Islam that I was personally familiar with and realized immediately that none of them suited his needs well. I then searched Muslim bookstores and found a few books that would be somewhat helpful, but they were either narrow in their scope or intended for children. As we began to meet and talk, I started compiling a list of the things I thought essential for new Muslims to know early in their Islamic learning.

And so, this manual before you was born, out of the realization that beginner English-speaking Muslims, whether new or returning, were underserved with regards to written materials to help them learn and practice their faith. These Muslims face multiple obstacles in their quest for knowledge. First, the information they need is scattered in multiple books that one would have to already know in order to find what one is looking for. Even if one knew how to find these books, they contain information beyond a novice's level and needs, which could be distracting and overwhelming. Second, these books presume a level of background knowledge that these readers lack. Third, many books introduce Arabic words without consistent translation, which often leads to the reader becoming focused on memorizing terms rather than understanding them.

To be clear, this work is by no means an original production. Rather, it is a compilation of concepts, explanations, and wisdom from the works of multiple luminaries, past and contemporary, brought together into one manual. The function I attempted to serve is analogous to that of a cloudy lens—although it inevitably distorts and diminishes the light—it at least focuses the separate beams upon one point. Anything of value found in this work testifies to the radiance of the beams of light that could penetrate such a lens—for the lens generates no light of its own. This work is firstly indebted to those luminaries who preserve for us all the light that came forth from the Holy Prophet Muhammad ﷺ. It is my hope that this manual makes the vital and revivifying knowledge they preserve and teach more easily accessible to the eager learner. I pray that, by striving to gather light for others, I too, despite the reality, by God's grace, am counted among those illuminated.

"Whoever has not thanked people, has not thanked God."
— **PROPHET MUHAMMAD** ﷺ

After thanking and praising God, without Whom nothing is possible, I would like to thank others whose contributions were vital to the completion of this work.

While this work is influenced by many, it is most indebted to a man whose contribution to Islam in the West is arguably unparalleled. His writing, teaching, and lecturing has inspired countless Muslims over the last twenty years (including myself), shifting paradigms and rectifying cognitive frames. Shaykh Hamza Yusuf, a great master of two traditions, has revived Islam in the West by helping Western Muslims rediscover traditional Islam while making it immediately relevant to the context of the modern world. In describing his contributions to Islam in the West, one can only remember, "God suffices as a witness!" (Quran 48:28).

I would like to thank my parents, Dr. Mahmoud Tarsin and Dr. Fawzia Bariun for their unyielding love and support. We are all who we are because of your love. May Allah grant your children the ability to serve you well. To my brother and friend, Amjad Tarsin, thank you for your constant support and for staying on me. A very special thanks to Aftab Malik for encouraging me in the early phases of this project—you tolerated me and were there with your experience and invaluable advice at every turn. To my partner in this project, Zahid Ahmed, thank you for always being there. To my dear friend Feraidoon Mojadedi, thank you for your urging me across the finish line. To my dear sister, Aisha Subhani, thank you for all of your support. For editing content and advice, my deep appreciation to both Imam Zaid Shakir and Faraz Khan. For diligently editing and really helping bring this to completion, I want to thank you, Tom Devine, for all of your work—it made all the difference. I am grateful to Mariam Jukaku, Sadia Shakir, and Zaynab Salman who helped proofread the manuscript. This work is indebted to Brad Brennan, a good friend who inspired me with his courage to leap towards the light without hesitation. Lastly, my deep appreciation to my supportive and understanding wife, Imaan Youssef, and my children, Yaseen, Maryam, and Ahmed Zarruq.

Below are a few points of reference for the reader:

Quotations from the Quran are referenced by their chapter (*sūrah*) and verse (*āyah*) number. For instance, a quotation followed by "(2:136)" refers to Chapter 2, verse 136. For the translation, I have relied almost exclusively on the work of M.A.S. Abdel Haleem. However, for a few verses, when it better illustrated the point being made, I used the translation of Thomas Cleary.

For some of the transliterated Arabic terms, I sometimes added an "-s" to denote the plural instead of transliterating the linguistically correct Arabic plural form. I did this for terms that English-speaking Muslims commonly use as though they are anglicized. For example, in Arabic the plural form of *masjid* (mosque) is *masājid*. However, for the sake of simplicity, I used the term *masjids*.

Lastly, this work presents Islam from the Sunni orthodox perspective and does not compare or contrast with other sects of Islam for the sake of clarity.

The erring servant of God, ever in need of His mercy,
Asad Tarsin
Ramadan 1436
June 2015

CHAPTER 1

Starting Point

... A light has now come to you from God,
and a Scripture making things clear,
with which God guides to the ways of peace
those who follow what pleases Him,
bringing them from darknesses out into light,
by His will, and guiding them to a straight path.

QURAN 5:15–16

1. THE BEGINNING

بسم الله الرحمن الرحيم

In God's Name (*Bismillāh*);
Praise belongs to God (*Alḥamdulillāh*);
O God: Bless and Send Peace Upon Our Master, Muhammad!
(*Allāhumma ṣalli wa sallim ʿalā sayyidinā Muḥammad*)[1]

The feeling of disorientation can be one of the greatest challenges to any new experience. It can lead to a distraction of energies, insecurity, unease, and confusion. If you are new to practicing and learning Islam, it can be a dizzying task to orient yourself to the landscape of the religion with all its concepts and terminology.

This book endeavors to bring together the elements of Islam that are most necessary for developing a basic understanding of the religion. It should serve as a starting point, and should give you most of what the average practicing Muslim would know. It is by no means comprehensive—it is not meant to give you all that you must know as a Muslim; but neither is it minimalistic—in some aspects, it gives you more than the bare minimum you need to know.

ADVICE FOR THE JOURNEY

Before you set out to learn and practice the material contained in this manual, some advice may prove helpful.

First, consciously think about your reasons for wanting to learn this material. Prophet Muhammad ﷺ taught us the fundamental precept, "actions are [judged] according to intentions." So it is essential that we examine our motivations for the things we do, especially before beginning such an important endeavor.

Also, keep in mind that you are in this for the long run, so pace yourself. Take things in gradually, internalize them at a pace that is appropriate for you, and do not feel that you need to figure it all out immediately. On the other hand, do not become complacent; use your enthusiasm to push yourself ever higher.

1. To begin in God's name is the best method to commence any act of importance. Connecting an act to God brings divine grace and blessings (*barakah*). After that, the optimal formula for beginning any discussion of Islam is to then praise God and send blessings upon His Beloved, the last prophet, Muhammad ﷺ.

As you grow in your practice of Islam, try not to make too many changes too quickly. Some people adopt the religion and then, within a few short months, change their entire social circuit and even marry someone new—likely unwise! Adopting a new faith is a sign that you are growing, and thus changing, as a person. Growth is a gradual process, and you may grow into someone different from the person you were at the outset. It may be useful to keep this in mind as you contemplate life-altering decisions. Before proceeding, allow yourself the time and space to process your new experiences fully.

Set for yourself appropriate expectations and anticipate a challenge. You may be elated that you have been guided to God's religion and are now committed to it. You may assume that the rest is easy. But know in advance that this is not the case! Growth is an intrinsically challenging and difficult process. You'll have good days and bad ones. Be patient and perseverant, and rely on God to take care of the rest.

As you progress, process new things, and grow, always strive to keep God first and foremost in your life. It can sometimes be easy to mistake the means for the end. Remember that everything in this handbook (and the entire religion) is simply about developing a healthy relationship with God. Never forget the purpose of the things you do as you practice your religion. You may feel that certain acts are more rewarding than others, but stay focused on what *God* wants, not what you may feel at some point in time. Talk to Him, call upon Him for help, and keep Him the center of your journey as you move forward.

In your long journey, you will find much benefit and comfort in a good support group. If you do not have one yet, make some good Muslim friends who can support you as you progress. They do not have to replace your current friends, but they can support you in the shared experience of being a Muslim. Books, CDs, and websites can be informative, but good friends to support your growth are invaluable.

As you learn and grow, be sure not to erase who you are at your core. Islam doesn't replace you with someone else; it enhances who you already are. Work towards becoming a devout Muslim who is still genuinely you. This will make you more sincere in your interaction with God and is absolutely necessary for sustained growth.

The simple advice given above won't be the only kind you will need, but it may be helpful to hear it early in your development as a Muslim. As a general rule, it would be wise to look at the experiences of others and learn from them, to help make your transition into a new faith, and way of living, as smooth as possible.

2. ISLAM IN CONTEXT

To more fully understand the message of Islam, it is helpful to appreciate its place within the greater human story. In this way, you will understand the bigger picture and keep it in mind as you navigate new ideas and concepts. It is also important to understand the general layout of the religion, and so we will examine an outline of Islam provided by the founder himself, Prophet Muhammad ﷺ.

THE HUMAN STORY

To start at the beginning: At a time before time, every human soul ever created was gathered before God. During that existence, which is detailed in the Quran, God asked us all, "Am I not your Lord?" To which every last one of us responded, "Oh yes! We bear witness."[2] In the Islamic understanding, each of us has this knowledge on some subconscious level.

Through this Grand Covenant, each of us sealed our moral responsibility to acknowledge the Lordship of God. Throughout our lives here on Earth, we have the challenge of living according to this acknowledgement. In fact, this is one of the implications of the Two Testimonies of faith. The first part, "There is nothing worthy of worship except God," is a reaffirmation of our bearing witness to God's Lordship over us at a time before our time here. The second testimony, "Muhammad is the messenger of God," is a statement that God's lordship over us necessitates that we live in line with His will. It is as if to say, "We remember the covenant we made before life here, and we still honor it, and we will live our lives according to it."

After testifying to God's Lordship over us, we as a species were charged with the weighty responsibility of being His delegates in the world. We are responsible for setting its affairs right, ensuring justice and security, and acting so as to make the conditions of society conducive to knowing and worshipping God.

Then, God created the first humans, the vessels of the souls that were gathered before Him. Tempted by Satan, Adam and Eve both disobeyed God, but when they realized what they had done, they repented, and God accept-

2. The complete verse reads: And when your Lord brought the descendants of the children of Adam from their loins, and made them testify about themselves: *'Am I not your Lord?'* They said, 'Oh, yes! We bear witness.' Lest you should say, on the day of resurrection, 'We were heedless of this!' (Quran 7:172)

ed their repentance. Still, He decreed that they and all of their offspring were to be expelled from the Garden down to Earth to live their destined worldly lives. Along with this exile came God's promise to send us guidance so that we may again find our way back to Paradise.

God then sent a succession of prophets and messengers, reminding people of their covenant before creation and their duty to God. Each was sent to a particular people, sometimes with a message particular to them, but always with a core message to surrender to the Lord of all creation, the One, the Almighty. Most people were selfish and resistant, while a number believed in and followed God's prophets. With the passage of time, sustaining the authenticity of the message became more and more difficult. People began to alter the scriptures brought by the messengers of God. The ideas of men were sold as truths from God, and yet still, each time, God renewed His guidance to us to help us find our way home to the Garden.

The divine guidance that God sent through these messengers concluded and culminated in the most eminent of His messengers, Prophet Muhammad ﷺ. He came not to replace previous versions of the message, but to perfect and complete them. Each of God's prophets taught the same essential truths, but only the teachings of Prophet Muhammad ﷺ survived unaltered over history. This protection from distortion, along with the universality of its teachings, is what makes Islam the religion of God for all people everywhere.

THE DIMENSIONS OF THE RELIGION

To better understand the final message from God to humanity, we will examine a concise yet comprehensive summary of the religion by Prophet Muhammad ﷺ. These words were spoken at one of the most famous and significant historical events in Islam, on a day when the messenger of God ﷺ was sitting with some of his closest companions (*Ṣaḥābah*).[3] The story is narrated by ʿUmar ؓ who tells us the following:

> One day, while we were sitting with the messenger of God, there appeared before us a man whose clothes were exceedingly white and whose hair was exceedingly black; no signs of journeying were to be

3. A **companion** (sing. ***Ṣaḥābī***, pl. ***ṣaḥābah***) is a person who met the Prophet Muhammad ﷺ, believed in his message, never apostated during his lifetime, and died as a believer. A **follower** (***tābiʿī***) is a believer who met a companion of the Prophet. The companions are the best generation of believers overall, while the followers are the second best generation.

seen on him, and none of us knew him. He walked up and sat down by the Prophet. Resting his knees against his and placing the palms of his hands on his thighs, he said, "O Muhammad, tell me about *islām*".[4]

The messenger of God said: "*Islām* is to testify that there is nothing worthy of worship except God and that Muhammad is the messenger of God, to perform the prayers, to pay the purifying alms, to fast in Ramadan, and to make the pilgrimage to the Sacred House if you are able to do so."

He said, "You have spoken rightly." And we were amazed at him asking him and saying that he had spoken rightly. He then said, "Then tell me about *imān*."

He replied, "It is to believe in God, His angels, His books, His messengers, and the Last Day, and to believe in divine decree, both the good and the evil thereof."

He said, "You have spoken rightly." He then said, "Then tell me about *iḥsān*."

The Prophet said, "It is to worship God as though you are seeing Him, for even if you cannot see Him, He indeed sees you."

He said, "Then tell me about the Hour."[5]

The Prophet replied, "The one questioned about it knows no better than the questioner."

He then said, "Then tell me about its signs."

He replied, "That the slave-girl will give birth to her mistress and that you will see the barefooted, naked, destitute herdsmen competing in constructing lofty buildings."

Then [the man] left and I stayed behind for a time. Then [the messenger of God] said, "O ʿUmar, do you know who the questioner was?"

I said, "God and His messenger know best."

He said, "He was Gabriel (Jibrīl), who came to you to teach you your religion."

With four questions, the Archangel Gabriel (Jibrīl) brought forth a summary of the foundational elements of the religion from God's final prophet to humanity. The religion, we learn, is comprised of three elements: *islām*, *imān*, and *iḥsān*. The fourth aspect mentioned, namely the signs of the Hour, provides us with the understanding that there is a downward trend

4. For the purposes of the discussion presented, the Arabic terms have been retained and not translated, because their definition is the purpose of the dialogue and follows shortly thereafter.

5. The Last Day and the Hour are other names for the Day of Judgment.

of the human story, and thus of the believing community as well. There are many such statements from Prophet Muhammad ﷺ which indicate the moral decline of the latter days, and the consequent need for believers to hold more tightly to their principles, values, and beliefs, despite increased difficulty in doing so.

These three elements are called the **dimensions of Islam**. The first of the three dimensions discussed was *islām*, which is presented as a sub-category within the religion itself, Islam. In Arabic, the word *islām* means "to surrender" or "to submit." We see from the definition laid out by Prophet Muhammad ﷺ that it is the dimension of our religion involving the external actions of our bodies, acts of surrender. To state the Testimony of Faith,[6] to pray, to fast, to pay alms, and to make pilgrimage are all acts we perform through the medium of our bodies. These are called the **Five Pillars of Islam**. We understand from them that actions of external conformity, which include ritual worship and more, are absolutely indispensable to a complete characterization of the religion.

Next, we heard about *imān*. In Arabic, *imān* means "to believe." Prophet Muhammad ﷺ starts his definition by using that phrase exactly: "It is to believe…." What follows is a series of beliefs that a person must affirm in order for their faith to be complete. Unlike the dimension of *islām*, these are not acts, but convictions of the mind which settle in the heart. We thus learn that the affirmation of realities as they truly exist is also essential to the characterization of the religion of Islam.

Lastly, we learn about *iḥsān*. The word in Arabic means "to make beautiful or good." We are told that *iḥsān* involves the internal constitution of a believer's heart—his or her spiritual state. This is the basis of your relationship with God Almighty. Here, Prophet Muhammad ﷺ defines this dimension by telling us its result. So, to attain a particular spiritual constitution, that of complete awareness of and reverence for God ﷻ, is an indispensable component of the religion, the one that gives it purpose.

Each of these components speaks to an aspect of human experience. The first is action—of the body; the second is belief—of the mind; and the third is purity—of the soul. And so Islam is a religion that speaks to every element of our humanity. Only when all three of these dimensions—faith, conduct, and character—are fulfilled simultaneously and harmoniously is the religion truly being practiced. To neglect any one of these will lead to imbalance and misplaced emphasis, a sure path to misguided religiosity. For example, to neglect the affirmation of our beliefs would make Islam

6. Scholars explain that stating the Testimony of Faith (Shahādah) is a precondition to the other four pillars.

a kind of cultural tradition void of its main purpose. To neglect the external conformity to God's commands leads to an abstract religion guided by personal whims, with no arena within which to prove faith through application. And lastly, a neglect of the spiritual leads to a version of the religion that, void of reverence and love of God ﷻ, becomes rigid, cold, and legalistic. It is thus only with the complete surrender of our minds, bodies, and spirits to God ﷻ that the complete vision of Islam can be realized.

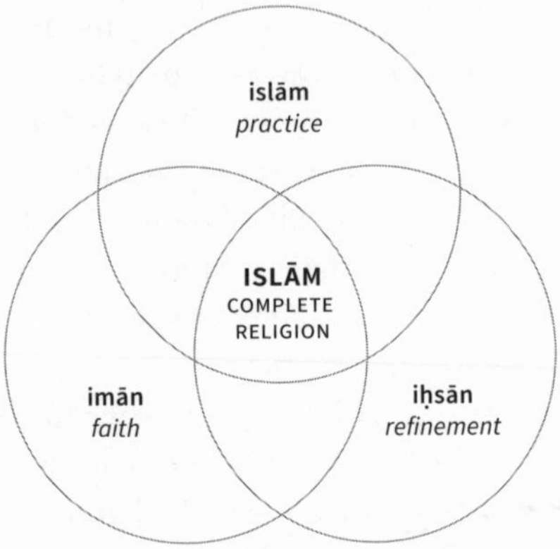

Figure 1: The Three Dimensions of Islam

ISLAM: SURRENDER TO GOD

From the above narration (*ḥadīth*) and from the Quran, we can develop a more complete understanding of the term *islām*. It has meanings on various levels, and by appreciating them we can gain a deeper understanding of the concept itself.

On the grandest scale, all created beings are in a state of surrender (*islām*) to God by the very nature of our dependence upon Him and subjugation to His will. We can only do whatever God allows us to do. A second use refers to voluntary submission: deliberately living in accordance with God's will. In this sense, Islam has existed from the beginning of the human story and has been the message of all of God's prophets. All of them ultimately called for submission to God and were themselves in a state of submission, and thus could be called *muslims*.[7] The third use, the one which most know

7. The term "*muslim*" means "one who surrenders." It is the title of those who follow the religion of Islam brought by Prophet Muhammad ﷺ (i.e. Muslims), but more generally can

best, refers to the religion brought by Prophet Muhammad ﷺ in the seventh century CE. Those who follow the religion of Islam, the final form of the ultimate submission taught by all prophets, are properly called Muslims: We are not named after a person, ethnicity, or region, but after our chosen relationship with God. Lastly, as a sub-category of the final religion of Islam, *islām* is the dimension of surrender to God through devotional practices, as discussed above. These general and specific meanings of the word *islām* enhance our understanding of submission to God and His final religion.

THE ARABIC LANGUAGE

It was part of God's divine wisdom that His final message to all of creation would be revealed to Prophet Muhammad ﷺ in seventh century Arabia. This has many implications, and for these reasons and more, the historical events and circumstances surrounding the life of Prophet Muhammad ﷺ are a necessary and inseparable context for understanding revelation.

Perhaps the most central and permanent of these implications is the revealing of the Quran, God's word, in the Arabic language.[8] For believers, Arabic is thus the sacred language of Islam: It alone is to be used for ritual worship, such as the recitation of the Quran and the daily prayers. However, for other activities, such as supplication (*duʿā'*), reading translations of the Quran, sermons, or study of Islam, any language may be used. Many scholars of Islam believe that, since the Quran is in Arabic, to understand aspects of the Arabic language may even provide insights into the realities of the world as God ﷻ created it.

To develop a basic understanding of how we can gain profound insights from Arabic itself, it would help to examine the root-word system of the language. In Arabic, words are derived from root bases. With rare exceptions, these root words are made up of three letters. The arrangement and alteration of the letters of a root word follow specific patterns that tell you something about the intended meaning of any word based on it. You can derive many insights from studying the root-word relationships among

indicate those who followed the message sent by God throughout history and surrendered to Him. So, in the Islamic view, those who followed Prophets Jesus (ʿĪsā), Moses (Mūsā), Noah (Nūḥ) ﷺ and others, were *muslims*.

8. There are translations of the meaning of the Quran, but only the original Arabic revealed text can be considered the Quran proper. Translations of its meaning can be used to enhance one's understanding and develop a deeper relationship with the Book, but only the original is used for devotional purposes. Although this close relationship to the religion applies to the Arabic language, it does not apply to all other things Arabic, such as the culture, dress, or food.

words that otherwise seem unassociated. All this may seem abstract at first, but it will become clearer as you learn some basic vocabulary.

Throughout this handbook, Arabic terms that you should eventually learn will be transliterated in parenthesis after the English translation. This is to help you understand the concepts and learn the words. When such a word is used for the first time in a paragraph, a reminder of the Arabic equivalent will follow, even if the term has already been introduced.

A standard Arabic transliteration key is provided at the beginning of this book to aid you in pronouncing the Arabic terms.

3. LEARNING ISLAM

The first task for every Muslim is to learn the things he or she will need to practice the religion and fulfill his or her duties to God ﷻ. In Islam, there is a very close correlation between religious knowledge and increased piety, since knowledge of God ﷻ and His religion brings you closer to Him, if you apply what you learn. Prophet Muhammad ﷺ said, "To seek knowledge is an obligation upon every Muslim man and Muslim woman." Learning should be an essential part of every Muslim's life, and you should commit yourself to becoming a lifelong learner and applying what you learn.

The contents of this handbook are just an introduction to the various subjects it contains. After studying the material provided here, you should further your learning by exploring the "Recommended Reading" section in the back.

ISLAMIC SCHOLARSHIP

The purpose of Islamic scholarship is to derive, refine, and preserve the guidance found within Islam. When Prophet Muhammad ﷺ passed on from this world, he did not leave gold or land to be inherited. He left knowledge of God's last message of guidance to humanity. An indication of this is found in a famous narration (*ḥadīth*) where he stated that "the scholars are the inheritors of the prophets."[9]

The guidance that God ﷻ sent through Prophet Muhammad ﷺ is preserved in two primary sources of knowledge: the Quran and the Prophetic Way (*Sunnah*). The **Quran,** the direct word of God ﷻ, is the first source of Islamic teachings. In the Quran, some verses are explicit and easy to understand, while others are more ambiguous in meaning. To interpret God's words requires specialized training in various disciplines; the scholars capable of such interpretation are called *Quranic exegetes.*

The **Prophetic Way (*Sunnah*)** of the Prophet Muhammad ﷺ is unanimously accepted as the perfect interpretation of the Quran, and it is used by scholars as an explanation and commentary of the Quran, and thus of the religion itself. The Prophetic Way is understood from the life of Prophet Muhammad ﷺ: some parts of it consist of his own statements, while others

9. While the qualifications for Islamic scholarship are extensive, it is something any believer can attain. The greatest scholars of Islam were men, women, Arab, non-Arab, rich, poor, from educated families, and orphans. There are no social prerequisites to becoming a scholar.

are based on his actions—either actions he performed himself or his reactions to what others did in his presence. For most scholars, the primary, but not only, source of understanding the Prophetic Way is through the body of narrations (*ḥadīths*) about Prophet Muhammad ﷺ.[10] These narrations have been compiled over time, and each has been evaluated as to its level of reliability. Despite the modern misconception that only the most rigorously verified narrations can be used, how to use the various types of narrations is actually the realm of scholars; laypeople should simply strive to make use of the basic guidance we can derive from them.

These sources then provide scholars with **proof-texts** from which to derive particular religious understandings or legal rulings. Proof-texts are usually in the form of a Quranic verse, a prophetic narration (*ḥadīth*), or a secondary source, such as analogous legal reasoning, the consensus of the jurists, or the words of an authoritative scholar.

The scholars of Islamic law laid out the legal methodologies by which a proof-text is processed and used in developing the overall picture for an issue. The methodologies are complex, but they include linguistic analysis, historical contextualization, chronological assessment, and juristic examination, among many other disciplines. Some of the great Islamic jurists differed somewhat in the methodologies and processes they used for reaching legal conclusions; this led to the development of different **legal schools (*madhhabs*)** in Islam today. However, the schools of law all agree on the primary sources of law, differing mainly in their analysis and utilization of them. As a result, all of the schools agree on the essential issues and differ only on finer details that are secondary in nature.

Jurists use proof-texts to derive **legal rulings**. It is an oversimplification and an error to treat a proof-text as a ruling in and of itself—it must be processed by jurists using the legal methodologies, including a global analysis of all relevant proof-texts. The result of such a process may be a conclusion that seems quite different from the apparent meaning of the original verse (*ayah*) or narration (*ḥadīth*) on which the ruling is based, but this should not be mistaken as "contradicting" the proof-text. With an understanding of these concepts, you will have an overall appreciation for the complexity of deriving religious rulings and be less likely to fall into confusion or oversimplification.

---

10. Narrations (*ḥadīths*) are verified accounts of Prophet Muhammad's words, actions, and tacit approvals and disapprovals. Hadīths come in various forms. Some are reports of statements he made, while others are stories of things he did or things done in his presence. Each of these gives an indication of part of his Prophetic Way (*Sunnah*).

Each legal school (*madhhab*) is both a particular methodology for deriving law and a corpus of centuries of scholarship contributing to the analysis of issues based on that methodology.[11] The very existence of the schools (*madhhabs*) clues us in to an essential reality in Islam: Differing positions can each be legitimate and valid, and believers can legitimately hold different positions, as long as each position is backed by qualified scholarship. Scholastic pluralism is a source of strength and divine mercy for the religion. It is the acknowledgment that in the absence of an infallible prophet, no one can be so certain of their interpretation that everyone else is morally bound to follow them. The holder of each position genuinely feels that they are correct, but each respectfully allows for differences to coexist harmoniously. When the allowance for scholarly differences is combined with the agreed upon standards and methodologies of religious scholarship, the result is a rich pluralism which avoids both religious monopoly and religious anarchy.

This should give you at least some idea of the complexity of definitively concluding that the religion says "A" or "B" on a given subject. Jurists of the past spent their entire lives working out the finer points of the religion so that it may be more easily practiced by the rest of us. Each of us is, thus, not expected to start over and figure everything out for ourselves. We are, however, expected to follow qualified scholarship. For centuries, this has taken the form of following one of the legal schools, affirming widely-accepted works of creed, utilizing the works of masters of the spiritual disciplines, and deferring to the scholars when we encounter unknown religious territory. These parameters still allow for a vast array of opinions under the same methodologies listed above.

In addition to respecting the complexity of the scholarly process, we should develop a deep respect for "the inheritors of the prophets." In the Islamic view, there is a strong correlation between knowledge and piety, since knowledge predisposes one to increase one's commitment to God ﷻ. This is one of the reasons Prophet Muhammad ﷺ taught that we should all be lifelong students of Islam. We should strive to develop in ourselves a deep respect for the scholars, great men and women who spent their lives preserving the guidance we need to succeed in the next life.

11. As a point of interest, it is actually not uncommon for the dominant position on a specific ruling within a legal school (*madhhab*), using the founder's methodologies, to be different from the founder's original position.

MISINTERPRETATIONS

As with all religious texts, just as there is the possibility of coming to different valid interpretations, so there is the danger of misinterpreting the primary sources of Islam. The reasons for this are many. One reason is the fact that the Arabic language conveys meaning in a very concise way. In the Quran, for example, many pronouns are used, and these frequently require an in-depth analysis to determine what they are referencing. Also, in Arabic a particular term can have different meanings based on its context. To understand its meaning in a particular sentence requires both a deep knowledge of the many meanings of the word and a clear understanding of that particular context. There are also phrases and statements in the Quran which have become proverbial in nature: When these are quoted in isolation from the words or verses that come before and after them, a naïve listener may end up with a serious misunderstanding of their intended meaning.

In addition to these intrinsic challenges, there is the modern trend of untrained and unqualified individuals attempting to derive their own understandings directly from primary texts. Historically, even to gain access to scholarly works, a person had to study under a trained authority. With the advent of the information age, however, practically anyone can access scholarly works without any guidance, training, or supervision. Some have likened this situation to people having access to medical textbooks and presuming they can diagnose conditions or perform surgery, without training under qualified physicians.

All of the above issues combined can make interpreting the primary sources of Islam quite complex. Hopefully, this brief sketch illustrates the dangerous potential that exists of misunderstanding the divine guidance.

BEING MUSLIM: AN OVERVIEW

Now, with the appropriate framework in place, you will be able to process the contents of this manual, and the religion, more properly. To fully understand the religion of Islam requires knowledge of several fundamental subjects within it, and the chapters in this manual attempt to reflect them.

First, you must understand the *beliefs* of the Muslims, since our belief is the cornerstone of our religion and is why we need the remaining knowledge to begin with. Next, you need to learn the essential devotional practices by which Muslims *worship* God. These are the five pillars of the dimension of *islām*. You must also understand human nature, recognize the importance of *spiritual refinement*, and learn the virtues and vices associated with that process. In this manner, you can attain sincerity in your relationship with God.

Beyond these, a proper understanding of the religion is inseparable from knowing the prophet of Islam, *Prophet Muhammad* ﷺ. It is essential to know about him, his life, his relevance in our lives, his merits, and his miracles. Also central to the religion is the final revelation from God to all of humanity, the *Quran*. It is the scripture of the Muslims and a source of guidance for all time. Finally, any Muslim who desires to embody the principles of the religion must live a *lifestyle*—in all elements of life, personal, social, and otherwise—that reflects the guidance set forth by God and His prophet. This includes observing the *holy days* in Islam, which are described in another chapter devoted to them.

At the end of this manual, you will find a glossary of the bolded terms used throughout the book. Important terms will be bolded and explained when they are first introduced. Terms followed by their transliterated Arabic equivalents should also be learned in Arabic. Each time such a term recurs, the Arabic will follow.

Appendix 1 contains several short chapters (*sūrahs*) of the Quran in both Arabic and English, for use in devotional worship.

Appendix 2, "Recommended Readings," points you towards other resources in each of these essential subjects, and more.

When you eventually learn the material this handbook contains, you should, if God wills (*inshā' Allah*), have a solid foundation of religious understanding, on which you can continue to build.

CHAPTER 2

Belief

Say, "We believe in God and in what was sent down to us and what was sent down to Abraham, Ishmael, Isaac, Jacob, and the Tribes, and what was given to Moses, Jesus, and all the prophets by their Lord. We make no distinction between any of them, and we devote ourselves to Him."

QURAN 2:136

It was He who made His tranquility descend into the hearts of the believers, to add faith to their faith—the forces of the heavens and earth belong to God; He is all knowing and all wise.

QURAN 48:4

1. THE TESTIMONY OF FAITH (*SHAHĀDAH*)

As Muslims, our beliefs are the bedrock upon which our entire religion is built. They are our key to entering the faith and, God willing, Paradise. The Muslim creed, or statement of beliefs, consists of many tenets that a Muslim must accept and affirm for soundness of faith, all of which are implied and contained in the two testimonies:

Ash-hadu an lā ilāha ill-Āllāh
I testify that nothing is worthy of worship except God,

Wa ash-hadu anna Muḥammad-an rasūl Allāh
And I testify that Muhammad is the messenger of God.

It is the belief in and uttering of these two proclamations, otherwise known as the **Testimony of Faith (*Shahādah*)**, which formally enters one into the religion.[1] They indicate that God is the only one worthy of worship and devotion and that the final and most complete pathway to God came in the person and message of Prophet Muhammad ﷺ.

A close reading of the first half of the Testimony (*Shahādah*) illuminates its profound meaning. Absolute negation—"nothing is worthy of worship"—is followed by the powerful affirming statement "except God!"[2]. It is the formula of pure monotheism—the message of all of God's prophets. The second half of the Testimony teaches that we must live in accordance with the reality of the first Testimony and that God ﷻ taught us how to do so through the life and teachings of His prophets, the last of which was Prophet Muhammad ﷺ.

In an era in which religious traditions are constantly pressured to deny the possibility of anything beyond human perception and to accept only the palpable and measurable, Muslims find respite in their creed, with its clear, unadulterated, non-negotiable tenets. We will now examine, more closely, the six objects of faith described in the previously mentioned narration (*ḥadīth*) which outlined the definition of faith: "It is to believe in God, His angels, His books, His messengers, and the Last Day, and to believe in divine decree, both the good and the evil thereof."

1. Scholars of Islam also conclude that only by negating the Testimony of Faith, and its inherent implications, can one be considered outside the pale of the religion.

2. This is what is referred to in religious studies as "radical monotheism." It is not simply the affirmation of one supreme deity, but the denial of any other supposed deities.

2. GOD (ALLĀH) ﷻ

THE ONENESS OF GOD (TAWḤĪD)

Muslims believe with conviction that **God (Allāh)** ﷻ is the Creator and Sustainer of the universe, and that He alone is worthy of worship.[3] He is the One Who sent Noah, Abraham, Moses, Jesus, and Muhammad, and indeed all of His prophets ﷺ.[4] He is incomparable and beyond the bounds of time and space.

The unity or **oneness (*tawḥīd*)** of God ﷻ is the most central tenet of faith. Anything that violates this oneness constitutes ***shirk***, or **associating partners with God** and setting up another as "worthy of worship." This is the one and only unforgivable sin in Islam. God has stated that He will not forgive anyone who dies in a state of *shirk* (associating partners). For normative Islam, to believe anything has power or ability *independent* of God, no matter how great or small that power or ability, constitutes a type of *shirk* (associating partners). That is why rejecting God altogether, or atheism, is considered to be in the same category as believing in multiple gods or divisions of God. This concept is summarized in the famous prophetic invocation, "There is no strength, nor power, save by God" (*Lā ḥawla wa lā quwwata illā billāh*).

This basic tenet—the oneness of God ﷻ and negation of any partners—was universal to all the prophets throughout history. To more fully illustrate what constitutes a proper understanding of divine oneness (*tawḥīd*), the chapter (*sūrah*) of the Quran that encapsulates it all is given here:

Chapter 112: Purity of Faith
Say, "He is God the One,
God the complete.[5]
He begot no one nor was He begotten.
No one is comparable to Him."

---

3. Allāh is the proper Arabic name for God. It is a unique term with no plural or gender. Using the English word "God" in English is a perfectly valid translation for the Arabic word Allāh. Of all words for the divine in the English language, "God" most closely approaches the loftiness of the Arabic word Allāh. For more on this refer to *One God Many Names*, by Dr. Umar F. Abd-Allah, Nawawi Foundation, http://www.nawawi.org/downloads/article2.pdf.

4. Although God transcends gender, language does not. In Arabic, there is no genderless pronoun, and in the Quran, God uses the default masculine gender, which linguistically is used to be inclusive of both genders, or when the gender is unknown. Throughout this book, God will be referred to through masculine pronouns using the Quranic convention.

5. The Arabic word is "*ṣamad*," which, according to the great interpreter of the Quran, al-Razi, has other interpretations, including "eternal," "self-sufficient," and "sought by all."

The tenets presented in these few lines are a summary of the Muslim belief in the absolute and unqualified oneness (*tawḥīd*) of God. They clarify the concept of God's oneness as excluding certain possibilities, namely: that there could be more than one god or that He is made of composite parts; that God could have any deficiency or be in need of anything; that anything could be born out of Him or that He could be born out of something before Him; or that He could have any peer or bear any similarity to created beings. There is a sharp distinction between the Creator and everything He created, and that dichotomy is what defines Islam's radical monotheism. There is no divinity in the creation, nor any createdness in the Divine.

FAITH BUILT UPON REASON

There are three types of judgments, or ways of knowing. First, we may know something empirically, that is, through observation of the world around us—for example, that water freezes at 0° Celsius. Alternatively, we can know something through some sort of convention, such as law or revelation—that is, through a construct laid out which assigns certain values to things. An example of this is the minimum driving age in a country or the number of prayers prescribed per day. Lastly, we can know something logically, that is, through reason alone. For example, we know logically that two is greater than one, or that something cannot both be and not be at the same time.

Because a person's faith must be firm, Islamic scholars stated that it should be, at its root, grounded in reason. Otherwise, one's faith could be circular—believing in the message of the Prophet Muhammad ﷺ because the Quran affirms it, and believing in the Quran because the Prophet ﷺ brought it. Alternatively, it could be the result of simply concurring with another's belief and adopting it, but that is not enough; the nature of faith is that it must be our own. For these reasons, Islamic theology is a rational discipline utilizing logical proofs to serve as the foundation for believing those things we can only know from revelation. For example, we can use reason to know that God exists, and upon that basis, believe in His revelation that tells us of angels and the resurrection. As such, reason becomes both the basis of faith and the framework within which it is initially understood.

There are three categories of logical propositions, and knowing them is a prerequisite to understanding basic Islamic theology.

- A **necessary proposition** is one the mind cannot conceive of as being false. Some describe it as something "that must be true in all possible worlds." So when we say something is necessary, it means that, rationally, it could be no other way.
- A **conceivable proposition** is one that the mind can see as being either true or false.
- An **inconceivable proposition** is one that the mind cannot conceive of as being true. It is false in all possible worlds.

Some logicians use the following example to illustrate these three categories. Three propositions can be made about the attributes of a triangle: it is *necessary* that it has three angles and three sides; it is *conceivable* that its sides be of equal length or that it have a right angle as one of the angles; and it is *inconceivable* that it have four angles or five sides.

It is important to keep in mind that propositions of this type are statements about the logical conceivability of something, not about whether or not it actually exists in that way. It is conceivable that "in another possible world" God could have made some humans with purple skin, but that proposition does not affirm that such a human actually exists; it just affirms the logical conceivability of it.

NECESSARY ATTRIBUTES OF GOD

There are a number of *necessary attributes* that a Muslim must know and believe about God ﷻ, many of which are intuitive to our concept of God. They are listed below.

- Being is essential to God, and His Being is both pre-eternal (has no beginning) and perpetual (has no end).
- God has life and is Living, incapable of dying.
- God is absolutely independent, not in need of anything else to exist.
- God is unique from and absolutely dissimilar to His creation.
- There is a oneness in His attributes, acts, and essence—God does not have parts or divisions.
- God has omniscience and is the Omniscient; nothing escapes his knowledge.
- God has omnipotence and is the Omnipotent; He is capable of and justified in doing anything He wills.

- God has hearing and is the All-Hearing, has sight and is the All-Seeing, and has the attribute of speech and indeed speaks.
- God has volition and is Willing; whatever He wills is, and whatever He does not will, is not.
- The lack or opposite of any of these attributes is inconceivable of God.

As a result of these attributes, of His independence and our dependence upon Him, God ﷻ has absolute authority over us and is intrinsically worthy of worship. The relationship is thus laid out: He is our Lord, and we are His servants.

THE UNIVERSE IS A PROOF OF GOD

The most fundamental questions of life center around the concept of existence. Why are we here? How did we get here? How did *all* of this get here? Why is there something as opposed to nothing? Existence, in and of itself, must then be examined.

With respect to existence, at least philosophically, there are two types of beings. The first type is a **contingent being**, one that could either exist or not exist. Since it could have either existed or not existed, something had to tip the scales towards its existence, that is, cause it. The second is a **necessary being**, one that by its nature exists in and of itself, not requiring a cause.

When we look at the world around us, we see a world full of temporal and changing things that live and die, grow and decay—contingent beings. Permanence is not a part of the contingent world around us. And, as we intuitively know, contingent beings are brought into existence by another being—that is, they have a beginning. This reality leads to two main problems and one ever-important conclusion.

First, if there is no necessary being to initiate existence, there would have to be an infinite chain of contingent beings, each caused by a previous set of contingent beings, going back through all time in an *infinite regress*, something that is self-contradictory, since each being has a beginning and is finite by definition. The second possible explanation without a necessary being is *circularity*, another logical problem—that C was brought into existence by B, and B was brought into existence by A, and that A was brought into existence by C. In the end, with a finite group of contingent beings, each of which had a beginning, there must be a cause that brought them into existence which itself is uncaused. This is one aspect of the Kalām Cosmological Argument for the existence of God:

1. Everything that has a beginning of its existence has a cause of its existence.
2. The universe has a beginning of its existence.[6]
Therefore:
3. The universe has a cause of its existence.

Therefore, we conclude, through reason, that a necessary being without a cause or beginning—that is, God—exists and brought about the existence of all of creation.

THE NINETY-NINE NAMES OF GOD

With respect to the nature of God ﷻ, it was best stated by one of Islam's great theologians, Imam Abū Isḥāq al-Isfarāyīnī: "All that theologians have said concerning the unity of God can be summed up in two statements: First, God is other than any concept that comes to mind. Second, while the essence of God is utterly unlike other essences, it is, nonetheless, not devoid of attributes."[7] In other words, God ﷻ is an incomprehensible reality beyond the limits of our minds but still manifests attributes that we can comprehend, at least analogously. Although His mercy is different from human mercy, for example, our lives give us glimpses into the divine mercy, the limits of which are beyond us.

This brings us to another important gift from God ﷻ to His creation: the revelation of His Most Beautiful Names. They are ninety-nine in number and help us, as God's servants, to more fully know our Lord and Creator. Essentially, the "names of God" are His attributes. The Ninety-Nine Names also illustrate to us both the complete transcendence of God ﷻ and His immanence. These realities are both essential aspects of Muslim belief.

The Most Beautiful Names of God ﷻ are: the Gracious, the Merciful, the King, the Holy, the Flawless, the Faithful, the Guardian, the Mighty, the Compeller, the Proud, the Creator, the Producer, the Fashioner, He Who is Full of Forgiveness, the Dominator, the Bestower, the Provider, the Opener,

---

6. The eternality of the universe used to be a matter of debate, but now modern science has affirmed an actual beginning to the universe in the event that became known as the Big Bang.

7. Hamza Yusuf, *The Creed of Imam Tahawi* (Sandala, 2007), 7.

the All-Knowing, He Who Contracts, He Who Expands, the Abaser, the Exalter, the Honorer, He Who Humbles, the All-Hearing, the All-Seeing, the Judge, the Just, the Subtle One, the Totally Aware, the Mild, the Tremendous, the All-Forgiving, the Grateful, the Most High, the Most Great, the All-Preserver, the Nourisher, the Reckoner, the Majestic, the Generous, the Watchful, the Answerer of Prayers, the Vast, the Wise, the Lovingkind, the All-Glorious, the Raiser of the Dead, the Witness, the Truth, the Trustee, the Strong, the Firm, the Patron, the Praised, the Knower of Each Separate Thing, the Beginner and Cause, the Restorer, the Life-Giver, the Slayer, the Living, the Self-Subsisting, the Resourceful, the Magnificent, the Unique, the One, the Eternal, the All-Powerful, the Determiner, the Expediter, the Delayer, the First, the Last, the Manifest, the Hidden, the Ruler, the Exalted, the Doer of Good, the Accepter of Repentance, the Avenger, the Effacer of Sins, the All-Pitying, the King of Absolute Sovereignty, the Lord of Majesty and Generosity, the Equitable, the Gatherer, the Self-Sufficient, the Enricher, the Protector, the Punisher, He Who Benefits, the Light, the Guide, the Absolute Cause, the Everlasting, the Inheritor, the Guide to the Right Path, and the Patient.

Each name is a rich facet of the Divine and could have a full book devoted to its explanation; still, there is benefit even in a reflective reading of the names themselves.

3. ANGELS

Muslims affirm the existence of the angels, creatures whose original material of composition was light (just as the human race was created from water and earth). The angels were not given free will to disobey God ﷻ and can only do as God commands them, always obeying. These genderless beings require neither nourishment nor rest. They are the intermediaries by which God ﷻ interacts with His creation. A number of notable angels are described below.

Gabriel (Jibrīl), God's most exalted archangel, is the Angel of Revelation. He was the messenger through whom God ﷻ revealed the Quran to Prophet Muhammad ﷺ. He also interacted with Prophet Muhammad ﷺ, and other prophets, in human form in many non-revelatory circumstances. He accompanied Prophet Muhammad ﷺ on the Night Journey and Ascension. He is the same angel that came to tell Lady Mary (Maryam) of her miraculous conception of the Prophet Jesus (ʿĪsā) ؑ.

Michael (Mikā'īl) is another of God's most exalted archangels. He plays a supportive role to Gabriel and is associated with providing sustenance to God's creation.

Raphael (Isrāfīl) is a mighty archangel whose charge is to blow the Trumpet to signal the commencement of the Last Day. One of the blowings will destroy all of creation; another will awaken the dead, summoning them for resurrection.

Azrael (ʿIzrā'īl) is the Archangel of Death, who is charged, with the aid of his helpers, with ensuring the seizing of souls from their host bodies at a time appointed by God ﷻ.

Munkar and **Nakīr** are two angels who interrogate a soul in its grave. They make the soul sit up, and then they ask him or her three questions: "Who is your Lord? What is your religion? What do you say about the messenger that was sent to you?" The soul's ability to answer these questions while being interrogated in the grave depends upon the person's strength of faith during his or her life.

Raqīb and **ʿAtīd**, also titled the Honorable Recorders, are two angels who sit on our shoulders and whose charge it is to record each good and evil act we perform.

Also worth noting here are Mālik, the angel charged with the guardianship of Hell, may God protect us from encountering it, and Riḍwān, the angel charged with the guardianship of Heaven, may we all enter it joyfully.

THE JINN AND THE STORY OF HUMANITY'S CREATION

Another creation of God ﷻ, in addition to the humans and angels, is the jinn. They are free-willed and sapient creatures, created long before humans, whose original materials of composition were air and smokeless fire. The forefather of this species was **Iblīs**, the proper name of the **Devil (*Shayṭān*)**, may God curse him. A species of devils descended from him, but, because they have free will, not all jinn disobeyed God ﷻ and followed Iblīs; some followed the prophets and messengers of God.

When God ﷻ created Adam, the forefather of humanity, He commanded those in the divine presence (both angels and jinn) to bow in reverence before Adam. All obeyed, except Iblīs, who objected to the command, feeling he was superior to Adam based simply on the materials from which he was created. This arrogance and envy led to Iblīs' expulsion from the divine presence, after which he requested God to grant him a reprieve of his punishment, delaying it to the Last Day. After God granted Iblīs this request, Iblīs vowed to devote himself to leading astray as many of Adam's offspring as he could. Iblīs, the Devil, is the Great Liar, who whispers suggestions[8] to God's servants. Prophet Muhammad ﷺ has taught us a prayer by which we can rid ourselves of his whisperings:

Aʿūdhu billāhi min ash-shayṭān ar-rajīm
(I seek refuge in God from the accursed Devil!)

---

8. Unlike some other religions, Islam teaches that the devil has no power to coerce or actually "do" anything. His method is suggestion. Our ability to choose, and thus our moral accountability, is always in place.

4. SCRIPTURES

Divine scripture, in the form of books, is revealed from God ﷻ to humanity through the Archangel Gabriel (Jibrīl). These are a series of editions of God's message to His creation. Muslims believe each of them originally contained guidance for humanity, but those that preceded the Quran—the final revelation—were altered by men, distorting God's message, so that the current versions of those scriptures are imperfect sources of divine guidance.

There are four divine scriptures Muslims believe in, each listed below.

The **Torah (*Tawrāt*)** was revealed to Prophet Moses (Mūsā) عليه السلام. It contained laws for the Children of Israel and was a source of light and guidance for them. But it has fallen victim to the distortion of men.

The **Psalms (*Zabūr*)** of Prophet David (Dāwūd) also is mentioned in the Quran as being a revelation from God.

The **Gospel (*Injīl*)** was revealed to Prophet Jesus (ʿĪsā) عليه السلام. Muslim creed includes belief in divine revelation from God ﷻ to Prophet Jesus عليه السلام as a mercy and source of guidance to His creation. Unfortunately, the Gospel suffered the fate of distortion by men, the most tragic and significant of which was the insertion of the fabrication of the divinity of Prophet Jesus عليه السلام.

The **Quran**, literally "the often recited," was revealed to Prophet Muhammad ﷺ. Revealed in the Arabic language in the 7th century CE, the Quran is the verbatim word of God ﷻ that will be protected from distortion by God Himself eternally. This protection is considered to be a miracle for Muslims, affirming the prophecy of Muhammad ﷺ throughout the centuries. Today, there is little dispute amongst theologians and religious critics alike that the Quran present today is the same exact one that the Prophet Muhammad ﷺ taught his companions (*ṣaḥābah*). God began revealing the Quran to Prophet Muhammad ﷺ when he was forty years old, and revelation continued until shortly before he passed on at the age of sixty-three.

5. MESSENGERS

There are servants of God ﷻ, indeed His very best, that He selected to receive revelation from Him and to guide their people. Throughout the ages God has sent to each people a messenger, both to warn them of the grave consequences of denying God and to encourage believers with promises of Paradise and divine forgiveness. The Quran often recounts the amazing events of these messengers' lives so that believers today can take lessons and guidance from their acts of faith and righteousness in the face of adversity. They all came with essentially the same message, which differed only in particular details. All of them ultimately called their people to submission (*islām*) to God, and were themselves in a state of submission, and thus could be called *muslims*.

Scholars clarify a difference between the terms "messenger" (*rasūl*) and "prophet" (*nabī*). For most, the term **prophet** refers to a person who received revelation from God ﷻ and was sent to a people with a message from God. The term **messenger** indicates that the revelation included a scripture, and a consequent legal system. Therefore, every messenger is a prophet, but not every prophet is a messenger. With respect to both categories, there are a number of necessary attributes—requirements for being a prophet—that a Muslim must believe in:

- Prophets and messengers alike are always truthful and incapable of lying.
- They are always loyal and have the highest moral integrity (towards God and other people).
- They are always endowed with great intellect and cannot be stupid or foolish.
- They convey the message given to them by God and are incapable of concealing any part thereof.
- They may experience human conditions such as hunger, illness, or fatigue; however, this cannot entail any deficiency or imperfection, such as insanity and the like.
- They are examples to be followed because they are **infallible**—a word that describes the protection that God spread over them, rendering them incapable of making mistakes in conveying, obeying, and perfectly embodying God's message. So Muslims believe sins and acts of immorality are impossible for prophets to commit.

In addition to the above tenets, Muslims affirm the prophethood of the twenty-five confirmed prophets[9] of God ﷻ, who are, in chronological order: Adam, Enoch (Idrīs), Noah (Nūḥ), Hūd, Ṣāliḥ, Abraham (Ibrāhīm), Lot (Lūt), Ishmael (Ismāʿīl), Isaac (Isḥāq), Jacob (Yaʿqūb), Joseph (Yūsuf), Job (Ayyūb), Jethro (Shuʿayb), Moses (Mūsā), Aaron (Hārūn), Ezekiel (Dhul-kifl), David (Dāwūd), Solomon (Sulaymān), Elijah (Ilyās), Elisha (Il-Yasaʿ), Jonah (Yūnus), Zechariah (Zakarīyyah), John the Baptist (Yaḥyā), Jesus (ʿĪsā), and finally, their paragon, seal, and the closer of prophethood, Muḥammad—God's blessings and peace be upon them all .

THE PROPHETS OF RESOLVE

Five messengers have a special rank with God ﷻ and are given the title "the Possessors of Resolve." Each has a unique place with God and was bestowed specific and unique bounties by God.

Prophet Noah (Nūḥ) ﵇ was given the title "The One Rescued by God." He was sent to his people and called them to God's way for a miraculous 950 years. They rejected and ridiculed him and his followers. God ﷻ commanded him to build an ark to carry away the believers before God sent a storm that would flood and destroy the people of Prophet Noah ﵇.

Prophet Abraham (Ibrāhīm) ﵇, the father of the three monotheistic religions of the world, was given the title "The Intimate Friend of God." He showed resolve when his people violently lashed out in rejection of God's message, attempting to burn him alive. God ﷻ commanded the fire to cool itself for Prophet Abraham ﵇, miraculously saving him. Later in Prophet Abraham's life, God would test his faith again. In a dream, Prophet Abraham saw himself sacrificing his son for God. Prophet Abraham asked his son how he felt about it. His son replied that his father should do as he felt God had commanded. To reward Prophet Abraham and his son for their unwavering faith and obedience, God miraculously substituted a lamb in place of the son, so that Prophet Abraham could sacrifice the lamb in his stead. Muslims commemorate this occasion of faith and its reward every year with the Festival of the Sacrifice (*ʿĪd al-Aḍḥā*).

Prophet Moses (Mūsā) ﵇, to whom God ﷻ gave the title "The One with Whom God Spoke," was sent by God to save the children of Israel from

---

9. These are the *confirmed* prophets of God, those that we can definitively say were sent by Him with divine messages. We also were told that God has sent a total of one hundred and twenty-four thousand prophets. It is thus conceivable, although one could not say definitively, that figures like Confucius and the Buddha could also have been prophets.

the slavery and oppression of Pharaoh. Prophet Moses, himself a Jew, was saved from Pharaoh only to be raised by him in his home. When God ﷻ spoke directly to Prophet Moses and sent him to warn Pharaoh, He sent with him miracles, including a staff that transformed into a serpent, to prove his prophethood to Pharaoh. The arrogant Pharaoh commanded his subjects to continue to worship him and rejected God and the warning of Prophet Moses. The children of Israel escaped with the miraculous splitting of the Red Sea, which Pharaoh and his men witnessed but in which they drowned as rejecters of God.

Prophet Jesus (**ʿĪsā**) ﷺ, given the title "The Spirit of God," was sent by God ﷻ to the children of Israel, bringing with him a message of spiritual purification and love of God. He was born of a virgin birth to the Blessed Virgin Mary (Maryam), a pious woman of noble descent. God ﷻ created him without a father simply by commanding the matter to be so, just as he created Prophet Adam with neither father nor mother. His miracles began in infancy, when he spoke from the cradle to defend the honor of his noble mother. His miracles continued on throughout his life, all occurring by the leave and permission of God, including the healing of lepers and the blind, bringing the dead back to life, and also the miraculous gift of a feast for him and his followers. When the enemies of Prophet Jesus conspired to kill him, God ﷻ protected him from crucifixion and gave them the illusion that they had succeeded in killing him.[10] God raised him up to the heavens, preventing any harm from befalling him.

Later, some serious problems surrounding the person of the noble Prophet Jesus (ʿĪsā) ﷺ arose. There were some who attributed divinity to Prophet Jesus as the literal offspring of God ﷻ Himself, Who is transcendent and above having offspring. Others created a trinity of deities to be worshipped, distorting the pure monotheism taught by Prophet Jesus himself. Yet there were others that maintained the prophethood of Jesus and did not ascribe any divinity to him. Muslims do believe that he is the Messiah whom the children of Israel still await, and we believe he will return to this world before the end of time to battle and defeat the Antichrist, and eventually to die, as do all mortal men, including prophets.

---

10. The Quran is very explicit in clarifying that historically it was not the person of Prophet Jesus (ʿĪsā) that was crucified, although the exact details surrounding what happened are a subject of some debate. Those who worked to crucify him were made to believe that they had succeeded in doing so. In mainstream Christian thought, his return (thought to be resurrection after death) is the basis of ascribing divinity to a man. In the Muslim belief, Prophet Jesus never died, and the resurrection of a dead man, well within the ability of God, makes the Resurrector, not the resurrected, divine.

Prophet Muhammad ﷺ, "The Beloved of God," was the last and final messenger of God ﷻ to all of humanity, the final seal of prophecy and revelation. Prophet Muhammad was born in Mecca, Arabia, in the 6th century CE. His life is known about in more detail than the life of any other prophet of God: We know how he interacted with his wives, friends, and neighbors, how he reacted to adversity, how he performed daily activities such as eating and sleeping, as well as how he lived countless other aspects of the human life we all experience. His life is a perfect model for believers to follow and find guidance in. He was born of noble lineage and his reputation for integrity was known long before his prophethood began. At the age of forty, while he was in a devotional retreat in a secluded cave, the Archangel Gabriel (Jibrīl) brought him the first revelation from God. The revelations, which would make up the Quran, would continue for twenty-three years until shortly before he passed on. Like all prophets, he was rejected by his people, who fought violently against him and his followers, although he asked only for the freedom to call people to God. He and his followers migrated to the city of Medina, where he founded a new community of believers who would live in peace. Eventually, he and his army conquered Mecca in a shining exhibition of his mercy and compassion—no blood was spilled, no revenge was sought. He left behind men who were forever changed and teachings that would forever change others.

6. JUDGMENT DAY

As a central tenet of faith, Muslims must believe that everyone will eventually die and be resurrected for judgment by God ﷻ as the beginning of a never-ending life. For Muslims, earthly life is the capital with which we work towards success in the next life. Although earthly life is not an illusion, the life of the next world is considered the *real* life. The purpose of earthly life is simply for God to test us to see if we will choose righteousness over selfish vice. All of it culminates in one moment in the human story—the day we are resurrected and judged.

This momentous day has several titles, all of which are interchangeable. They include the Hour, the Last Day, the Day of Reckoning, the Day of Resurrection, and many more. Below is some of what Muslims believe regarding that day, although many more details are known:

- In the grave, the dead are questioned by the two angels Munkar and Nakīr.
- After dying, God will resurrect us back to life.
- We are questioned by God and held accountable for our actions in this life.
- God created the Scale, which weighs the worth of our deeds, both good and bad, against each other, to determine our fate.
- The Pathway is a bridge over Hell—those burdened by sin and disbelief will fall into the fire below.
- Paradise is an actual place to which believers will go as a reward from God, as He has promised.
- Hell is an actual place to which some people will go as a punishment from God, as He has warned.

It should become clear from this that Muslims believe in both reward and punishment as possibilities in the afterlife. **Paradise (*Jannah*)** is a place with which God ﷻ rewards His servants. Its inhabitants dwell therein forever, with peace, joy, and serenity. They know no pain or suffering, nor any unfulfilled wish. The joys of Paradise dwarf the transient pleasure of the senses we can experience here in this life.

On the other hand, those who reject and rebel against God ﷻ, and die in such a state, are punished. God places them in **Hell (*Jahannam*)**, an abode of blazing torment. Its inhabitants suffer immense pain and know no joy. As the Owner and Creator of all creation, God does with us as He pleases—all is within His right and justice.

As for Muslims, no guarantee of direct entry into Paradise (*Jannah*) is given simply by believing. Their fate is unknown to a certain extent. However, we are told that Prophet Muhammad ﷺ fulfills the very important role of **intercessor (*shafīʿ*)** for Muslims on the Day of Judgment. On that day, God ﷻ will grant Prophet Muhammad ﷺ, His Beloved, the ability to intercede with Him. Prophet Muhammad ﷺ will prostrate himself before God in a series of events, and in the end, Prophet Muhammad ﷺ will beseech God until anyone who believed in the Testimony of Faith (*Shahādah*) is removed from Hell (*Jahannam*).

The Prophet of Mercy gives us hope that each of us, if we sincerely believe in the Testimony of Faith, will eventually enter Paradise. From this we know that even Muslims can spend a period of time in Hell, to purge them of their sins, with an eventual entry into Paradise. This should remind us all that we are not "saved" beyond the point of being called to account; on the contrary, each of us will be taken to task for our actions in the world. Even though it is only by God's mercy that we enter into Paradise, it is through both faith and works that we strive to earn His grace, with proper faith as a prerequisite. Such an understanding instills in a believer both hope in the mercy of God ﷻ and fear of His just punishment, a perfect balance that instills in us the desire to work for more piety without a false sense of security.

7. DIVINE DECREE (*QADR*)

All matters in the entire history and future of the cosmos—both good and evil—are known to God ﷻ and are a direct result of His willing them, decreeing them, and, through His power and ability, bringing them into existence. Nothing can alter the command of God. This means that anything that happened could not have been prevented, and anything that didn't happen was never going to. God has determined the measure of it all: our lifespans, our financial provisions, and our destinations in the next life. This is what is referred to as divine decree (*qadr*).

At the same time, humans and jinn alike have been given free will: the ability to choose their actions. We are all morally responsible for the decisions we make and the things we do. We are free to choose our actions within the limits set by the divine decree, and we are held accountable for those choices.

Islam thus presents a harmonious balance between free will and divine predestination: neither of them is absolute. We are neither absolutely free to do anything we wish, nor are we compelled to act by divine decree, without any will of our own. One famous scholar used the game of chess as a metaphor to explain this: predetermined rules dictate what movements can be made, while the player is free to choose within that predetermined framework. Both the predetermined rules and the player's freedom are preserved.[11]

In the end, it is important to recognize that completely reconciling these two realities (free will and divine predestination) is beyond the capacity of the human mind, which, as great as God ﷻ has made it, has its inherent limitations. Attempting to delve into the inner workings of the decree of God, the secret of it, is an exercise that is discouraged in the Islamic tradition, as it is God's domain and not to be questioned, nor can it be fully grasped by anyone. We are reminded by God that "He cannot be questioned for what He does—it is they who will be questioned" (Quran 21:23). Believers are to accept His decree with gratitude for the sweetness it brings and with patience for its bitter moments.

For Muslims, belief in divine decree (*qadr*) is a source of comfort in an era that is losing its ability to deal with tragedy and disaster, always asking "Why?" Our faith in divine decree provides us with both reliance upon God and contentment with what He decrees. We find solace in the fact

---

11. Hamza Yusuf, "Chess and the Divine Decree," *Seasons*, Spring 2006: 16-17.

that things could not have been any other way and are reminded that we will be called to account before God not for what happens to us, but for our own actions in response to it.

CHAPTER 3

Worship

Even those who live in the presence of your Lord are not too proud to worship Him: they glorify Him and bow down before Him.

QURAN 7:206

"He is Lord of the heavens and the earth and all that is between, so worship Him: be steadfast in worshipping Him. Do you know of anyone equal to Him?"

QURAN 19:65

Surrendering or "submission" to God (*islām*) infuses everything Muslims do. Whatever your occupation, social relationships, or personal interests, everything can be done in a manner that is ultimately in surrender to the Divine. To make this easier, God ﷻ has revealed a set of devotional practices upon which to build and expand. The most essential of them are the five pillars of the dimension of *islām* in the previously mentioned narration (*ḥadīth*) from Prophet Muḥammad ﷺ: "To testify that nothing is worthy of worship except God and that Muhammad is the messenger of God; to perform the ritual prayers (*ṣalāh*); to pay the purifying alms (*zakāh*); to fast (*ṣawm*) in Ramaḍān; and to make the pilgrimage (*ḥajj*) to the House if you are able to do so." These practices, which are performed through the medium of the physical body, illustrate the Islamic view of the mutual relationship between the body and the soul—that the actions of each directly affect the other, a concept all but lost in the modern world.

The devotional practices of a Muslim are guided by divine instructions, providing Muslims with both standardization and insight in their surrender to God ﷻ. These instructions reach us as a part of **Islamic law (*sharīʿah*)**, a set of codes and principles derived by the jurists from divine revelation and used as a guide for all important matters of Muslim life. Islamic law is generally described as having two realms: the devotional, which governs the interaction between people and God, and the social, which governs human interaction. The first of these realms, consisting of the laws related to ritual devotions, is the subject of this chapter.

Always keep in mind the interdependence of the three dimensions of Islām: *islām* (acts of the body), *imān* (beliefs of the mind), and *iḥsān* (purity of the spiritual state). Although a subject may technically fall under one specific dimension, you should remember that it can both affect and be affected by the other two dimensions as well. And so, the physical acts of worship that we will examine have spiritual implications and meanings; they result from and strengthen one's faith and certitude. Performing these practices consistently and properly will impact your faith, your spiritual state, and your entire constitution.

RELIABLE SCHOLARSHIP

As previously discussed, the process of deriving legal rulings from the sources of law is a complex process. Over time, jurists eventually settled on methodologies that serve as the foundation of the four legal schools (*madh-*

habs). All the schools are based on the same sources and are equally valid in their methodology. For the most part, their differences are minor.

The details surrounding the devotional acts presented here are from the perspective of one of the four schools of orthodox law.[1] There are other valid and correct methodologies, and you may find other Muslims who do things slightly differently. Do not jump to the conclusion that one method is correct and the other mistaken. Just be sure that your actions are based on one of these sound methodologies.

This chapter provides a basic outline of the essential devotions of Islam. It will help you get started, but it is by no means a comprehensive presentation of the subject. After learning these basics, seek to learn about these practices in greater depth and detail.

1. This legal school is named after its founder, Imam Mālik ibn Anas (711 - 795CE). The Mālikī school of law, like the other schools of law, is a legal tradition which is based upon the methodologies of its founder and to which some of the greatest jurists of Islamic history have contributed their insights.

1. THE LEGAL RULINGS

Islamic law (*sharīʿah*) is concerned not with objects and materials, but with actions. For example, it does not forbid alcohol itself; it forbids *consuming*, or *selling*, or *serving* alcohol. Every conceivable action a Muslim could take is assigned a particular **legal ruling** in Islamic law. This ruling tells us how good or bad an act is, or how important it is to perform or refrain from. The ruling also defines the metaphysical consequences, good or bad, of that action.[2] The five basic rulings form a spectrum of virtue and vice, and a good understanding of them will help you develop an understanding of the worldview of the sacred law.

1. **Required (*farḍ*)** acts are those that a Muslim must do. In terms of consequence, they are rewarded by God ﷻ and are recorded by the angels as good deeds if you do them, thereby fulfilling your duty to God. Conversely, if you fail to perform these acts, you accrue sin for disobeying God's commandment. Examples of required acts are performing the five daily prayers and showing deep reverence and good manners towards one's parents.
2. A **commendable (*mustaḥab*)** act is an optional good deed. Commendable acts earn reward from God ﷻ, but failing to perform them, although a missed opportunity for serving the Divine, does not result in sin. A subcategory of this ruling is a **prophetic practice (*sunnah*)**: a commendable act that was performed by Prophet Muhammad ﷺ quite regularly. It is a higher grade of commendable act, as the Prophetic Way (*Sunnah*) is an illuminated source of guidance for us.[3] One example of a commendable act would be feeding a needy person.

2. In Islamic theology, proper faith is a prerequisite to attaining salvation. Actions play a role in attempting to attain salvation in that they have divine consequences attached to them. So in the broader theological discussion of "salvation," "faith," and "works," the Islamic view holds that no one can really secure their salvation with certainty: it is only by the grace of God. If one's life gives evidence of both proper faith and righteous actions, one may hope that God will show His mercy and grant ultimate salvation in the afterlife (*ākhirah*).

3. The specific meaning of the term *Sunnah* depends on the context in which it is used. In the context of Islamic law, it means the category of deeds mentioned here. In the broadest sense, *Sunnah* means the Prophetic Way of Prophet Muhammad; it includes the aforementioned category and much more. The third usage of *Sunnah* is as a synonym for narrations (*ḥadīths*) of Prophet Muḥammad. (It is worth noting that some commands contained within the

3. A **permissible (*mubāḥ*)** act is one that has a neutral quality to it: one is free to do or not do it, with no preference for either one. In terms of divine consequences, performing the act or refraining from it results in neither sin nor reward. The vast majority of acts fall under this category, and it is important to note that jurists consider this the baseline ruling for any act, unless and until some divine or prophetic guidance indicates otherwise. A noble intention, however, has a transformative effect on acts that are merely permissible. To engage in such an act with the intention to remember God or help a neighbor, for example, can transform it into a commendable act.
4. Opposite the commendable acts on the other side of the spectrum are **disliked (*makrūh*)** acts, which we are encouraged *not* to do. One is rewarded for refraining from these acts but is not punished for doing them (although some scholars hold that performing them consistently is forbidden). This category is a reminder that not doing something *is* an act, in and of itself. An example of a disliked act is wasting water while performing ritual washing or taking a ritual bath.
5. The dark counterpart of the required act is the **forbidden (*ḥarām*)** act—an action a Muslim must never do. In performing a forbidden act we accrue sin, while refraining from the act is a duty to God ﷾ that begets His generous reward. Scholars consider avoiding the forbidden acts even more important than performing the required acts. Of course, it is best that the former be avoided and the latter performed, but the priority given to avoiding forbidden acts is meant to highlight the dangers of that darkness. Examples of such loathsome acts are lying, stealing, and the like.

For the broad category of acts that are not forbidden (*ḥarām*), the term **lawful (*ḥalāl*)** is used. ***Ḥalāl*** implies that an act falls under one of the other four rulings (disliked, permissible, commendable, or required). However, this term is sometimes also used as a synonym for the permissible (*mubāḥ*) acts.

While developing an understanding of what is required of us and what is forbidden for us, it is important to remember this narration (*ḥadīth*) from Prophet Muhammad ﷺ: "Each child of Adam makes mistakes, and the best of those who err are the repentant." Repentance is a gift from God ﷾ by

narration literature create rulings that do not necessarily carry the legal ruling of a prophetic practice (*sunnah*), but can be required (*farḍ*) or permissible (*mubāḥ*).)

which, when human weakness makes us fall short of our duties to God, we can have our sins erased.

REWARD AND SIN

As you can see from the description of the rulings, in four out of the five categories, the believer does not incur sin. This highlights the mercy and compassion with which God has graced His servants. Furthermore, a famous narration (*ḥadīth*) from Prophet Muhammad states that the reward of one good deed is multiplied by ten, while each bad deed carries only one sin.

As you study Islam, you will find that different acts may carry different amounts of reward, differing even by an order of magnitude. For example, we have been taught that prayer (*ṣalāh*) in congregation confers twenty-seven times the reward of a prayer performed alone. This multiplication of rewards reveals to us the level of importance God has assigned to particular acts. This ensures that we do not follow our personal whims when trying to grow closer to God; rather we follow the path He has laid out before us.

	FORBIDDEN	DISLIKED	PERMISSABLE	COMMENDABLE	REQUIRED
PERFORM	Sin	Nothing	Nothing	Reward	Reward
ABSTAIN	Reward	Reward	Nothing	Nothing	Sin

Table 1: The Five Legal Rulings and Their Consequences

THE MORALLY ACCOUNTABLE

God, through Islamic law, has defined what type of person is subject to Islamic law (*sharīʿah*). Such an individual is termed a morally accountable individual. The conditions for moral accountability (itself a legal status) are that a person must:

1. Be of sound mind, with the ability to exercise good judgment;
2. Reached puberty;
3. Have received the message of God's final guidance for humanity, Islam.

The age of puberty is determined by presence of menstruation, pregnancy, the ejaculation of fluid, the presence of pubic hair, or reaching eighteen years of age if none of the other signs show. This means that prepubescent children, the mentally ill or challenged, the insane and unconscious, and those who have not received the message of Islam are not held accountable for following the sacred law of Islam.

2. THE PRAYER (*ṢALĀH*)

The most important task for you as a newly practicing Muslim is to learn the prayer (*ṣalāh*), which will remain the central pillar of your practice for the rest of your life, the one around which the rest are built. Every day, a Muslim arranges his or her daily activities around making time to remember God ﷻ in the form of the five-time daily prayer. This is a devotional act, structured and formalized, given to us through Prophet Muhammad ﷺ. Previous prophets also prayed in a similar manner, but over time their followers failed to maintain the practice, until it disappeared from their traditions almost completely. Muslims all over the world, throughout the history of Islam, have prayed and continue to pray in the same manner, towards the same direction, and in the same language as the last and final prophet of God, Prophet Muhammad ﷺ.

The Term "Prayer"

The term "prayer" can mean two different things, based on the context in which it is used. It can mean the five-time daily ritual devotion that is a pillar of Islam, or it can mean addressing God to ask for a need. For purposes of this manual, the structured devotion that is performed daily will be termed **the prayer** (*ṣalāh*). The second usage, the beseeching of God for a need or request, which can also be called "prayer" in common parlance, will be termed **supplication** (*duʿā'*). The vast majority of Muslims will call both these practices "prayer" in English; usually, it is easy to tell which is meant based on the context, with the default use being that of the ritual devotion.

An Overview of the Prayer (Ṣalāh)

At five points during the day, based on the position of the sun in relation to the Earth, a Muslim joins the universe's perfect order of obedience to God ﷻ by performing the prayer (*ṣalāh*). You begin by ensuring that your clothing is clean; then you wash your limbs to purify yourself in preparation for standing before God. Next, you stand facing the direction of the sacred house of worship built by Prophet Abraham ﷺ, the *Kaʿbah*, and formally commence the ritual prayer. Through a series of divinely revealed positions—including standing, bowing, prostrating on the floor, and sitting—we perform an act of worship and devotion that creates a connection between ourselves and the Divine. The prayer itself includes recitation of the Quran, invocations and praise of God ﷻ, and supplications of different kinds. Finally, we conclude the ritual prayer by uttering a greeting of peace.

The following pages present a detailed set of instructions for performing the prayer (*ṣalāh*), along with explanations of the concepts underlying its methodology.

PREPARATION FOR THE PRAYER

Before entering the prayer (*ṣalāh*), you must observe four prerequisites for the prayer to be valid, each of which we will examine more closely:

1. Ensuring the ritual cleanliness of your body, clothes, and place of prayer
2. Being in a state of ritual purity
3. Facing the proper prayer direction
4. Covering the body appropriately

The first two prerequisites, ritual cleanliness and ritual purity, are related to the process of purification. **Purification** refers either to: a) the process of *removing filth* to attain ritual cleanliness, or b) the *performance of the ritual washings* to attain the status of ritual purity. Both modes of purification require the use of pure, unaltered water.

Unaltered water is water that is colorless, tasteless, and odorless. Water that is contaminated to the point where any of these three qualities is altered is considered unfit for ritual purification. Some water, however, has a perceptible taste, smell, or color in its natural state, such as water from a reddish stream. Such water is still considered unaltered and can be used for purification. Water taken from the sea, a swamp, a river, or directly gathered from rain, is also considered unaltered.

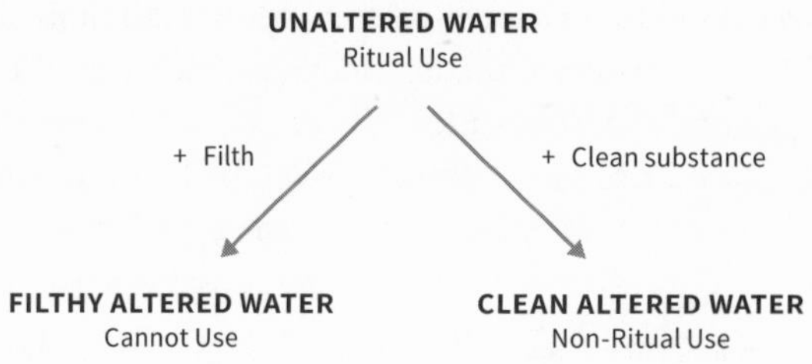

Figure 2: The Types of Water and Their Uses

Note: The prerequisites are not components of the prayer itself but occur outside of it altogether.

Ritual Cleanliness of Body, Clothing, and Prayer Area

Ritual cleanliness is the absence of certain substances designated by Islamic law (*sharīʿah*) as **filth** (***najāsah***). These substances are:

- liquid intoxicants (e.g., wine)
- vomit
- pus
- pre-seminal fluid
- semen
- blood
- human feces and urine
- the feces and urine of animals that we are forbidden (*ḥarām*) to eat by Islamic law

Filth, according to sacred law, is different from a purely hygienic lack of cleanliness. For example, if a man's trousers were splattered with mud, they would certainly be dirty, but they would not be considered filthy by Islamic law.

For a prayer (*ṣalāh*) to be valid, the clothing you are wearing during the prayer and the immediate area upon which you will pray and prostrate must both be completely free of any filth (*najāsah*). If they are free of filth, nothing needs to be done. But if either your clothing or the area upon which you will pray is tainted with filth, you must wash it with unaltered water until the filth is removed.

You must also be sure that your body is free from any filth (*najāsah*) after using the bathroom. Men must gently squeeze and shake the penis after urination to ensure complete removal of any urine. For both sexes, the bodily openings should be cleaned after either urination or defecation to remove any filth. The preferred method of cleansing yourself is: First, wipe the opening (urethra or anus) with a clean, dry substance, such as toilet paper, until it is clean. Use your left hand to do so.[4] Next, use water to wash the body part (either urethra or anus), again using the left hand to wash the

4. In Islamic etiquette, following Prophet Muhammad's teaching, we use our left hand to carry out less refined actions, and our right hand for other activities, including those that entail interaction with others (e.g., shaking hands). This applies regardless of whether one is right- or left-handed when performing tasks requiring fine motor skills, such as writing.

area clean. Dry the area if possible when finished. Then wash your hands to make sure they are clean.

If you are unable to clean the impurities in the above manner, then washing with water alone is the next best method, and if that is not possible, then wiping with a clean, dry substance until nothing remains is permitted for both genders after defecation and for men (but not for women) after urination. However, if after either urination or defecation the filth (*najāsah*) has spread beyond the bodily opening, you must wash the area with water.

State of Ritual Purity

Attaining a **state of ritual purity** is an important prerequisite to the prayer (*ṣalāh*). While the ritual cleanliness of the prayer area and attire have to do with the absence of certain physical substances, the state of ritual purity is an immaterial *ritual status*. This status can be invalidated by certain actions, just as a valid driver's license can be invalidated by violating driving laws. If you are in a state of ritual purity and do something that invalidates that state, you must ritually purify yourself again before performing the prayer.

To better understand ritual purity, you must understand the state of ritual *impurity*—since the former is obtained by removing the latter. Ritual impurity has two types, major and minor.

Minor Ritual Impurity

A person in a state of ritual purity may fall into **minor ritual impurity** through certain actions, called **causes of minor ritual impurity**, listed below:

1. Urination
2. Defecation
3. Passing gas
4. Deep sleep (more than just a "nodding off" in which you still sense things)
5. Lustful emission of pre-seminal fluid[5]
6. Intoxication or a state of insanity
7. Loss of consciousness
8. Sensual touching and kissing: acts in which sensual pleasure is typically felt, even if no pleasure is actually felt at the time.

---

5. There is also a non-lustful fluid that can be emitted under some circumstances. In the end, the emission of anything from either the urethra or the anus will result in, at least, minor ritual impurity. For the instances that lead to major ritual impurity, refer to that section.

Even if you touch someone without intending such pleasure but happen to feel it nonetheless, ritual purity is invalidated. (Non-sensual touching, where sensual pleasure is neither intended nor experienced, does not invalidate the state of ritual purity.)

9. A man touching his penis with the inner part of the hand or fingers (palm side)

If any of these actions occurs, the state of purity is invalidated and minor ritual impurity results. A person in a state of minor ritual impurity needs to perform *wuḍū'* (ritual washing) to enter into a state of purity again.

If you are in a state of minor ritual impurity, certain rulings of Islamic law come into effect. There are three acts for which ritual purity is a prerequisite and which, therefore, are forbidden (*ḥarām*) to perform in a state of ritual impurity:

1. Prayer (*ṣalāh*)
2. Circling (*ṭawāf*) of the Sacred House (*Kaʿbah*) in Mecca (see page 84)
3. Touching a **hard copy (*muṣḥaf*)** of the Quran—that is, a copy of the scripture itself in the original Arabic.[6]

Figure 3: A Hard Copy (*muṣḥaf*) of the Quran

6. This rule does not apply to translations of the Quran into other languages or to works that include selected passages of the Quran along with other text.

Wuḍū'—Ritual Washing

Wuḍū',[7] a ritual washing,[8] a process of purification in which different parts of the body are washed with unaltered water in preparation for standing before God ﷻ in prayer or another devotion. To perform *wuḍū'*:

1. Begin by saying the phrase ***Bismillāh*** (In the name of God) while consciously intending to perform *wuḍū'*.

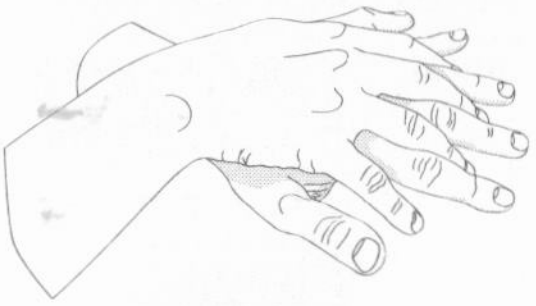

2. Wash your right hand three times, up to and including the wrist; then your left hand.

3. Rinse your mouth three times, swishing the water around.

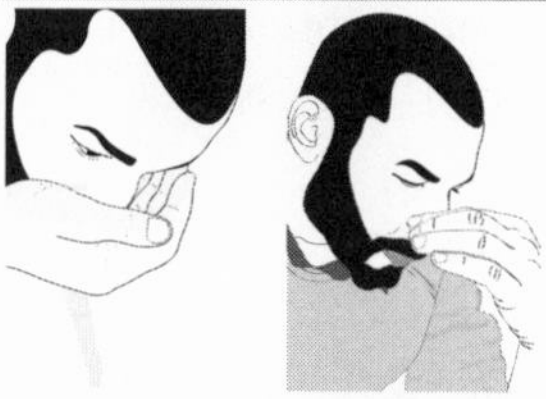

4. Then, with your right hand, bring water to your nose and lightly sniff it in, immediately blowing out and wiping downward on your nose with your left hand. Do this three times.

7. This is the first of a few exceptions to the practice of using an English word with the Arabic equivalent in parentheses afterwards. This will only be done for those things that English-speaking Muslims always refer to by the Arabic word, because the Arabic word is considered its name or title. While English-speaking Muslims use the words "God," "heaven," "hell," "piety," etc., they still call many ritual acts, such as *wuḍū'* (ritual washing) or particular daily prayers, by their Arabic names.

8. I have chosen to use the phrase "ritual washing" for my rendering of *wuḍū'*. Most translations of the word use the unfamiliar term "ablution," which does not convey much meaning to most English-speaking Muslims, but becomes a title in and of itself.

5. Wash your face three times, from the natural hairline to the chin and from ear to ear. For men: If your facial hair is so dense that the skin beneath is not visible, then wash over it as if it were skin (rubbing the hand over it). If your facial hair is sparse, so that the skin beneath is visible, use your fingertips to comb the water through and rub the skin below.

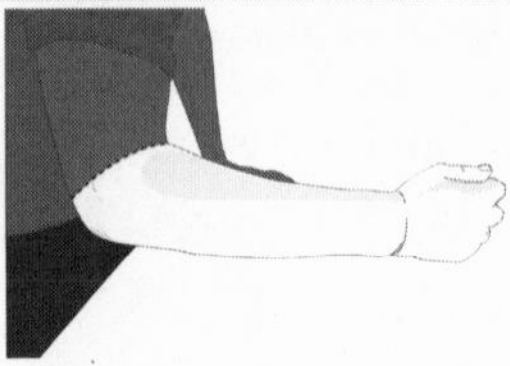

6. Wash your right arm three times, from the fingertips up to and including the elbow, and comb the fingers with the fingers of the other hand, to wash in between them; then do the same for the left arm.

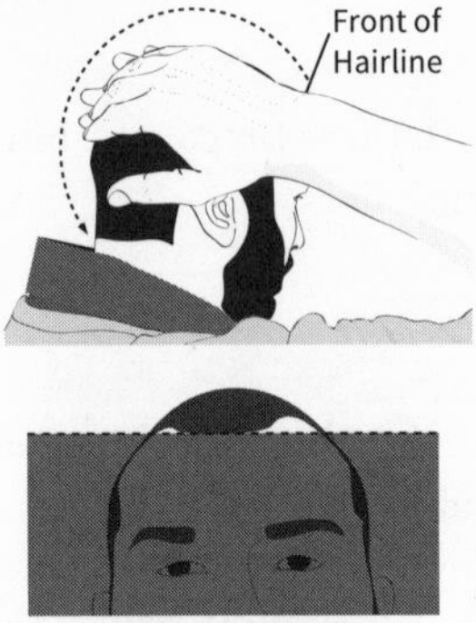

7. With wet hands, wipe your hair just once from the front of the natural hairline to the back of it, pulling any long hair through the wipe as well. Now, repeat the same motion in reverse, from back to front. Do this once.

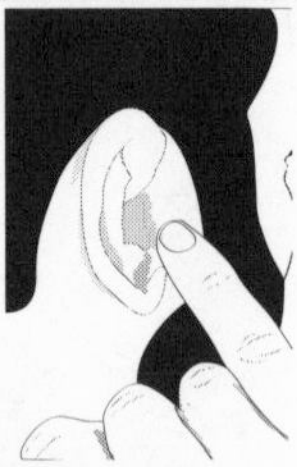

8. Rewet your fingers and wipe your ears just once.

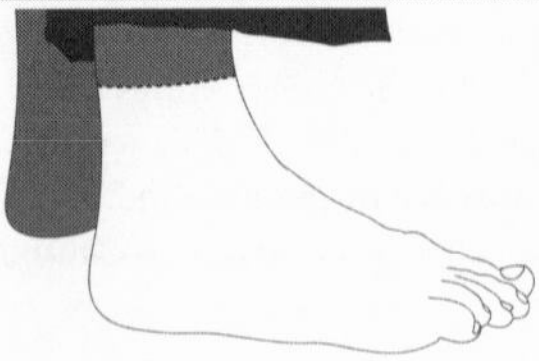

9. Wash your right foot three times, up to and including the ankle, combing through the toes with either the index finger or the smallest finger; then do this for the left foot.

Washing means pouring water directly onto a body part and then rubbing it; *wiping* means rubbing a body part with a wet hand, without having previously poured water directly onto it.

At the conclusion of the *wuḍū'* (ritual washing), it is a prophetic practice (*sunnah*) to say the two testimonies of faith:

Ash-hadu an-lā ilāha ill-Āllāh, wa ash-hadu anna Muḥammadan rasūl Allāh
(I testify that there is nothing worthy of worship except God, and that Muhammad is the messenger of God).

The scholars of Islamic law have determined which components are essential for *wuḍū'* (ritual washing) to be complete and valid. If an essential component is missed, then the whole process is invalid. The essential components of *wuḍū'* are: to bring the intention to mind at the outset; to wash once your arms, face, and feet; to wipe your head; and to perform these actions without a long interruption. If anything else is forgotten it is best to redo it afterwards, but your *wuḍū'* (ritual washing) is still valid.[9]

Any barriers that might prevent the water from penetrating the areas to be washed or wiped, such as nail polish or paint, must be removed for the water to reach the body and for the *wuḍū'* (ritual washing) to be valid.

The ritual purity that is brought about by *wuḍū'* (ritual washing) is nullified by the minor violators of ritual purity listed above. If you are in a state of ritual purity and one of the causes of minor ritual impurity occurs, then you must perform *wuḍū'* again before performing the prayer.

RITUAL IMPURITY VERSUS FILTH (*NAJĀSAH*)

The state of ritual impurity is *immaterial*—it is caused by an action and cannot be seen: it is a legal status. It can only be removed through *wuḍū'* (ritual washing).

In contrast, filth (*najāsah*) is *material*. A person can literally see, feel, or smell it and thus remove it. If filth is on your body or clothes, it does not invalidate *wuḍū'*—it only needs to be washed off.

9. If a prayer was performed with an invalid *wuḍū'* (ritual washing), the prayer must be repeated.

Major Ritual Impurity

There is a greater level of ritual impurity which cannot be removed by *wuḍū'* (ritual washing) alone—**major ritual impurity**. A person can fall into this state through one of the four **causes of major ritual impurity of ritual purity**:

1. Menstruation
2. Postpartum bleeding
3. Ejaculation
4. Penetration of the head of a man's penis into a woman's vagina (this causes major ritual impurity for both parties)

With the major ritual impurity caused by these events, certain rulings of Islamic law (*sharīʿah*) come into effect. If a woman is in a state of major ritual impurity caused by either menstruation or postpartum bleeding, sexual intercourse is forbidden (*ḥarām*) for both husband and wife until the bleeding has ended and the woman has ritually purified herself. During the time of bleeding, prayer (*ṣalāh*) and fasting (*ṣawm*) are not required (*farḍ*) for a woman.[10] If a man or woman's state of major ritual impurity comes from ejaculation or from penile penetration, then verbal recitation of the Quran is forbidden for them. If you are in a state of major ritual impurity from any of the four causes, it is forbidden to enter the designated prayer area of a mosque, although you can enter other parts of the building.

Note that for a woman with menstrual or postpartum bleeding, it is permissible to recite the Quran verbally, although, as mentioned above, it is forbidden (*ḥarām*) for her to touch a hard copy (*muṣḥaf*) of the Quran, since that requires a state of ritual purity, which she cannot attain. She may, however, touch other materials, such as a commentary on the Quran, even if they contain Arabic verses from the Quran.

10. A woman with menstrual or postpartum bleeding is in a state that prevents her from undergoing purification. Therefore, for a woman in this state, prayer is not required, nor does she owe the prayers as a debt to God to be made up later—she is entirely excused. This is not the case for the required fasting of Ramadan, where she owes the days missed.

	QURANIC RECITATION FORBIDDEN	INTERCOURSE FORBIDDEN	ENTERING PRAYER AREA OF MOSQUE FORBIDDEN
MENSTRUATION		✔	✔
POSTPARTUM BLEEDING		✔	✔
PENETRATION	✔		✔
EJACULATION	✔		✔

Table 2: Restrictions of Major Ritual Impurity According to Cause

The Ritual Bath (Ghusl)

A person who falls into a state of major ritual impurity needs to perform a **ritual bath** (***ghusl***) in order to attain a state of ritual purity. To perform a ritual bath:

1. Begin with a conscious intention to perform this ritual act of purification.
2. Next, wash your private parts, ensuring that any filth (*najāsah*) is washed off.
3. Then, as in *wuḍū'* (ritual washing), wash your hands, rinse your mouth, sniff water to cleanse your nose, and wash your face and arms, but do each washing only once.
4. Then wash your head three times. (In *wuḍū'* you only *wipe* the head, but in the ritual bath you *wash* your head, rubbing your fingertips down to the roots of your hair, three times.)
5. Then, starting at the top of your body and working your way down, wash your ears, neck, chest, shoulders, upper arms, torso and back, buttocks and thighs, calves, and feet. Always wash the right limb or body part before the left (i.e., right ear, then left ear, then right side of the neck, then left side of the neck, and so on).

You will wash your entire body (in contrast to *wuḍū'*, there is no wiping), making sure to penetrate all hair to the root, washing it, and washing even the hard to reach places (navel, gluteal cleft, between the toes, etc.).

As in *wuḍū'* (ritual washing), certain acts are essential for a ritual bath (*ghusl*) to be valid. The essential components are: to bring the intention to mind at the outset; to wash the entire body, washing and penetrating all hair to the root; and to do all of this without an interruption (i.e., a break long enough to air-dry the body).

Once you have performed a ritual bath (*ghusl*), you are in a state of ritual purity.[11]

Some important differences between *wuḍū'* (ritual washing) and the ritual bath (*ghusl*) are:

- In *wuḍū'* you must wash in between the fingers (in the webs), and doing the same for the toes is recommended but not required. In a ritual bath, you *must* wash in between *both* the fingers and toes.
- In *wuḍū'* most limbs are washed, while some are wiped. In the ritual bath the entire body is washed, and there is no wiping.
- Performing the ritual bath (*ghusl*) can replace the need for *wuḍū'*, but *wuḍū'* cannot replace the need to perform the ritual bath.

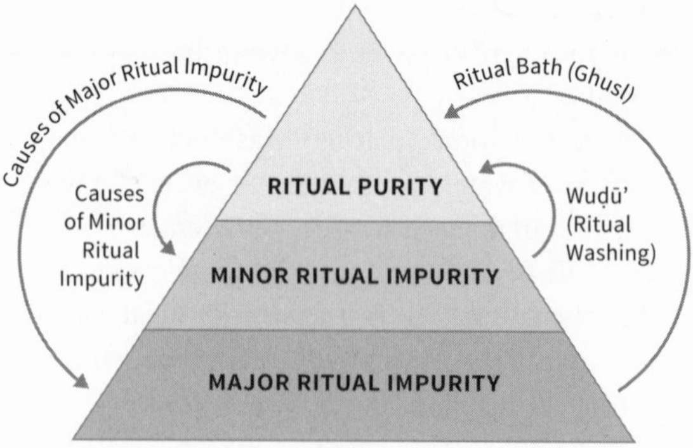

Figure 4: The Levels of Ritual Purity and the Modifiers

11. After performing a ritual bath (*ghusl*) as outlined above, you do not need to perform *wuḍū'* (ritual washing) to be in a state of ritual purity, unless you do something in the ritual bath by which *wuḍū'* would be invalidated *after* you have washed the limbs of *wuḍū'*. For example, if a man touches his penis with his palm, or a man or woman passes gas, after washing the limbs of *wuḍū'*, the ritual bath is valid, but a subsequent *wuḍū'* must be performed to attain a state of ritual purity. (However, if you do something that invalidates *wuḍū' before* you have washed the limbs of *wuḍū'*, an additional *wuḍū'* is not necessary.)

The Prayer Direction (Qiblah)

For the five-time-daily prayer (*ṣalāh*), Muslims face the Sacred House (*Kaʿbah*) in Mecca from wherever they are in the world. The Sacred House was built by Prophet Abraham (Ibrāhīm) ﷺ as a house of worship of the One God.

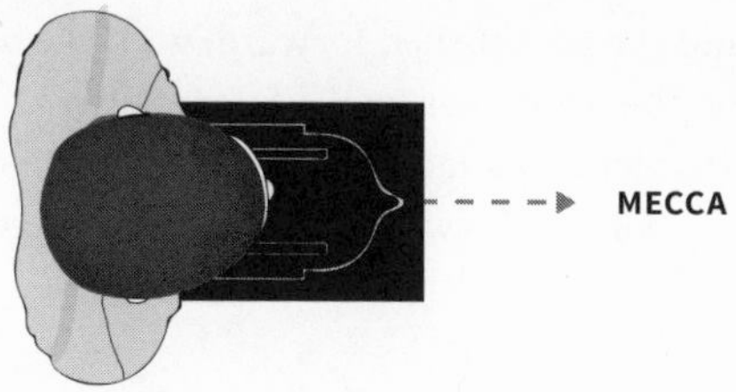

Figure 5: Person Praying Facing the Prayer Direction (Qiblah)

Covering Appropriately

For the prayer, God ﷻ has commanded that Muslims cover their bodies in a particular manner. This manner differs for men and women, as God has fashioned their bodies differently. For men, the minimum that has to be covered is the area between the navel and the knees. For women, the face, hands, and soles of the feet can be exposed, but the rest of the body must be covered in prayer (this includes the arms, legs, torso, head, and the top of the feet), even when all alone.

Now, with an understanding of the proper preparation for the prayer, we will move on to the prayer itself.

THE FIVE DAILY PRAYERS

It is a requirement (*farḍ*) for every morally accountable Muslim to perform five prayers (*ṣalāh*) daily. The required daily prayers have specified times, as well as specified lengths and contents. Every ritual prayer is composed of a specific set of actions, performed in a particular sequence repeated multiple times throughout the prayer. The specific set of actions makes up a **prayer-unit (*rakʿah*)**.

There are four positions in the ritual prayer (*ṣalāh*), each present in the prayer-unit (*rakʿah*):

1. **Standing** straight, facing the prayer direction (*qiblah*).
2. **Bowing** (***rukūʿ***): bending at the waist and resting the palms above the knees, to make the back parallel to the ground, as much as one can.
3. **Prostration** (***sujūd***): placing the forehead and nose to the ground, palms resting on the ground on either side of the shoulders, and the toes turned forward, with the balls of the feet placed on the ground as well.
4. **Sitting** (***julūs***) with the feet tucked beneath the buttocks and the knees pointed forward, with the palms gently resting upon them.

During each of these positions, one recites Quran or says a certain Arabic supplication (*duʿāʾ*) or invocation, depending on where in the prayer-unit (*rakʿah*) the position falls.

In order to perform the prayer (*ṣalāh*), you will have to memorize a number of supplications, invocations, and chapters (*sūrahs*) from the Quran in the original Arabic. The prayers and invocations are included below, with their transliterations, to help you memorize them. This book also contains an appendix of short chapters from the Quran to memorize and recite in prayer. In a short amount of time, God willing, you will become very comfortable with reciting these pieces from memory.

The Prayer-Unit (Rakʿah)

The instructions below are for a basic prayer-unit (*rakʿah*), the building block of every prayer (*ṣalāh*). Depending on the specific prayer you are performing, you will perform two, three, or four prayer-units—with some additions at various points in the prayer. We will discuss these additions after describing the basic structure of the prayer-unit.

Before starting a prayer-unit (*rakʿah*), you must first begin the prayer (*ṣalāh*) by raising your hands from your sides to the height of your shoulders, palms down, and saying, aloud, the opening proclamation, *Allāhu akbar* (God is greater), which marks entry into the sanctified state of the prayer. Do this while consciously intending to perform the particular prayer that you are about to pray.

Then, to perform the prayer-unit:

1. Stand straight, hands folded above your navel, right over left.[12]

12. Actually, the dominant opinion within the Mālikī school of law (*madhhab*) is to place the hands at the sides, similar to the standing position after coming up from bowing position.

2. In this position, recite, in Arabic, the first chapter of the Quran, "The Opening" (*al-Fātiḥah*).

CHAPTER 1: THE OPENING (AL-FĀTIḤAH)	
Bismil-lāhir -Raḥmānir-Raḥīm	*In the name of God, the Lord of Mercy, the Giver of Mercy*
Alḥamdu lillāhi Rabbil-ʿālamīn	Praise belongs to God, Lord of the Worlds,
Arraḥmānir-Raḥīm	the Lord of Mercy, the Giver of Mercy,
Māliki Yawmid-Dīn	Master of the Day of Judgment.
Iyyāka naʿbudu wa 'Iyyāka nastaʿīn	It is You we worship; it is You we ask for Help.
Ihdinaṣ-ṣirāṭal-mustaqīm	Guide us to the straight path:
Ṣirāṭal-ladhīna 'anʿamta ʿalayhim ghayril-maghḍūbi ʿalayhim wa laḍ-ḍāallīn.	the path of those You have blessed, those who incur no anger and who have not gone astray.

3. Finally, close the supplication it contains by saying *Āmīn* (Amen).
4. Next, say the proclamation, ***Allāhu akbar*** (God is greater), while transitioning to the bowing (*rukūʿ*) position. Once in bowing position, silently say ***Subḥāna Rabbil-ʿaẓīm*** (Glorified is my Lord, the Magnificent),[13] three times.
5. Next, transition from the bowing position back to standing straight a second time, and say, ***Samiʿ-Allahu liman ḥamidah*** (God listens to those who praise Him). Then standing

The reason the minority position of folding the hands is presented here is that most people are unaware of the dominant position of the school. This may lead people who are ignorant of this valid position to approach others to "correct" them. Because this lack of awareness is so widespread, it may be wisest for beginners to follow the minority opinion, which is also valid (and is, in fact, the dominant opinion in other schools). This will help new Muslims avoid becoming involved in complex discussions of legal philosophy which are likely beyond the scope of everyone involved. It is important, however, to be aware of this position, and to understand the degree of verification it has undergone—having been inspected and approved by countless scholars over the centuries—to become the dominant position of the school.

13. When referring to the prayer (*ṣalāh*), to recite something *silently* means to recite it so that you cannot hear your own voice (but you must still move your lips). To recite *aloud* is to recite a little louder than what would be just loud enough for you to hear your own voice.

straight, hands resting at the sides, say, ***Rabbanā lakkal-ḥamd*** (Our Lord, praise is yours alone).

6. Next, again proclaim, ***Allāhu akbar*** (God is greater), and transition to the prostration (*sujūd*) position. In prostration, silently say, three times, ***Subḥāna Rabbil-aʿlā*** (Glorified is my Lord, the Exalted).
7. Then, move to the sitting position, say again, ***Allāhu akbar*** (God is greater). In the sitting position, say, ***Rabb-ighfirlī war-ḥamnī*** (My Lord, forgive me and have mercy on me).
8. Then, while saying again, ***Allāhu akbar*** (God is greater), return to the prostration position and repeat the same invocation. This completes one prayer-unit (*rakʿah*).

To begin the next prayer-unit, say ***Allāhu akbar*** (God is greater) and return to the standing position: you are now in the next prayer unit.

Additions to the Basic Prayer-Unit (Rakʿah)

Prayers (*ṣalāh*) vary in length from two to four prayer-units (*rakʿahs*). Depending on which prayer-unit you are performing, you must add certain verses or supplications to the steps of the basic pattern. There are three types of addition:

a. In the first two prayer-units (*rakʿahs*) of any prayer (*ṣalāh*), after you recite "The Opening" (*al-Fātiḥah*) and say *Āmīn* (steps 2 and 3 above), you recite an additional selection of your choosing from the Quran. This recitation is done in the standing position, before moving to the next position (step 4). Remember that additional verses are recited only in the first two prayer-units of a prayer; in a third or fourth prayer-unit, only "The Opening" is recited.
b. In the second prayer-unit (*rakʿah*), when you rise from the second prostration (step 8), this time, instead of standing up for the next prayer-unit, proceed to the sitting position (*julūs*). At this sitting, called the **middle sitting**, you recite the **Testimonial Invocation (*at-Tashahhud*)**.

TESTIMONIAL INVOCATION (AT-TASHAHHUD)	
at-taḥiyyātu lil-lāh,	All salutations of authority belong to God;
az-zākiyātu lil-lāh,	All righteous actions are for God;
aṭ-ṭayyibātuṣ-ṣalawātu lil-lāh;	All good speech and the daily prayers are for God.
as-salāmu ʿalayka ayyuhan-nabiyyu wa raḥmatul-lāhi wa barakātuh; as-salāmu ʿalaynā wa ʿalā ʿibādil-lāhiṣ-ṣāliḥīn;	Peace be upon you, O Prophet, with the mercy of God and His blessings. Peace be upon us and upon all the righteous servants of God.
ash-hadu al-lā ilāha ill-Āllāh waḥdahu lā sharīka lah,	I bear witness that there is nothing worthy of worship except God, He has no partner,
wa ash-hadu anna Muḥammadan ʿabduhu wa rasūluhu	and I bear witness that Muḥammad is His servant and messenger.

c. In the last prayer-unit (*rakʿah*) of any prayer (*ṣalāh*) (for a two prayer-unit prayer, the second prayer-unit is the last), you will rise from the second prostration (step 8) and proceed to the sitting position (*julūs*). At this sitting, called the **final sitting**, you say the Testimonial Invocation, above, and then add the **Abrahamic Prayer** (***aṣ-Ṣalāh al-Ibrāhīmīyyah***).

ABRAHAMIC PRAYER (AṢ-ṢALĀH AL-IBRĀHĪMĪYYAH)	
Allāhumma ṣalli ʿalā Muḥammadin wa ʿalā āli Muhammad, kamā ṣallayta ʿalā Ibrāhīm wa ʿalā āli Ibrāhīm.	O God: Send blessings upon Muhammad and the family of Muhammad, as you sent blessings upon Abraham and the family of Abraham.
wa bārik ʿalā Muḥammadin wa ʿalā āli Muḥammad, kamā bārakta ʿalā Ibrāhīm wa ʿalā āli Ibrāhīm.	O God: Bless Muhammad and the family of Muhammad, as you blessed Abraham and the family of Abraham.
fil ʿālamīn innaka Ḥamīdun Majīd.	In all the worlds, surely, You are the Praised, the All-Glorious.

Ending the Prayer

After the last prayer-unit (*rakʿah*), after you finish reciting the Abrahamic Prayer (*aṣ-Ṣalāh al-Ibrāhīmīyyah*) in the sitting position, you conclude the prayer (*ṣalāh*) by turning your head to the right, then the left, and after each turn saying the greeting of peace (*salām*), ***as-salāmu ʿalaykum wa raḥmat Allāh***.[14]

The Prayer Positions

ENTERING THE PRAYER

Raise your hands from your sides to the height of your shoulders, palms down, and say, aloud, the opening proclamation, *Allāhu akbar* (God is greater).

STANDING

Stand straight, with feet about shoulder width part with your hands folded above your navel, right over left.

After rising from bowing, stand straight, resting your hands at your sides.

14. It is common to hear other variations of the greeting of peace (*salām*) used to conclude the prayer.

BOWING (*RUKŪʿ*)

Bend at the waist and place your hands on your knees, elbows out, keeping your back straight and your head in line with your body; do not tilt it upwards or downwards.

PROSTRATION (*SUJŪD*)

Place your hands, forehead, nose, knees, and the balls of your feet against the ground. Men should have a moderate amount of space between the stomach and thighs, and the elbows should be slightly spread. Women should bring the chest towards the thighs and bring the elbows in towards the sides.

SITTING (*JULŪS*)

Between prostrations: Place the hands over the knees.

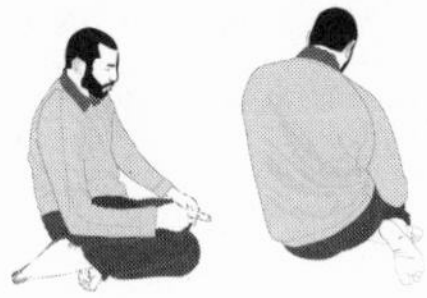

In the Middle and Final Sitting: Tuck the left leg under the right shin; keep the thumb and index finger of the right hand straight while folding the other three fingers; place the left hand over the left knee.

ENDING THE PRAYER

Conclude the prayer (*ṣalāh*) by turning your head to the right, then the left, and with each turn say the greeting of peace (*salām*), ***as-salāmu ʿalaykum wa raḥmat Allāh***.

A Two Unit Prayer

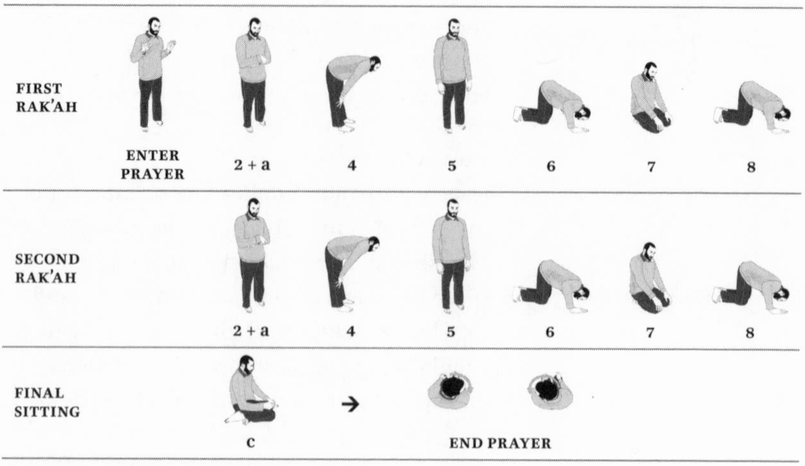

A Three Unit Prayer

A Four Unit Prayer

Note: The letters and numbers in these diagrams refer to the actions detailed on pages 56–59.

The Times and Lengths

There are three things you should know about every prayer (*ṣalāh*): its timeframe, its length (i.e., how many prayer-units (*rakʿahs*) it contains), and whether the passages of Quran in the first two prayer-units are recited silently or aloud.[15] (If a prayer is longer than two prayer-units, Quran recitation after the first two prayer-units is always silent.)

The timeframe for a prayer is the period of time within which you must perform the prayer—neither before it, nor after it. Although the vast majority of Muslims depend on calculated prayer times available online and at local mosques, these times are based on the position of the sun in relation to the earth, as described below.

Now we will look at the five daily ritual prayers (*ṣalāh*) individually.

The first prayer is the ***Ẓuhr*** **(Midday) Prayer**. Its timeframe begins when the sun moves past the zenith. It must be performed before the entry time for the next prayer,[16] the *ʿAṣr* (Afternoon) prayer. The ***Ẓuhr*** Prayer consists of four prayer-units (*rakʿahs*), in each of which the Quran is recited *silently.* Since it is four prayer-units long, the second prayer-unit will have a middle sitting in which the Testimonial Invocation is recited, and in the last prayer-unit, in the final sitting, you will recite both the Testimonial Invocation and the Abrahamic Prayer.

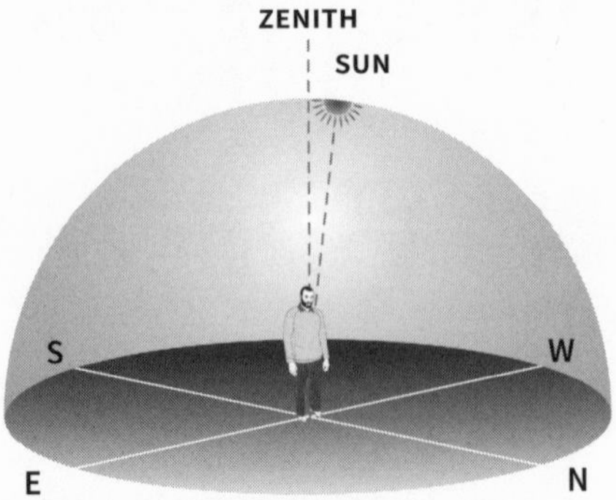

Figure 6: Timeframe for *Ẓuhr* (Midday) Prayer begins when the sun moves past the zenith.

15. The rules given here as to reciting the Quran aloud or silently apply if you are praying alone or if you are the prayer-leader (*imām*) leading a congregational prayer. For following along in a congregation, see below.

16. It is common to use the phrase "the prayer time has *entered*" to indicate that the timeframe for a prayer has begun.

Next, when the sun is at the position that makes an object's shadow equal to its own length,[17] the timeframe for the *ʿAṣr* **(Afternoon) Prayer** begins. Its timeframe ends when the disc of the sun touches the western horizon, so it must be prayed before then. It is otherwise identical to the *Ẓuhr* (Midday) Prayer in length and in silent Quran recitation.

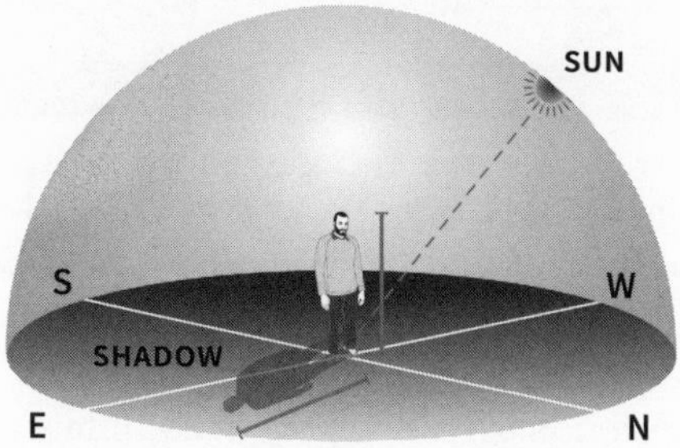

Figure 7: The end of the timeframe for *Ẓuhr* (Midday) and the beginning of *ʿAṣr* (Afternoon) is when the sun is at the position that makes an object's shadow equal to the sum of its length and the length of its shadow at the zenith.

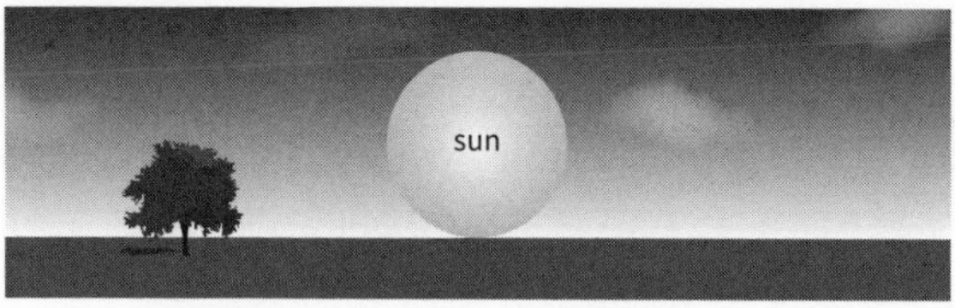

Figure 8: The end of the timeframe for *Aṣr* (Afternoon) is when the the disc of the sun touches the western horizon.

The timeframe for the ***Maghrib*** **(Sunset) Prayer** begins when the disc of the sun falls completely below the horizon and the eastern horizon grays. For this prayer, you should perform this prayer as soon as the timeframe begins, taking only the time needed to prepare for the prayer and perform it. It consists of three prayer-units (*rakʿahs*): In the first two, the Quran is recited aloud. Since it is three prayer-units long, the second unit ends with the Testimonial Invocation (a middle sitting), and the third and last ends

17. To be accurate, one must add the residual shadow length, which is the length of the shadow of an object with the sun at its zenith.

with a final sitting and recitation of both the Testimonial Invocation and the Abrahamic Prayer.

Figure 9: The timeframe for the *Maghrib* (Sunset) Prayer begins when the disc of the sun falls completely below the horizon.

Next, when the western horizon loses the reddish hue of twilight, even if some white twilight remains, the timeframe for the ***ʿĪshā'* (Night) Prayer** begins. One must perform it before light begins to appear along the eastern horizon—the time of the *Fajr* (Dawn) Prayer. The *ʿĪshā'* Prayer is four prayer-units (*rakʿahs*) long. In the first two units, the Quran is recited aloud. Otherwise, the pattern of sitting and invocating follows that of the *Ẓuhr* (Midday) Prayer.

The timeframe for the ***Fajr* (Dawn) Prayer** starts when light begins to appear along the eastern horizon. It must be performed before sunrise, when the disc of the sun begins to appear above the horizon. It is composed of two prayer-units (*rakʿahs*), in both of which Quran is recited aloud in the first standing of a prayer-unit. Since it is composed of only two prayer-units, the sitting after the second prayer-unit is the final sitting, and so you recite both the Testimonial Invocation and the Abrahamic Prayer.[18]

Figure 10: The *Fajr* (Dawn) Prayer must be performed before sunrise, when the disc of the sun begins to appear above the horizon.

18. The Dawn (*Fajr*) Prayer also has an additional supplication, recited just before bowing (*rukūʿ*), called the *Qunūt*. It is included in the appendices at the end of the book. Because it is a recommended act, if omitted, it does not invalidate the prayer.

NAME	UNITS	RECITATION OF 1ST TWO RAKʿAHS	BEGIN TIME	END TIME
Fajr	2	Aloud	Break of dawn	Start of sunrise
Ẓuhr	4	Silent	Sun moves past zenith	Shadow=length of object
ʿAṣr	4	Silent	Shadow=length of object	Start of sunset
Maghrib	3	Aloud	End of sunset	Time to prepare & perform
ʿĪshā'	4	Aloud	Red twilight disappears	Break of dawn

Table 3: The Five Daily Prayers. Recite al-Fātiḥah + Selection of Quran in first two prayer units of every prayer

The Prayer Call (Adhān) and Call to Rise (Iqāmah)

The **Prayer Call** (***Adhān***) is a series of invocations, in Arabic, that a designated person (the *muezzin*) calls out loudly in a chant-like fashion. It has the dual purpose of announcing the beginning of a new prayer time and calling believers to congregate for the prayer (*ṣalāh*). It is common to see it called at a mosque, but it is commendable (*mustaḥab*) to give the call whenever a group of believers is present (e.g., in a home). After the Prayer Call, a period of time is allotted to allow believers to perform *wuḍū'* (ritual washing) and congregate for the prayer. The Prayer Call is:

THE PRAYER CALL (*ADHĀN*)	
Allāhu akbar (Four times)	God is greater! (Four times)
Ash-hadu al-lā ilāha illā-llāh (Twice)	I testify that there is nothing worthy of worship except God. (Twice)
Ash-hadu anna Muḥammad-ar-rasūl-ullāh (Twice)	I testify that Muhammad is the messenger of God. (Twice)
Ḥayya ʿalāṣ-ṣalāh (Twice)	Hasten to the prayer! (Twice)
Ḥayyah ʿalā-l-falāḥ (Twice)	Hasten to success! (Twice)
Allāhu akbar (Twice)	God is greater! (Twice)
Lā ilāha illā-llāh	There is nothing worthy of worship except God.

When it is time to begin the prayer (*ṣalāh*), the **Call to Rise (*Iqāmah*)** is given, telling believers to rise and line up for the prayer (*ṣalāh*). The Call to Rise (*Iqāmah*) is given for every required (*farḍ*) prayer, regardless of where it is performed and how many people are praying. Even someone praying a required prayer at home alone should say the Call to Rise before starting the prayer—that is, it is a commendable (*mustaḥab*) act.

The Call to Rise (*Iqāmah)* is similar in content to the Prayer Call (*Adhān*), but it varies in the number of repetitions and includes one additional statement. It is:

CALL TO RISE (*IQĀMAH*)	
Allāhu akbar (Twice)	God is greater! (Twice)
Ash-hadu al-lā ilāha illā-llāh	I testify that there is nothing worthy of worship except God.
Ash-hadu anna Muḥammad-ar-rasūl-ullāh	I testify that Muhammad is the messenger of God.
Ḥayya ʿalāṣ-ṣalāh, Ḥayyah ʿalā-l-falāḥ, qad qāmatiṣ- ṣalāh	Hasten to the prayer! Hasten to success! The prayer is starting.
Allāhu akbar (Twice)	God is greater! (Twice)
Lā ilāha illā-llāh	There is nothing worthy of worship except God.

During the Prayer

Once you begin the ritual prayer (*ṣalāh*), you enter into a sanctified state, communing with the Divine and standing before God ﷻ. Because of the sanctity of the act, you must perform it in a state of ritual purity, and you must preserve the sanctity of the prayer throughout its performance. Acts that violate the sanctity of the prayer, and thus invalidate it, include the following:

1. Intentional extraneous speech
2. Missing an essential component of the prayer[19]

19. In brief, the essential components of the prayer are: (i) standing and saying the opening proclamation while intending to perform the particular prayer; (ii) performing the prayer positions properly, coming to complete bodily stillness at each, and performing them in the proper order: standing, bowing (*rukūʿ*), rising back to a standing position, prostrating (*sujūd*), sitting, and then prostrating again; (iii) concluding the prayer from the sitting position by saying the greeting of peace (*salām*). Distinguishing between the essential components, the prophetic practices (*sunnahs*), and the commendable acts, and what to do

3. Violating one's ritual purity
4. Audible laughter
5. Swallowing anything (e.g., regurgitated food, large food particle in mouth, etc.)

Any of these will violate the sanctity of the prayer, and the prayer will have to be started anew.

THE CONGREGATIONAL (*JAMĀʿAH*) PRAYER

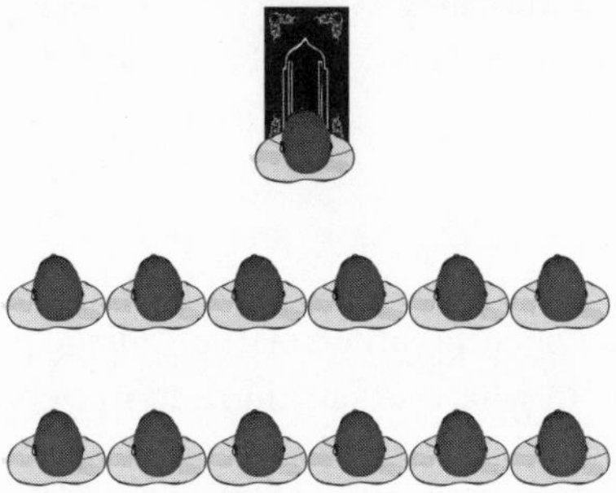

Figure 11: Congregation Praying Behind a Prayer Leader (*imām*)

The Prophet Muhammad ﷺ taught us that the reward for praying in a congregation (*jamāʿah*) is twenty-seven times greater than the reward for praying alone. For this reason, Muslims exert effort to pray in a congregation, whether by going to the mosque, meeting with other Muslims, or waiting for a fellow believer to come along.

In a congregational prayer, one morally accountable male is designated the **prayer leader** (***imām***). The prayer leader conducts the prayer, standing in front, with the other worshippers standing behind him, shoulder to shoulder in horizontal rows, as they face the prayer direction (*qiblah*). Those following the prayer leader transition to the next prayer position only *after* the prayer leader has done so (even if they have finished a recitation before him and even if they haven't finished their own recitation). Also, followers should recite silently to themselves when the prayer leader is silently

if those are omitted, are beyond the scope of this overview. For a more detailed exposition, see the forthcoming publication from Sandala Publications, *The Helping Guide*, by Shaykh Hamza Yusuf.

reciting Quran. For prayer-units in which the Quran is recited aloud, the followers listen to the prayer leader's recitation. The only other difference from praying alone is that, when transitioning to the second erect standing of a prayer-unit, after the prayer leader says *Samiʿ -Allahu liman ḥamidah* (God listens to those who praise Him), the follower does not say it himself, but goes directly to the response, saying *Rabbanā lakkal-ḥamd* (Our Lord, praise is yours alone).

There are, of course, situations in which only women gather to pray. In those situations, when a there are no men to lead a congregation, according to some schools of Islamic law (although not the Mālikī school), a woman may be designated as the prayer leader (*imām*) for a group of women. The format of such a prayer would be the same as described above, except that the woman leading the prayer stands in the middle of the first row of congregants.

Joining Late

If you come upon a congregation (*jamāʿah*) that has already started to perform a prayer, say the opening proclamation, *Allahu akbar* (God is greater), join the congregation in whatever position and prayer-unit they are in, and follow the prayer leader (*imām*) in whatever he does afterwards. If you join the congregation before the end of the bowing position of a prayer-unit (*rakʿah*), the prayer-unit counts towards the total needed for the prayer. If you come in after that point, you should still follow the prayer leader in the rest of that prayer-unit, although it will not count towards the total needed for that prayer. After the prayer leader concludes the prayer with the greeting of peace (*salām*), you would rise and make up the leftover prayer-units to complete the total needed.

PRAYER AND TRAVEL

Because God ﷻ desires to lighten the burden upon His servants, He has given certain allowances to be made in particular circumstances. Among these dispensations is the alteration of the length and timing of the ritual prayer (*ṣalāh*) while traveling.

The definition of travel in Islamic law (*sharīʿah*) is to journey a distance of at least 48 miles (77.25 kilometers) from the limits of your city of residence. When you travel that far, certain divine allowances with respect to praying and fasting apply. Because this pertains to devotional acts that are ritual, they still apply in our times, even though travel has become somewhat easier than in the time of the Prophet. As it pertains to prayer, traveling is considered to have two parts: the journey to the destination, and the time spent at the destination.

Shortening the Prayer

When you are traveling farther than the distance noted above, you should shorten the four prayer-unit (*rakʿah*) prayers (the *Ẓuhr* (Midday), *ʿAṣr* (Afternoon), and *ʿĪshāʾ* (Night) prayers) to two prayer-units. The *Fajr* (Dawn) and *Maghrib* (Sunset) prayers remain the same length.

Joining the Prayers Together

Another allowance applies only to the journey itself—that is, to the time when you are actually traveling between your point of origin and your destination. During this time, you are allowed to join certain prayers together, either by delaying a prayer or by praying it earlier.

There are two pairings of prayers with shared timeframes: the *Ẓuhr* (Midday) and *ʿAṣr* (Afternoon) prayers share a timeframe, and the *Maghrib* (Sunset) and *ʿĪshāʾ* (Night) prayers share one. The *Ẓuhr* (Midday) and *Maghrib* (Sunset) prayers may be delayed to the next prayer time, so that you may pray the *Ẓuhr* and *ʿAṣr* (Afternoon) prayers during the timeframe for the *ʿAṣr* prayer, and the *Maghrib* and *ʿĪshāʾ* (Night) prayers during the time for the *ʿĪshāʾ* prayer. Likewise, the *ʿAṣr* (Afternoon) and *ʿĪshāʾ* (Night) prayers may be brought forward, so that you may pray the *Ẓuhr* and *ʿAṣr* prayers during the *Ẓuhr* (Midday) timeframe (as long as you will still be on the journey until *Maghrib* (Sunset)), or the *Maghrib* and *ʿĪshāʾ* prayers during the *Maghrib* (Sunset) timeframe (as long as you will still be on the journey until *Fajr* (Dawn)).

Upon Arrival

Once you have arrived at your intended destination, you should shorten the prayers in the manner mentioned above but pray each in its own prayer time—delaying or bringing prayers forward does not take place.[20] The time spent traveling away from home also affects the divine allowance for shortening prayers. If you intend on staying at the destination for less than the duration of twenty prayers (four days' worth of prayers), you can shorten

20. Another school of law (*madhhab*), the Shāfiʿī school, does permit joining prayers even after arriving at your destination. The position above, like the rest of the material here, is based on the Mālikī school.

the prayers for your entire stay. However, if you intend on staying there for more than the duration of twenty prayers, you must begin to pray the full lengths of the prayers upon arriving at your destination.

THE SPIRITUAL DIMENSION OF PRAYER (*ṢALĀH*)

The prayer (*ṣalāh*) combines spoken words and bodily movements, but its ultimate purpose is to alter your soul. The movements are essential to the prayer, as are the words, but the true objective of the prayer is to develop the spiritual state of *worshipping*—sensing and expressing, with humility and awe, your absolute need for and gratitude to God ﷻ. The following spiritual insights, gifted to us by Imam Abū Ḥāmid al-Ghazzālī,[21] will aid you in adding the spiritual dimension of true submission to the words and movements of your prayer.

Perfecting Your Prayer (Ṣalāh)

Six qualities of your inner being must be nurtured in order to perfect the devotional act of the prayer (*ṣalāh*): concentration, comprehension, reverence, awe, hope, and shame. Each expresses a necessary component of your servanthood to God ﷻ; you should bring each quality to mind during the prayer, and in turn, each will be enhanced by the prayer itself.

A state of focused *concentration* means that your thoughts and feelings are not distracted from what you are doing and saying. This will protect you from heedless and distracted prayer, which, although it technically fulfills your obligation, bears no spiritual fruits.

Beyond being focused in your concentration, you must develop reflective *comprehension* of the words you are saying. This is more than simply learning the meaning of the Arabic words; it includes internalizing the magnitude of the words you utter.

In addition to concentration and comprehension, you should say the invocations of prayer with a sense of *reverence* for the One before Whom you stand, God Almighty. To take it further, you must develop *awe*—a type of fear brought about by a sense of the majesty of God. Alongside awe, you should

21. Imam Abū Ḥāmid al-Ghazzālī (d. 1111 CE) is the most influential medieval Muslim theologian, philosopher, jurist, sage, and thinker. He was given the title "the Proof of Islam," and his most famous work, "The Revivication of the Islamic Disciplines," is considered the greatest work of its kind. In it, Imam al-Ghazzālī presented the clearest exposition we possess of the balance of the inward and outward dimensions of Islam.

have *hope* for His grace, mercy, forgiveness, and reward. Lastly, aware of your shortcomings and sins, you should feel a sense of *shame* before your Lord.

Spiritual Reflections on the Prayer (Ṣalāh)

Each of the outward acts of prayer (*ṣalāh*) has symbolic meaning that you should reflect on to further develop your spiritual state within the prayer.

When you hear the Prayer Call (*Adhān*), you are in effect being summoned by God ﷻ. You should reflect on the willingness with which you respond to His call, and in doing so, prepare for the greatest of His calls, when we are all resurrected on the Day of Judgment to stand before Him.

When you purify the things around you in progressively closer layers—the area of prayer, your clothes, and finally, through *wuḍū'* (ritual washing), your person—reflect on what is innermost, the state of your soul, and be reminded of its need for inner cultivation and refinement.

When you face the prayer direction (*qiblah*), turning away from all other directions, remind yourself of the need to commit yourself to God, pulling your heart away from all other distractions and attachments.

When you stand in prayer, remember your need to be upright in character.

When you bow, renew your sense of submission and humility before God Almighty. The invocations in this position assist you in confirming this reality in your soul.

When you perform prostration (*sujūd*), realize that this is the supreme symbol of submission and the point in prayer at which you are closest to God ﷻ. In it, you bring the noblest part of your body, your face, to the lowest of places, the earth. When doing so, reflect on your humility before God and your immeasurable debt to Him. The invocations will help you internalize this reality. Then, while still in this position, hope for the mercy of God, for it descends on those who are humble.

When you are in the sitting position and recite the Testimonial Invocation (*at-Tashahhud*), reflect on its meanings and the reality they describe. Bring to the forefront of your mind that all you do is for God ﷻ, and be aware of Prophet Muhammad ﷺ as you send blessings (*ṣalawāt*) upon him.

Conclude the prayer (*ṣalāh*) with a sense of gratitude to God ﷻ for having enabled you to obey Him, and remorse for the inherent deficiencies we suffer in our attempts to concentrate, comprehend, show reverence and awe, have hope, and feel a sense of shame before God.

3. PURIFYING ALMS (*ZAKĀH*)

The third pillar of practicing Islam is the practice of giving **purifying alms (*zakāh*)**. This is a required (*farḍ*) tax on certain types of wealth and assets that must be distributed to the needy. Behind the requirement for giving the purifying alms (*zakāh*) are two important principles.

First, members of society have a moral responsibility to provide for the less fortunate. The needy have a right to part of the wealth present in their society, even if God ﷻ has allotted it to others.

Second, society's money has become tainted through greed, corruption, and theft, and, as a result, its spiritual blessing is decreased. The only means to purify the entire mass of wealth is to pay out the purifying alms (*zakāh*) to its rightful recipients.

Although we will not provide a thorough legal examination of the purifying alms (*zakāh*), it is important to understand the central concepts behind it, as that will enhance your understanding of this pillar of our faith.

THE LIABILITY MINIMUM AND RATE

Not all members of a society are expected to pay the purifying alms (*zakāh*). Only those whose wealth is greater than the **liability minimum** are legally obligated to pay the purifying alms. The liability minimum was set by Prophet Muhammad ﷺ based on the units of currency of his society. Thus, the liability minimum is an amount of wealth and assets equivalent in value to 85 grams of pure gold or 595 grams of silver.

For a Muslim's wealth to be liable to the purifying alms (*zakāh*), he or she must have met the liability minimum for one full lunar-year—if at any point in the year your wealth falls below the liability minimum, no purifying alms is owed. (In some Muslim societies, the liability minimum is used as a sort of assessment of the poverty line.)

In pre-modern societies, monetary wealth consisted of gold and silver pieces, but in our times it is our cash, bank account balances, stocks, mutual funds, and other monetary equivalents. A portion of this wealth—two-and-a-half percent (one-fortieth)—is owed as purifying alms (*zakāh*). Note that not all of our income is subject to this tax: only the amount of accumulated wealth that goes unused for a full year. The concept is that a small contribution from many members of society is all it will take to bring about a type of economic balance and provide temporary relief for the poor.

ELIGIBLE RECIPIENTS

There are eight categories of people that are eligible to receive the money from another's purifying alms (*zakāh*):

1. *The indigent*: those who are in imminent danger of dying from lack of resources.
2. *The poor*: those below the poverty line but not in danger of dying. Since they do not have enough to provide for their needs for the next year, dying from lack of resources is still a possibility for them.
3. *Those struggling for the cause of God*: people working to promote God's cause, including those justly fighting to protect the innocent or free the oppressed.
4. *Slaves*: Although it is less common today, purchasing the freedom of a slave is a highly regarded act in Islam, worthy of immense reward from God. Modern forms of slavery do exist, and Islam provides many incentives to eliminate them.
5. *Purifying alms distributors*: the administrators and employees needed to distribute the collected wealth to its rightful recipients. In some Muslim societies, there was a centralized system of collecting and distributing the purifying alms (*zakāh*), and its workers were paid from a portion of the alms.
6. *Debtors*: those with legitimate debts who are not able to pay them off with their own assets.
7. *Those whose hearts are to be won over*: This category includes recent converts or those for whom conversion to Islam is hoped. Through it, Islam recognizes the immense courage needed to face the challenge of beginning anew. Gifts to a new or potential convert, whether to alleviate an existing burden or simply to bring them joy, are seen as making a bit easier this major transition of mind, body, and soul, strengthening that person's bond with the faith itself.
8. *Stranded travelers*: those who have lost access to their wealth and are therefore unable to return home.

In cultures where capitalism has become excessive and greed has created perhaps the most disproportionate distribution of wealth our world has ever seen, the purifying alms (*zakāh*) is especially needed. God ﷻ has given us the tools with which to better ourselves through helping others in these times; we need only to give of what God has given in the first place and to remember that nothing is truly ours.

4. FASTING RAMAḌĀN

The fourth pillar of practicing Islam is fasting the month of Ramaḍān. We will examine both the month of Ramaḍān and the particulars of the practice of fasting.

Ramaḍān is the ninth month of the Islamic calendar, which is a lunar calendar (see Chapter 7). As a natural phenomenon, lunar months vary in length, containing either twenty-nine or thirty days.

Methods to Identify the Start of Ramaḍān

A subject of much debate and controversy in recent times is the method of marking the start of Ramaḍān. There are a number of legally valid ways of doing so, and also a number of newer ways whose validity is a subject of much discussion. What is most important for you to understand is that these differences should not lead to disputes or divisions. Such disputes rarely lead to anything productive, and it is wise to avoid them altogether.

There are two parts to the question of when to commence the lunar month of Ramaḍān. The first is *how to sight the new crescent.* Muslim classical scholarship indicates that the crescent must be actually sighted (with the human eye) by two Muslims on the eve of the potential first day of Ramaḍān (i.e., the night after the 29th day of the eighth month). If it is sighted, which would happen at the time of sunset, that night and the next day are considered the first of Ramaḍān. If nothing is sighted, the previous month, called Shaʿban, continues to the maximum of thirty days, and the day after is the first of Ramaḍān.

With the advent of technology, some Muslims now consider scientific calculation to be a legitimate replacement for actual sighting. However, even the proponents of calculation fall into two different groups: those who commence based on the birth of the invisible new moon, and those who calculate when the moon would theoretically be visible to the human eye, regardless of whether or not it was actually sighted.

The second part of the question is how far (geographically) the implications of starting Ramaḍān reach, once a sighting is established. There are two legally valid sighting methods, according to classical Muslim jurists: global and regional. As implied by its name, the global sighting method states that a new crescent sighting anywhere in the world can be used to mark and conclude the month of Ramaḍān everywhere. In contrast, the regional method divides the world into regions, roughly based upon continents, and maintains that the new crescent must be sighted within one's own region to start Ramaḍān. Because the sighting of the moon depends upon varying natural phenomena, it is possible for the moon to be sighted in one region while being impossible to sight in another. So, with this method, different regions can legitimately start and conclude Ramaḍān on different days, as often happens in different parts of the Muslim world today.

The purpose of describing these methods is not to dizzy you with unnecessary details, but to prepare you for the inevitable pluralism that you will encounter within the Muslim community. Based on the different combinations of sighting methods and sighting distances, a community may decide to start and conclude the holy month in several different ways. What is important for you, as a new Muslim, is to avoid entering such technical discussions and disputes and to focus instead on the gifts that are forthcoming from the experience of fasting Ramaḍān.

Themes of Ramaḍān

Like most holy days and religious occasions, the month of Ramaḍān has a few central themes that define its spirit. It is the combination of these themes that leads to the full experience and benefit of the month.

Generosity in charity is the first of these themes. Being a time of self-deprivation and abstaining, Ramaḍān reminds us of what the less fortunate experience, and consequently impels us to come to their aid.

Another theme of Ramaḍān is an intensified level of *worship and devotional servitude to God* ﷻ. We are told that devotional acts performed on one particular night in the month of Ramaḍān, the **Night of Glory** (***Laylat al-Qadr***), are rewarded more than the same acts performed for a thousand months of ordinary time—but the exact date of this night is unknown! (For more information about the Night of Glory, see Chapter 7.)

Yet another central theme of Ramaḍān is *studying, reciting, and reflecting upon the Quran*. Muslims attempt to complete one entire reading of the Quran during the month. This intense focus on the word of God provides Muslims with a renewed clarity with which to guide their hearts and affairs throughout the year.

FASTING (*ṢAWM*)

How to Fast

Once the month of Ramaḍān has commenced, it is required (*farḍ*) that a Muslim fast it in its entirety. The legal rulings of fasting have three elements: the preparation for the fasting, the duration of the fast, and what the actual fasting entails.

In preparation for the fast, as for all devotional acts in Islam, a conscious intention is required (*farḍ*) at the outset of the act. A conscious intention to fast the month must be formulated the evening prior to the day of fasting. An intention at the beginning of the month, suffices for all of the fasts therein.[22] Without the conscious intention, the fast is invalid.

During Ramaḍān, a daily preparation for fasting is the **pre-dawn meal (*suḥūr*)**. This is to eat some food, even if just a small amount, before dawn's light strikes the horizon and the time of the fast enters. Although this is not required (*farḍ*), it is highly commendable (*mustaḥab*) and is considered an important prophetic practice (*sunnah*).

The duration of the daily fast is based on the position of the sun, and this correlates to the prayer (*ṣalāh*) times. The time of fasting begins when the dark night sky is broken by the first rays of dawn before sunrise—the time of the *Fajr* (Dawn) Prayer. Fasting ends, and the time to break the fast enters, when the entire disc of the sun falls below the horizon in complete sunset—the time of the *Maghrib* (Sunset) Prayer. At this time, it is a prophetic practice (*sunnah*) to break the fast with three dates, or even just one. If dates are not available, the prophetic practice is to break the fast with a drink of water. If neither is available, one can break the fast with something else. Another prophetic practice of breaking the fast is to *hasten to break it.* Once a Muslim is sure the time of the fast has ended, he or she should break the fast without unnecessary delay.

Fasting, according to the legal rulings, requires abstaining from: eating, drinking, sensual acts (that lead to release of pre-seminal fluid), and sexual relations.[23] Anything that reaches the stomach—even from the nose, ear, or eye, such as nosedrops—invalidates the fast. The inhalation of smoke (such as from cigarettes), or dense particles in the air, also invalidates the fast. Also, intentionally induced vomiting (as opposed to unintentional vomiting) invalidates the fast.

22. The exception to this is if the days of fasting Ramadan are interrupted, such as for a legitimate excuse. In the case of interruption, a renewal of the conscious intention is required at the outset of resuming the fast.

23. Sensual touch that would not lead to the release of pre-seminal fluid is disliked (*makrūh*).

The Spiritual Fast

In addition to the outward aspect of obeying God سبحانه وتعالى by abstaining from food, drink, and sexual relations, the fast has an inward, spiritual dimension. Fasting (*ṣawm*) is meant to weaken the ego (*nafs*), by depriving it of its nourishment—the fulfillment of its desires. Weakening the ego is essential to the work of self-purification. In essence, the spiritual fast is the real point of the physical one.

The internal dimension of fasting (*ṣawm*) comprises several elements. The first is to abstain from deliberately looking at things God has forbidden us to look at, as in looking desirously at the opposite gender. To lower the gaze is an essential component of the fast. The second element is to abstain from any kind of speech that would be displeasing to God: You must not lie, slander, backbite, or be rude or argumentative. Instead, you should preoccupy your tongue with invocation (*dhikr*) of God. Likewise, you should not listen approvingly to any such forbidden type of speech. Either speak out against it, or leave its presence.

In summary, although these vices are always forbidden (*ḥarām*), while you are fasting, you should work even harder to avoid them and to be righteous in your behavior. With the added spiritual serenity of fasting, you should find it easier to be kind to others, extending patience and forgiveness more readily. This inner purity and nearness to God سبحانه وتعالى are the intended results of fasting.

Exemptions from Fasting

Fasting is only required (*farḍ*) of Muslims who are morally accountable individuals and who are free of menstrual or postpartum bleeding at the beginning of a day's fast.

If you fulfill these prerequisites, you may break the fast for two broad categories of reasons: fear that your *health* will be harmed as a result of fasting, or *traveling* a distance of at least 48 miles—the same distance required to be permitted to shorten the prayer (*ṣalāh*).

Fear that one's health will be harmed applies to four general categories of people—the ill, the elderly, pregnant women, and breastfeeding mothers. The elderly, if they are frail and fear the fast would harm their health, may break the fast. The ill, if they fear that fasting will delay recovery or worsen their illness, may also break the fast. A genuine concern for actual harm must exist, however, as hardship and fatigue are intrinsic to fasting and are not in themselves a reason for exemption.

Pregnant women are given the same legal status with respect to fasting as those who are ill. Therefore, if a pregnant woman fears for her well-being, or for her child's, she should break her fast. There is still a debt owed to God, and at a later time, she must make up the days of which the fast was broken.

If a nursing mother fears excessive fatigue for herself or harm to her child, she too should break her fast. The difference between her and the pregnant woman is that the nursing mother must make up the missed days and also pay a minor expiation.

If you are either exempted from fasting, or are in a situation that, by Islamic law, prevents you from observing the fast (e.g., menstruation), you still owe the days of fast as a debt to God ﷻ and you must make them up by fasting an equal number of days, before the next Ramaḍān.[24] If the next Ramaḍān arrives before you have made up the owed days from the previous Ramaḍān, you also owe a **minor expiation** for each overdue day, in addition to fasting those days. The minor expiation consists of giving a poor person approximately 0.51 liters (based on measurements used by Prophet Muhammad ﷺ) of food, from the predominant staple of the community. For example, in some regions rice is the staple food, while in others it may be lentils or dried beans.

If a person intentionally breaks the fast and has no valid excuse, he or she owes the day of fasting, as well as a **major expiation** of either feeding sixty needy Muslims or fasting sixty days consecutively.[25]

Parting with Ramaḍān

Ramaḍān closes the way it began, with the sighting of the new crescent moon of the next month, Shawwal. The first day of Shawwal is the **Festival of Completing the Fast**, and it is thus forbidden (*ḥarām*) to fast on this day. Before the day of the Festival, it is a requirement (*farḍ*) upon every Muslim to pay the **Alms for Completing the Fast** (***Zakāt al-Fiṭr***). This is a gift, given to the needy, of a particular volume of food (roughly 2 liters, based on measurements used by Prophet Muhammad ﷺ).

For more information about Ramaḍān, see Chapter 7.

24. A terminally or chronically ill person, or a frail elderly person who does not regain the strength to fast, has no obligation to make up the fasting, because for them it is impossible.

25. The acts that necessitate a major expiation are intentionally eating, drinking, smoking, having intercourse, or ejaculation.

5. THE PILGRIMAGE (*ḤAJJ*)

The final pillar of practice in Islam is to perform the **pilgrimage** (***ḥajj***) to the Sacred House at the Sanctuary in Mecca at least once in your life,[26] if you are physically and financially able. The pilgrimage (*ḥajj*) is a convergence of three sacred things, each of which has become obscure to modern man.

The first is sacred time. With Ramaḍān we were exposed to sacred time: time favored by God ﷻ, into which He pours spiritual blessing and untold bounties. God selects these times: Fridays, Ramaḍān, the Night of Glory, the last third of the night, and many, many more.

The second thing that converges at the pilgrimage (*ḥajj*) is sacred space. Places that are honored and blessed by God ﷻ or His prophets can be of benefit to us through God's favor. The counting of a deed, good or bad, is multiplied in Mecca one-hundred thousand times. It is the Sanctuary; it is where we go to protect ourselves from God's wrath with God's mercy. "There is no escape from Him, except by fleeing to Him."

The third element that converges at the pilgrimage (*ḥajj*) is sacred ritual, acts whose outer forms are prescribed to us but whose inner realities are a secret to most. These sacred rituals, when performed in the sacred places in and around Mecca, during the sacred time set for the pilgrimage, constitute the Hajj.

A BRIEF LOOK

A detailed exposition of the legal aspects of the pilgrimage (*ḥajj*) is beyond the scope of this presentation. Instead, this section will try to give you some familiarity with the rite of the pilgrimage and, hopefully, an appreciation for it.

Traditionally, the pilgrimage (*ḥajj*) was literally the journey of a lifetime. Even today, in certain lands, the moment they are born, children are given bank accounts dedicated to saving up for the pilgrimage. All Muslims who are physically and financially capable of the pilgrimage must intend, plan on, and work towards performing it, rather than merely wishing or hoping for it to come about some day.

The sacred time during which one performs the pilgrimage (*ḥajj*) is the Month of Pilgrimage (*Dhul Ḥijjah*), the twelfth month of the Islamic calendar. If a Muslim who is physically and financially capable sets out on

26. Although the number of places imbued with spiritual blessing (*barakah*) are great, three places are generally considered the major sanctuaries of Islam: the Meccan Sanctuary, the Prophet's Mosque in Medina, and the Farther Mosque in Jerusalem.

the pilgrimage, he or she enters the **state of inviolability** (***iḥrām***) upon entering the greater zone of Mecca. Entering this state consists of performing a ritual bath (*ghusl*), forming a conscious intention to enter the state of inviolability to perform the pilgrimage, and for the men, putting on two white cloths, one covering the lower half of the body and the other, a shawl, worn over the shoulders. In this manner, princes and paupers stand side by side, indistinguishable by any worldly measure, reminded that their only value before God ﷻ lies in piety. While in the state of inviolability (*iḥrām*), the pilgrim may not harm any animals or insects, use foul language, show impatience, or disturb the sacred grounds of the Sanctuary of Mecca.

Figure 12: A Male Pilgrim in the Garb of Inviolability (*Iḥrām*)

The pilgrim then proceeds towards Mecca, and begins to say, repeatedly, the **Response of the Summoned** (***Talbiyah***):

> Here I am at Your service, O God! Here I am at Your service! Here I am at Your service! You have no partner! Here I am at Your service! Indeed, all praise and bounty are Yours, and all dominion. You have no partner!

This declaration of God's oneness and the pilgrim's active response to His call is the mantra of the pilgrimage (*ḥajj*). This is repeated until pilgrims reach the Sanctuary of Mecca, which encloses the Sacred House (*Kaʿbah*) built by Prophet Abraham (*Ibrāhīm*) ﷺ. In fact, when we examine both the sacred place and the sacred rituals of the pilgrimage, we find they were almost completely instituted and founded by Prophet Abraham ﷺ. The Sacred House was built by Prophet Abraham and his son, Prophet Ishmael (Ismāʿīl) ﷺ—an act that founded the city of Mecca itself, which was at the time a barren desert. Also, the call of God ﷻ to the pilgrimage itself came through the person of Prophet Abraham ﷺ, whom God instructed to call people to Mecca for the pilgrimage.

After arriving at the Sanctuary, the pilgrims perform **circling (*ṭawāf*)** around the Sacred House (*Kaʿbah*), making seven counter-clockwise circuits around the black cubic structure while in constant supplication and invocation. This ritual of circling (*ṭawāf*) was also instituted by Prophet Abraham ﷺ.

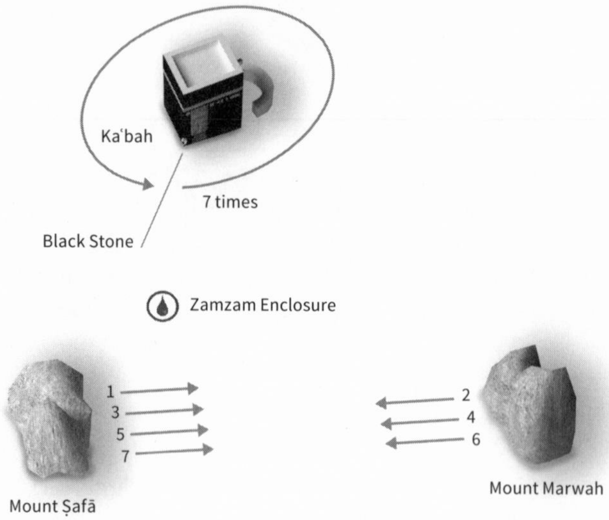

Figure 13: The Circling Around the Sacred House (Ka'bah)

Next, the pilgrim heads to the hill of Ṣafā. This is a hill upon which Lady Hagar, the mother of Prophet Ishmael ﷺ, once stood. The Prophet Abraham ﷺ was commanded by God ﷻ to leave them both in the barren valley of Mecca, a test of faith and reliance upon God. When the infant became thirsty, the concerned mother, whose trust in God never wavered, ran to Ṣafā and scanned the surroundings for any sign of water or help. She then ran back and forth between Ṣafā and another nearby hill, Marwah, looking for any help for her baby Ishmael. She did this seven times, until she heard the bubbling of water and saw that a spring had erupted from beneath the feet of the kicking babe. This well still runs today and is called the well of

Zamzam. Pilgrims drink from this sacred water, from which blessing, healing, and answered prayers are sought. The **Treading (*Saʿī*)**, a ritual of the pilgrimage based on the events of the life of Lady Hagar, consists of passing seven times between the two hills. This act is symbolic of a Muslim's soul, which should be filled with two complementary relationships with his Lord: fear of God's justice, and therefore, punishment; and hope for divine mercy, and therefore, reward.

Next is the single most important event of the pilgrimage (*ḥajj*)—the standing on the plains of **Mount ʿArafah** on the 9th day of the Month of Pilgrimage (*Dhul Ḥijjah*). On this day, on this mount on the outskirts of Mecca, all the pilgrims converge at once to stand before God ﷻ and beg for divine pardon and mercy. Millions of God's servants, clad in the simplest of garbs, each concerned only with their own shortcomings before God's immeasurable bounties, are given a preview of the scene of Judgment Day, when masses will be gathered, simply clad in the Muslim death shroud,[27] and all that can be hoped for is divine mercy. On this day on Mount ʿArafah, as tears of confession and hope pour forth, God promises the sincere repenter that He will, by His divine mercy, pardon every sin ever committed from birth until then. Now, the pilgrim has a fresh, new start on life.

From Mount ʿArafah the pilgrims move to a valley called Muzdalifah, where each pilgrim collects a group of small stones. After spending the night at Muzdalifah, the pilgrims move to the valley of Mina, which is home to the three **stoning pillars**. On this tenth day of the holy month, pilgrims pelt the largest stoning pillar seven times with the stones collected from Muzdalifah Valley. The first act after the great repentance of Mount ʿArafah is to repel the devil and proclaim him enemy number one. This act is also based on events in the life of Prophet Abraham ﷺ: When he obeyed God's command to sacrifice his son Ismāʿīl (Ishmael) ﷺ, the devil, under the guise of caring for the Prophet Abraham's family, worked to convince him to disobey God ﷻ. Prophet Abraham, in a display of his immense resolve and faith, remained unmoved by the devil's false pleas; God would care for his family. Instead, he pelted the devil away from him at three different places. The stoning pillars mark these places, and millions of Muslims reenact this display of faith every year.

Next, on the tenth day of the holy month, each pilgrim arranges the slaughter of a lamb, or a similar animal, in commemoration of an act of faith that Prophets Abraham and Ishmael ﷺ underwent. This is the day of the Festival of Sacrifice (*ʿĪd al-Aḍḥā*). The men also shave their heads (or trim

27. The death shroud of the Muslims is identical to the two white cloths of the pilgrimage (*ḥajj*).

their hair), perhaps symbolic of the purity of an infant, while women trim their hair. This act ends the state of inviolability (*iḥrām*) for the pilgrim, who continues to stone all the pillars for two more days.

The last event in the pilgrimage is the farewell circling (*ṭawāf*),[28] seven circuits around the Sacred House (*Kaʿbah*) that Prophet Abraham ﷺ built. After this, with strengthened faith and a renewed commitment to God ﷻ, the pilgrim returns home to infuse his life with servitude of God in preparation for the life to come.

SYMBOLISM OF THE PILGRIMAGE (*ḤAJJ*)

Much can be said of the spiritual dimension of the pilgrimage (*ḥajj*), which is full of deep rituals and constant devotional acts to God. A few concepts, extracted from narrations (*ḥadīths*), statements of prominent companions (*ṣaḥābah*), and scholarly commentary, provide a glimpse into the symbolism behind the event.

The Grand Covenant by which we declared our pledge to God and recognized His sovereignty is embodied on Earth by the **Black Stone**. A narration (*ḥadīth*) teaches us that the Black Stone is a heavenly stone, brought to Earth by the Archangel Gabriel (Jibrīl) and given to Prophet Abraham, who set it into the eastern corner of the Sacred House (*Kaʿbah*). Another teaching states that the Black Stone is to God what the ring on the right hand of a king was in some cultures: a place where we declare, again, our allegiance to God and assert His sovereignty over us. We come to God's house declaring, "Here I am at Your service, O God! ... Indeed, all praise and bounty are Yours, and all dominion." We come to the King, declaring His sovereignty in our lives, as if to say, "We honor the Grand Covenant we made before this life, O Mighty King!"

28. This is a recommended act, but it is not essential – omitting it does not make the pilgrimage (ḥajj) invalid.

6. OTHER COMPONENTS OF WORSHIP

All the acts of one's life can be infused with worship. In addition to the required five pillars of practice, there are optional devotional acts that help to bring the servant nearer to God ﷻ. These are called the **voluntary acts**. They are not required by God, but the reward for performing them is immense, and they make one's surrender more complete.

To help clarify the various levels of devotion to God, consider this famous narration (*ḥadīth*) of Prophet Muhammad ﷺ:

> God Almighty has said, "Whosoever shows enmity to an ally of Mine,[29] I shall be at war with him. My servant does not draw near to Me with anything more beloved to Me than the religious duties I have made required (*farḍ*) upon him, and My servant continues to draw near to Me with voluntary works so that I shall love him. When I love him, I am his hearing with which he hears, his seeing with which he sees, his hand with which he strikes, and his foot with which he walks. Were he to ask [something] of Me, I would surely give it to him, and were he to ask Me for refuge, I would surely grant it to him."

The hierarchy is thus established: first we must carry out our required (*farḍ*) devotions, and then we may draw ever nearer with voluntary acts until God ﷻ may grace us with His love. The previous sections elaborated upon the required (*farḍ*) acts of ritual worship. Now we will look at several voluntary acts of worship. Some of them are voluntary forms of the required pillars of devotion, while others are components of the required pillars performed independently.

VOLUNTARY FORMS OF THE PILLARS

For each of the pillars there exists a voluntary form of the act which a Muslim can opt to do in an attempt to receive the good grace of God ﷻ. Some of these have special times and manners of practice, while others are simply carried out whenever the opportunity presents itself.

29. A saint (*walī*), here rendered as an ally of God, is one whose purity of heart and righteousness of acts has granted him or her a close position with God, upon which God grants all the benefits listed in this narration (*ḥadīth*).

Voluntary Prayer (Ṣalāh)

This voluntary devotion has the same format as the required prayer (*ṣalāh*). There are a few types of the voluntary prayer worth noting here. These prayers are conjoined with the required (*farḍ*) prayers, either preceding them or following them. The table below outlines these prayers and their relationship to their corresponding required acts. Generally, these voluntary prayers are to be prayed silently.

VOLUNTARY PRAYER BEFORE	REQUIRED PRAYER	VOLUNTARY PRAYER AFTER
Two prayer-units	Fajr (Dawn)	None
Four prayer-units	*Ẓuhr* (Midday)	Two or four prayer-units
Four prayer-units	*ʿAṣr* (Afternoon)	None
None or two	*Maghrib* (Sunset)	Two or four prayer-units
	ʿĪshā' (Night)	Two, then one prayer-unit of the Even- and Odd-numbered (***Shafʿ* and *Witr***) Prayer

Table 4: Voluntary Prayers Conjoined with Required (*Farḍ*) Prayers

Although not obligatory, the ***Shafʿ* (Even-numbered) and *Witr* (Odd-numbered) prayer** is a highly emphasized prophetic practice (*sunnah*). It is performed by praying two prayer-units (*rakʿahs*)—the even-numbered—and closing out that prayer, and then praying a single prayer-unit—the odd-numbered. The Quranic recitation is aloud for both.

Another form of voluntary prayer is the **Tarawīḥ Prayer** of Ramaḍān. This special prayer is performed only during the holy month of Ramaḍān, after the *ʿĪshā'* (Night) Prayer. Also, on both of the Festivals (*ʿĪds*), there is the Festival Prayer, a two prayer-unit prayer that takes place in the morning. Both Festival prayers have the special status of a prophetic practice (*sunnah*). (For more information on these prayers, see Chapter 7.)

Lastly, the **Night Vigil Prayers (*Qiyām al-Layl*)** are perhaps the hallmark of those seriously desiring nearness to God ﷻ. Performed in the last half or third of the night, these voluntary prayers are performed at a time most beloved by God, for it is a time in which only those burning with the desire to draw nearer to Him would wake up to pray, and in which the heart and mind are at their clearest. The importance of these prayers increases even more during Ramaḍān.

Voluntary Fasting (Ṣawm)

There are a number of voluntary fasts with particular times. The 13th, 14th and 15th days of any lunar month are highly commendable (*mustaḥab*). Also, Mondays and Thursdays are blessed days to fast.

Additionally, certain days are especially good to observe by voluntary fasting. The tenth day of the first lunar month, Muharram, which is the day that Prophet Moses (Mūsā) عليه السلام split the Red Sea, saving the Children of Israel from Pharaoh, is a day on which fasting is commendable (*mustaḥab*). Also, for those who are not themselves pilgrims, fasting the first nine days of the Month of Pilgrimage (particularly the ninth, the day of standing on Mount ʿArafah) is commendable.

Charity (Ṣadaqah)

When it is voluntary and not required, the sharing of wealth with the needy is simply called **charity (*ṣadaqah*)**. This charity is given in excess of the requirement of purifying alms (*zakāh*) and can take many forms. In fact, Prophet Muhammad ﷺ has taught that it need not be financial in nature, and that "even a smile" can be rewarded as charity. In the Quran, God سبحانه وتعالى tells believers that for anyone who gives charity, He provides seventy times as much in return. While there are restrictions on who must give and who may receive purifying alms, voluntary charity permits believers to freely give to any cause they deem worthy of help.

The Lesser Pilgrimage (ʿUmrah)

At any time of the year, a Muslim may make a lesser pilgrimage (*ʿumrah*) to the Sanctuary of Mecca. The lesser pilgrimage is comprised of the first components of the pilgrimage (*ḥajj*). It begins with entering the state of inviolability (*iḥrām*), followed by the circling, and then the treading between the hills of Ṣafā and Marwah. It concludes with either shaving or trimming the hair to mark the exit out of the state of inviolability.

INDEPENDENT VOLUNTARY ACTS

These acts do not directly correspond to any required acts and might be viewed as components of the ritual prayer (*ṣalāh*) performed individually, in a focused and enhanced manner. Each of the two we will examine is absolutely essential to any Muslim's life as he or she strives to draw close to God ﷾ and to live a life infused with devotion to Him.

Supplication (Duʿā')

Your Lord says, "Call on Me and I will answer you." – Quran 40:60

Supplication (*duʿā'*) is a gift from God ﷾ by which Muslims can directly call upon Him, beseeching Him for any of their needs, whether worldly or spiritual. Unlike the prayer (*ṣalāh*), a formalized and structured ritual that must be in the Arabic language, your supplication can be in any language. However, there are particular etiquettes, detailed below, which make a supplication more likely to be fulfilled by God. These include a particular stance in which you should supplicate, special invocations with which you should begin your supplication, and special salutations with which you should close it.

Begin by facing the prayer direction (*qiblah*) while raising your hands, palms up and alongside each other, at about chest level. Then praise God ﷾ and send blessings (*ṣalawāt*) upon Prophet Muhammad ﷺ. Next, call upon God ﷾ using His Most Beautiful Names, and then ask Him for all your needs. Close with blessings upon Prophet Muhammad.

You should call upon God ﷾ for any need, whether significant or seemingly mundane. Common supplications include: asking forgiveness for sins; requesting guidance and faith, or patience and strength; asking for virtuous qualities and for refuge from vile ones; asking to be granted paradise and to be pardoned from the fire; and many others. The best supplications are those that were said by Prophet Muhammad ﷺ; it is best to ask for those things he asked for.

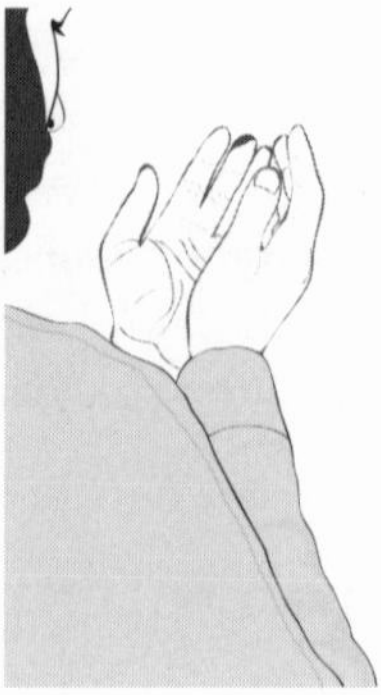

Figure 14: A Man Raising Hands in Supplication (*Duʿā'*)

Invocation (Dhikr)

Believers, remember God with unceasing remembrance! – Quran 33:41

God ﷻ created human beings with the essential quality of recurring forgetfulness—an absentmindedness about what we already know to be right, and about the bigger picture altogether. The Quran serves as a reminder to everyone of the realities we tend to neglect. In essence, the very purpose of religion is to remember these realities. **Invocation** (***dhikr***), which also means "the remembrance of God," is an action of the tongue and heart in which the name of God, or His praise, is mentioned repeatedly, with the purpose of bringing Him to the forefront of the heart and mind. Through the medium of invocation we remind ourselves of that which we too often forget. Invocation of God is a means of awakening from spiritual slumber, which humans are prone to by their very nature.

Invocation (*dhikr*) of God ﷻ is an essential component of a Muslim's daily life and is a broad category under which prayer, recitation of the Quran, and supplication all fall. It is an action of the tongue and heart that you should perform often and plentifully, for this transformative practice, if done consistently, will awaken your heart and sharpen your spiritual sight to be able to see truth and reality as they are. It will purify your heart from the tarnish caused by sin, negligence of God, and other spiritual pollutants.

Although the modes of invoking God ﷻ are potentially infinite, there are several modes that are central to Muslim practice and were handed down to us from Prophet Muhammad ﷺ himself:

- The invocation ***Subḥān Allāh*** (How transcendent God is!) is a form of praising God and an expression of wonderment at His creation.
- ***Alḥamdulillāh*** (Praise belongs to God!) is another invocation which is said as a means of expressing gratitude to God for bounties.
- The first part of the Testimony of Faith (*Shahādah*), the proclamation ***Lā ilāha ill-Āllāh*** (Nothing is worthy of worship save God!), is another invocation, one by which we may renew and strengthen our faith.
- ***Allāhu akbar*** (God is greater!) is an invocation that, by means of an incomplete phrase, exclaims God's supremacy over anything and everything.

- The invocation ***Astaghfir Allāh*** (I seek God's forgiveness!) is a means of repenting and rectifying shortcomings.

Lastly, sending blessings upon Prophet Muhammad is an invocation through which much divine benefit can be derived. It has particular significance and reward on Fridays. The simplest form is to say, ***Allāhumma ṣalli wa sallim ʿalā sayyidinā Muḥammad*** (O God: Bless and send peace upon our master, Muhammad!).

To take time out during your day to repeat these invocations will illuminate your heart and infuse your day with mention of God ﷻ, which is a source of blessing and grace. Invoking God and remembering Him elevates a mundane act, such as driving somewhere, into an act of drawing nearer to God.

It is quite common, and a practice of Prophet Muhammad ﷺ, to repeat a certain invocation a particular number of times. These prophetic practices are considered a kind of prescription or formula for attaining spiritual blessings. For this reason, Muslims all over the world carry prayer beads, usually one hundred beads on a looped string, to be able to count their remembrances of the divine wherever they go.

Figure 15: An Example of Muslim Prayer Beads

Invocation (*dhikr*) of God ﷻ and His messenger are actions of the heart and tongue. For most new to the practice, particularly those unfamiliar with the Arabic invocations and their meanings, the invocations are mostly from the tongue. But with frequent and consistent repetition, these meanings will gradually engrave themselves upon your heart, increasing the effect of the invocations and transforming your heart and psyche.

7. RULINGS PARTICULAR TO WOMEN

MENSTRUATION & POST-PARTUM BLEEDING

Within the realm of ritual purity are rulings of Islamic law (*sharīʿah*) particular to women. They all relate to the womb, which is considered a sacred organ in Islam. Of it, God said:

> I am God and I am the Merciful (*al-Raḥmān*). I created the womb (*raḥm*) and derived its name from My own. If someone connects the [ties of the] womb,[30] I will connect him with Me, but if someone severs the [ties of the] womb, I will cut him off from Me.

It is this organ, the seat of the creative force of God ﷻ in this world, among other things, that makes women so highly esteemed in the faith. Prophet Muhammad, God bless and grant him peace, said "Heaven lies beneath the feet of mothers."

With respect to ritual purity, there are two main kinds of uterine bleeding for women—menstrual periods, and post-partum bleeding (after giving birth to a child). According to Islamic law, either kind of bleeding causes a state of major ritual impurity and thereby prevents a woman from performing acts for which ritual purity is required. During either kind, a woman is relieved from the obligation of doing,[31] and it is forbidden (*ḥarām*) for her to do, any of the following:

- Praying the ritual prayer (*ṣalāh*)—she is not obliged to make them up.
- Fasting—she is required to make up the obligatory fasts of Ramaḍān.
- Touching an Arabic-language copy of the Quran, except for study or teaching
- Entering the prayer area of a formally designated mosque[32]
- Having intercourse with her spouse

---

30. The phrase "ties of the womb" refers to the ties of kinship, which Islam places great importance in maintaining.

31. This only applies to those items which are required (*farḍ*) for her to begin with.

32. If the area was intended as a mosque, this ruling applies; however if the place is a multipurpose room that is used for prayer, among other uses, the ruling does not apply.

After the bleeding ceases, a woman must perform a ritual bath (*ghusl*) to exit the state of major ritual impurity. The above rulings apply until she takes a ritual bath (*ghusl*), even if the uterine bleeding has ended.

For each of these two types of bleeding, there is a maximum duration. For menstrual periods, the maximum duration is a woman's typical cycle plus three days, the total of which should not exceed fifteen days. For post-partum bleeding, the maximum duration is sixty days. If bleeding of either type exceeds the maximum duration, it is considered dysfunctional uterine bleeding. A woman in such a case should then perform a ritual bath (*ghusl*) and consider herself free of the state of major ritual impurity. After that, if the dysfunctional bleeding occurs for less than half of the day, it would be considered a cause of minor ritual impurity, thus necessitating *wuḍū'* (ritual washing) in order to pray. If the dysfunctional bleeding is more than half of the day, it is recommended to make *wuḍū'* (ritual washing) between prayers, but not required.

Also, for the fasting of Ramaḍān, there are certain exemptions made for pregnant or nursing mothers (see above, page 81, for details).

CHAPTER 4

Spiritual Refinement

God has been truly gracious to the believers in sending them a Messenger from among their own, to recite His revelations to them, to make them grow in purity, and to teach them the Scripture and wisdom—before that they were clearly astray.

QURAN 3:164

The Quran teaches that God ﷻ created the universe with two planes of existence: the material, which we perceive with our senses, and the spiritual, which is beyond human perception. Among the many elements within the latter realm is the very essence that defines our humanity—the soul (***rūḥ***).[1]

Faith and practice—the first two dimensions of the religion—bring about the cultivation and beautification of the soul. That is the end to which their paths lead and the element which, in turn, transforms Islam from a set of codes and rituals to a living, vibrant path to the Divine. For "to worship God as though you are seeing Him" transforms ritual into piety and dogma into faith.

Iḥsān, the third dimension of Islam, is an intricate discipline concerned with the refinement of the human soul. One scholar of Islamic spiritual disciplines, Sīdī Aḥmad Zarrūq, succinctly summarized the process as "sincere inner direction" towards God, thus clarifying both the aim and the manner of such refinement. For Islam, at its essence, is about your relationship with your Creator, because religion devoid of a direct relationship with God ﷻ is incapable of bringing hearts to life.

1. The Arabic word *rūḥ* (from a root that can also mean "to breathe") can be translated as "spirit" or "soul." In this book, we will use these two terms interchangeably to designate the immaterial essence of a human being.

1. HUMAN CONSCIOUSNESS

There are several components that contribute to the human consciousness that we experience. These components co-exist and interrelate with one another. Having a basic understanding of them not only provides some self-knowledge, but gives us a necessary background for understanding the process of refining the soul.

THE PRIMARY NATURE (*FIṬRAH*)

God ﷻ created mankind with a **primary nature** (***fiṭrah***) that knows, recognizes, and inclines towards all that is good, beautiful, and pure. This nature is also, in its original form, opposed to evil and corruption. When we are in touch with our primary nature, it instills in us a sense of guilt when we do something we know to be wrong.

It is also this innately good primary nature that knows and yearns for God Almighty. It is the reason why, when we lack a connection to the divine, we sense a disturbing void, even if only on a subconscious level. Simply put, we are hardwired with a need to worship and know God.

In the Islamic view, therefore, our essential nature is good, and much of the process of cultivation involves removing the obstacles between us and our primary good nature. For this reason, Islam rejects the concept of "original sin." We are neither responsible for what others did before us, nor are we born in a state of sin; on the contrary, we are born with a subconscious recollection of our relationship with God ﷻ and an inclination towards Him and towards all that is pure and good.

THE EGO (*NAFS*)

Opposite to the primary nature (*fiṭrah*) is the **ego** (***nafs***). It is the part of our consciousness that resembles a wild animal—it is concerned primarily with the fulfillment of its desires to the detriment of our soul. It seeks the self-serving pursuits of pleasure, wealth, fame, and power. The most basic forms of pleasure that preoccupy it are eating, drinking, resting, leisurely pursuits, and sex. It also is dominated by the base characteristics, such as anger, jealousy, and arrogance.

The ego (*nafs*) and its desires are part of human nature and cannot be eliminated completely—rather, they are to be tamed. It is how we behave in response to desire that affects who we become as people. We can tame the ego through the use of reason and by weakening the intensity of its impulses. This is done by starving it of its proper nourishment—the fulfillment of its desires. Through exercises of conscious self-deprivation, such as fasting (*ṣawm*), we can weaken the grip of the ego, and then we will be freer to utilize the faculty of reason.

REASON (*ʿAQL*)

The faculty of **reason (*ʿaql*)** is another gift from God ﷻ in the complex composition of human consciousness. It is the "executive function" of the mind, which can sort through decisions and possibilities and subject the other components of consciousness to its decisions. However, if the faculty of reason is subjugated to the will of the ego (*nafs*), the soul is controlled by its base desires, steering itself towards immorality. While the faculty of reason has the ability to make wise decisions, many a person has turned decision-making over to the whims of the ego. But, by subjugating the ego to the faculty of reason, we can restore an appropriate hierarchy within our consciousness, thus ensuring our advancement in the process of refining our souls.

THE HEART (*QALB*) AND THE SOUL (*RŪḤ*)

The focal point of interaction for the components of consciousness is **the heart (*qalb*)**. The spiritual heart is the center of the soul (*rūḥ*), just as the physical heart is the center of the body. For this reason, the two terms "heart" and "soul" can be used interchangeably to refer to the center of our consciousness and spiritual being. The heart is the means by which we interact and connect to revelation and the Divine, and the portal through which we achieve piety in devotion.

2. THE PATH OF REFINEMENT

In summary, the path of refinement includes two complementary endeavors that lead to one objective. They are the acquisition of virtues and the expulsion of vices from the heart, until one's character resembles that of Prophet Muhammad ﷺ. The path of refinement is, in a phrase, to become Muhammadan.

THE PERFECT BALANCE

Every human quality exists on a spectrum of expression, ranging from non-existence to the fullest expression. Much of the process of refinement lies in finding the appropriate degree of expression for a particular attribute—what Aristotle called "the golden mean." Most attributes are neither absolutely good nor absolutely bad. The quest is to achieve the perfect balance in the two possible extremes of a given characteristic. This balance is best known by studying Prophet Muhammad ﷺ, because God said to him, "Truly you [possess] great character." (Quran 68:4)

For example, let's consider the generally negative attribute of anger. Anger is a character trait most of us have in excess of the perfect balance exemplified by Prophet Muhammad ﷺ, and so most of us must work to reduce the impact of this characteristic in our hearts. The two extremes for presence and absence of anger could be called *rage* and *spiritlessness*, respectively. While the error in rage is obvious, the misguided nature of spiritlessness requires further examination. If one were spiritless and therefore had no ability to be angered, one could not come to the aid of a defenseless person being attacked by a criminal. A proper degree of anger, in the appropriate situation, is what compels one to do what is best, whatever the difficulties may be.

It is the appropriate emphasis, between two extremes, at the appropriate time and place, that constitutes the perfect balance of a characteristic.

THE SPIRIT THROUGH LAW

We have previously discussed the interdependence of the dimensions of Islam. The practice of *islām*, that is, the dimension of performing devotional acts, has a direct impact upon our heart and spiritual state. Sins taint the heart, and devotions refine it. Likewise, a heightened spiritual state makes a devotional act a source of serenity and spiritual strengthening. It is a cyclical relationship, and devotional acts jump-start the process towards refinement of the heart.

For spiritual purposes, this means that the senses and limbs, the means by which we act in this world, are the main sources of input into the heart. Islamic scholars have identified seven **inroads to the heart**: the *tongue, eyes, ears, hands, feet, stomach* and *genitals.* For each of these, certain actions directly cause spiritual harm and are forbidden by Islamic law (*sharīʿah*). For example, using the hand to steal taints the spiritual state. Avoiding these actions enhances one's spiritual purity, and when combined with consistent invocation (*dhikr*), it awakens the heart and sharpens one's spiritual vision.

This inseparable marriage between law and spirit is what makes Islam the perfect balance between the revelations of old. It is the moderating completion between the rich legal tradition of Judaism and the vitalizing spirituality brought by the Prophet Jesus (ʿĪsā) ﷺ.

THE PATTERNS OF GOD

God ﷻ, the creator and fashioner of everything, tells us in the Quran that He created the universe with patterns to its organization. These patterns apply consistently across the many levels of God's creation. Therefore, with an understanding of these patterns, we can access deep insight into the workings of the spiritual realm itself. All religions speak by way of metaphors and parables precisely for this reason: A perceptive and reflective person can derive spiritual lessons from the physical world. This is summarized as one of the simplest, yet most helpful, spiritual maxims, noted in a poem by the great Shaykh Muhammad ibn al-Ḥabīb:

> "The whole universe is but meanings, into physical forms turned;
> Whoever can see this, will have many a lesson learned."

Whether we look at the principles of physics, biology, mathematics, or economics, in each field we find reflections of spiritual principles. We all have spiritual inertia, predispositions, growth-curves, and we all have basic spiritual needs that must be met before we can seek to go further. These reflections allow us to continue to draw spiritual reminders from our world, no matter how void of the spirit it may seem.

We are encouraged by God ﷻ in the Quran to reflect on His creation because it will both engender awe of God and provide us lessons which we can apply to our own lives, further enriching our piety. This contemplative reflection will have deeper implications when applied to the process of spiritual refinement.

SELF-PURIFICATION

God ﷻ describes the momentous Day of Judgment as a time when wealth and children will prove futile and of no benefit to those who stand before Him in judgment. He does however identify those who are able to save themselves:

> *"...those who bring to God an unblemished heart."* — *Quran 26:89*

The process of refining the heart to soundness involves the *acquisition of virtues* and *purification from vices.* This dual task reminds us that we all have inherent deficiencies and lack much-needed virtues.

This is why the great theologian, jurist, and sage Imam al-Ghazzālī divided his masterpiece on spirituality into two branches, which he called "the *saving* virtues" and "the *destructive* vices": because of the ability of virtues to save us from perdition and the ability of vices to spiritually destroy us.

3. DESTRUCTIVE VICES

The destructive vices are obstacles to tapping into our primary nature (*fiṭrah*) and are expressions of our ego (*nafs*) which must be removed. They are called such because if we allow them to overrun our lives, they will cause spiritual perdition. Only by ridding ourselves of these vices, while taking on spiritual virtues, can we be saved. An overview of some of the major destructive vices is below.[2]

RAGE

Rage is anger so intense that it causes one to lose control: one is taken over by it and loses the composure of good character. Anger, in itself, is a natural human energy that we should not eliminate completely, but rather harness and focus for productive ends. Appropriate anger is what compels people to courageous acts, giving them the strength to oppose tyranny and injustice despite the difficulty inherent in doing so.

Anger, like all other human qualities, varies in different people in the extent to which it dominates their character. We all know people who can be described as hot-tempered and others who are mild-mannered. What is important to understand is that we are not prisoners of our inherent dispositions; they are the means by which God calls us to a higher challenge. Prophet Muhammad ﷺ was once asked for spiritual guidance, to which he simply responded, "Do not become angry." The path of refinement rejects the excuse of "That's just the way I am," and instead calls us to work against our dispositions to become the way we all should be.

RESENTFUL ENVY (*ḤASAD*)

Oftentimes, when we see that others possess something we desire, we envy them and wish we had it too, but we do not wish for them to lose it. This form of simple envy can be noble or corrupt, depending on whether the object we are longing for is noble or corrupt. **Resentful envy (*ḥasad*)**, on

2. For a deeper exposition of these and more, see the modern classic on which this section is based, *Purification of the Heart: Signs, Symptoms and Cures of the Spiritual Diseases of the Heart* by Hamza Yusuf, Sandala Publications.

the other hand, is wanting to possess something that another has and also wishing for the other person to lose that thing.

To desire that another person lose a blessing and you be given it is to question God's allotment of blessings on Earth. It implies that God ﷻ did not know best where to place His blessings, and stems from a feeling that we deserve something that God has withheld. It is a malicious vice that opposes the virtue of desiring good for others.

It is best to remember that God ﷻ is the wisest and most merciful of allocators. He would only give you something if it were better for you to have it than not to. You must remember that your ego (*nafs*) has passions that are selfish and short-sighted, and that your proper spiritual state is gratitude for what God ﷻ has given you.

SUSPICION

We view the actions of others through the lens of our soul. To draw negative conclusions regarding what others do is both divisive to social harmony and a testament to one's own inner shortcomings. When others act, we have no ability to know their true intentions, nor can we judge their outward actions without at least a degree of investigation. In these situations, our spiritual challenge and obligation is to find the best possible interpretation of the appearance of things.

Even in everyday language we speak of giving someone "the benefit of the doubt" when circumstances and intentions are uncertain. A great scholar of Islam once said, "Make for your brother in faith seventy excuses." This means that we say to ourselves, "There must be a good explanation," rather than inclining towards a negative interpretation of what we see or hear. The ego (*nafs*) is always seeking to catch someone at fault, because doing so bolsters a false sense of our own righteousness, and because this preoccupation with the shortcomings of others blinds us to our own faults. We must resist this temptation. When there are sensible explanations other than a negative interpretation of an act, we should accept them, unless the facts clearly indicate misconduct. Of course, to ignore open misconduct could render one vulnerable to being taken advantage of or harmed—another extreme that should be avoided! Still, there is no need to be investigative; you should not wish for your brother or sister in faith to have a fault exposed. We learn from this that social harmony is much more important than catching someone making a mistake. It is the same in society at large: We know that to uphold the principle of "innocent until proven guilty" is more important than convicting every criminal.

In the end, we should remember that what we see is a reflection of what we are. If we suspect evil and malice in benign acts, it is because we are filled with those negative qualities. But if we see a suspicious act and immediately interpret it positively, that reflects a purity of heart that is to be sought by all.

ARROGANCE & VANITY

Arrogance, the belief that you are superior to others, can lead to mistreating and having contempt for people. This vice is especially easy to fall into in a society that places so much emphasis on social status vis-à-vis others.

The wise believer, on the other hand, knows that piety is the basis of true status, and keeps in mind that piety is truly known only to God ﷻ. The humble believer is also preoccupied with his or her own shortcomings and defects. With this outlook, it becomes clear that feeling superior to others simply because of career, race, or socioeconomic status is foolish; your assessment of greatness or insignificance alters radically, and you become more focused on your own flaws, in order to refine yourself to a higher level of spiritual purity.

As for **vanity**, it is closely related to arrogance. The difference is that it is not a sense of superiority in relation to another—it doesn't need a second person. It is self-admiration and a sense of self-accomplishment. A vain person forgets that whatever he has, he did not truly achieve it by his own efforts. In reality, all that we have is from God ﷻ, and the appropriate response is gratitude towards the Giver. Patting oneself on the back is a means to self-delusion that severs one from the blessings and bountiful increase granted to those who are grateful.

SHOWING OFF (*RIYĀ'*)

One of the most essential teachings of Islam is encapsulated in a narration (*ḥadīth*) of Prophet Muhammad ﷺ: "Actions are [judged] according to their intention." It defines the basis of our relationship with God ﷻ, as stated in the opening chapter of the Quran, which we recite daily in our prayers: "It is You we worship" (1:5). Everything we do, ultimately, is for God. We may have other noble motivations, but they must fall under the umbrella of seeking God's pleasure.

The opposite of this, **showing off (*riyā'*)**, is doing something for the purpose of gaining the admiration of other people. Prophet Muhammad ﷺ called it the minor form of *shirk* (associating partners with God). The desire to show off stems from an inappropriate love of praise and status, exceeding the appropriate degree. This does not mean that we should seek to have *no* status in the eyes of others: That too would be an extreme, and it would make us subject to self-humiliation and indignity—the antithesis of the ennoblement Islam provides us.

During adolescence, we tend to feel more intense inclinations towards showing off (*riyā'*), and while it is easier to recognize them then, those inclinations can persist well into adulthood. Our society is filled with people seeking validation from others, and societal pressures push us all to do so at times. Deep down, we know that this reflects a weakness in character; its motivation does not come from within but is dependent upon acceptance by others.

The most heinous form of this vice is showing off (*riyā'*) in our devotions to God. A trick of Satan (*Shayṭān*) is to point out our moments of showing off, so that we despair and stop doing the acts involved, even if the acts are essential to our spiritual development. Scholars of Islam teach that we should perform the devotion and rectify the misguided intention, redirecting it towards God.

HEEDLESSNESS

Planet Earth, because of its composition and sheer mass, exerts the force of gravity on any object within its reach. Likewise, worldly life exerts a spiritual gravity on our souls, pulling us away from heavenly endeavors and distracting us downward to temporal concerns. Heedlessness is the lack of concern for matters of prime importance and ultimate consequence because of preoccupation with the unimportant and temporary. We are in a world where change is the only constant, and we are constantly being given new ways to distract ourselves from the bigger questions of life. We can entertain ourselves to death, never opening a window of reflection through which a sense of our mortality can shine through. Heedlessness causes us to be spiritually out of touch with reality, living in an illusion of fleeting pleasures.

Heedlessness leads to a downward spiral that exacerbates all the other destructive vices. To counter this tendency, we must struggle against the spiritual gravity that draws us to this world, and awaken our hearts to our divine purpose and our accountability before God ﷻ. This will enable a state of heightened spiritual awareness, and this state, God willing, will allow us to focus our energies and endeavors on those matters that are most pleasing to God and most consequential to us in the next life.

AVERSION TO PONDERING DEATH

It is common, particularly in modern cultures, to shy away from discussions about our own death. It is seen as ruining the joy of life within that moment. To reflect on one's own demise, to some, seems morbid.

Contrary to this philosophy, Prophet Muhammad ﷺ encouraged his followers to remember their own mortality often, for in it lies the greatest clarifier of perspective. In essence, remembering death corrects one's loss of perspective, and, with that, the loss of one's sense of appropriate priorities in life. We all have heard stories of people who learn they have only weeks to live, and how that knowledge radically alters their lifestyle, values, and relationships.

For a Muslim, who sees death as a transition to the everlasting afterlife, the remembrance of death is a motivation to prepare to meet God ﷻ. It inspires repentance, rectification of errors, and intensified worship.

To forget where you are headed is to forget your purpose, which is the reason antipathy towards death is a destructive vice—it leads to a neglect of your duties to God. To remember our inevitable end often renders this life more sweet and fruitful. It is a constant reminder that pulls us away from heedlessness and towards "worshipping God as if you see Him."

4. SAVING VIRTUES

Opposite the destructive vices, which are expressions of the tendencies of our ego (*nafs*), are the saving virtues, which are inherent to our primary nature (*fiṭrah*). If we rid ourselves of the destructive vices, our primary nature will take over, and our saving virtues will be enhanced and displayed.

One of the greatest summations of the saving virtues comes from a sage in the 13th century, Imam Abu ʿAbbās al-Mursī. He summarized all of life's possibilities in four scenarios:

1. You can be in a state of **obedience** to God
2. You can be in a state of **disobedience** to God
3. You can be in a state of **ease**
4. You can be in a state of **adversity**

Each of these situations is from God ﷻ, and each necessitates an appropriate response—not of the body, but of the heart. The appropriate spiritual virtues to embody in response are:

1. If you are obedient to God, you must exhibit **awareness** of God's favor upon you, having guided you to obey Him.
2. If you are disobedient to Him, you must remorsefully **repent** to Him for your transgressions.
3. If you are in a time of ease, you must sense deep **gratitude** to God for his gifts.
4. If you are challenged by adversity, you must endure God's decree with **patience**.

To make use of this timeless wisdom requires a level of awareness and introspection regarding the states we are in. Too often we live our lives at so fast a pace that we do not reflect upon ourselves. With reflection and introspection, we will be more able to engender the appropriate virtuous response of heart. Now we will examine more closely these and other spiritual virtues one should strive to embody.

REPENTANCE (*TAWBAH*)

A sin is an act that defies the boundaries set by God ﷻ. The Islamic understanding of humanity includes sinning as an inescapable part of our makeup. God, in His mercy, has granted a simple resolution to our problem: the ability to directly ask God ﷻ for forgiveness and thus be forgiven. Fortunately, it really is that simple, for our Lord is the All-Merciful. There is no need to sacrifice animals, confess to clergy, or be punished in this life in order to be pardoned from punishment in the next life. Prophet Muhammad ﷺ said, "One who repents from sin is like one who has never sinned."

There are four preconditions to a complete repentance to God. The first and most central is feeling a sense of *remorse* for the sin. The second is *abandoning the sin* without delay. The third is *resolving to never return* to the act. The fourth is conditional—if you have harmed another person in the process, you must *rectify your harm* (e.g., return something stolen).

All that matters is the state of your heart at the moment you repent. If you are sincere in remorse and resolution, God ﷻ promises to accept your repentance. It does not matter whether or not you manage to keep true to your promise afterwards: that is, we can end up returning to the same sin one thousand times, as long as each time we repent sincerely, remorsefully, and resolutely. We must simply repent one thousand and one times.

Satan works to make us despair of God's mercy, by attempting to make us believe that our sins are so great that even the All-Merciful cannot forgive us. That is a lie, and we must constantly remind ourselves that God has promised to forgive our sins, if only we repent.

CONSCIENTIOUSNESS (*TAQWĀ*)

Conscientiousness (*taqwā*) is the very core of our religious existence—it is both the end and the means of spiritual refinement. The root word in Arabic implies more than simple awareness: It also includes a caution to protect oneself from harm—which in this case means protecting oneself from earning God's displeasure. Conscientiousness is an all-encompassing spiritual state that affects our actions and spiritual conditions; when we have conscientiousness, all that we do is imbued with a concern for what is pleasing and displeasing to God.

Conscientiousness (*taqwā*) is manifested in four ways:

- Acting in ways that fulfill God's commandment (i.e., doing)
- Avoiding acts that God has forbidden (i.e., not doing)

- Embodying spiritual virtues internally (i.e., being)
- Avoiding spiritual vices internally (i.e., not being)

These are both the means to attaining conscientiousness (*taqwā*) and the result of attaining it. Observing conscientiousness before God سبحانه وتعالى begets more conscientiousness. Conscientiousness is closely linked to one's strength of faith (*imān*), a spiritual standing that is in constant flux. Our strength of faith is dynamic: It is always either increasing or decreasing, never fixed. Our goal should always be to increase our strength of faith by observing and cultivating conscientiousness before God.

DETACHMENT (*ZUHD*)

One of the challenges of leading a life guided by religion is interacting with the world around us in a moderate and balanced manner. The material world is the bridge over which we pass on our journey to the next life. It is also the medium through which we strive to manifest our obedience to God سبحانه وتعالى and live piously.

The human ego (*nafs*), however, has an innate desire to indulge itself in this world. In modern times, the opportunities for self-indulgence and instant gratification are greater than ever before, strengthening these tendencies of the ego. Islam gives us a balance between the monastic lifestyle on the one hand and the indulgent on the other. This is achieved through the spiritual state of **detachment (*zuhd*)**, which allows us to use this world as a means to an other-worldly end. Simply put, detachment is the realization that material wealth should be in our hands, not in our hearts. When the heart is attached to possessions and material items, its spiritual yearning is suppressed.

HOPE & FEAR OF GOD

Human beings, unlike angels, are sinners who consistently fall short in their duties to God Almighty, Who is both the Merciful and the Just. Although the believer has much to fear in terms of divine punishment, our fear must be coupled with an equivalent hope for God's mercy. An overemphasis on either side is a spiritual imbalance in our relationship with God سبحانه وتعالى. So we must work to foster both of these spiritual virtues simultaneously. We should reflect on our sins, shortcomings, and debt to God, and feel grief and shame before Him. At the same time, we should remind ourselves of His divine mercy and throw ourselves at the gate of His forgiveness. Motivated by both fear of punishment and hope of forgiveness and reward, we can spiritually propel ourselves toward increased conscientiousness (*taqwā*).

RELIANCE UPON GOD (*TAWAKKUL*)

As sentient willful beings we have hopes and dreams, and we work hard to attain them. As Muslims, we know that God Almighty is capable of doing anything He wishes, and that in His divine mercy, He will give us what is best for us—whether or not that is readily apparent to us. **Reliance upon God (*tawakkul*)** involves putting our trust in God that He will guide our affairs, and that, ultimately, He alone is our protector and sustainer.

An elucidation of true reliance upon God ﷻ is found in a famous narration (*ḥadīth*). A man came and asked Prophet Muhammad ﷺ, "Should I rely upon God and leave my camel... or should I tie my camel and then rely upon God?" Prophet Muhammad ﷺ replied, "Tie the camel, and rely upon God." This teaches us that reliance upon God (*tawakkul*) does not entail inaction. It is action along with the proper placement of hope—in God, *not* in the rope. It is not the rope that binds the camel, but God *through* the rope.

Reliance upon God (*tawakkul*) does not go unanswered. God ﷻ says in the Quran, "And whoever trusts in God, God suffices him" (65:3). If you rely on God while working to accomplish something, God will aid you in your efforts. Reliance upon God is a source of much serenity and relief—when we realize that God ﷻ is the manager of our affairs, we can also trust that whatever the outcome of a situation, *that* is what God has deemed best for us in His infinite knowledge and wisdom. So in the end, reliance upon God is a source of much optimism in a Muslim's life.

GRATITUDE (*SHUKR*) & CONTENTMENT (*RIḌĀ*)

Remember that your Lord promised, "If you are thankful, I will certainly give you more and more." — Quran 14:7

A sense of indebted **gratitude (*shukr*)** is the main driving force behind devotion to God ﷻ. Each of us, if we reflect deeply upon our own situation, can acknowledge countless blessings that we take for granted. Beyond these immense blessings, which we do not deserve, is the generous offer of God: If we do the bare minimum—acknowledge a blessing and feel grateful—it will not simply suffice for that blessing, but will invite others as well. Conversely, ingratitude is one of the lowest states a person can be in towards their Creator, and it invites the removal of other blessings in our lives. The greatest blessing of all is faith and being guided by God to His religion, Islam. All other blessings pale in comparison. The best form of gratitude to God ﷻ is the kind manifested through obedience to Him.

Alongside gratitude (*shukr*) is a related spiritual virtue, **contentment (*riḍā*)**. As believers, we ask God ﷻ for certain things, but in the end all matters are for God to decree. To be content with God's decree means not objecting to it, not questioning divine wisdom, and not feeling that what has happened to us should not have happened. An obvious exception to this is our own sinning: we should not be content with it, but rather should feel remorse and be compelled to repentance.

The ego (*nafs*) tends to constantly desire more when it compares itself to others in worldly matters, while, in spiritual affairs, it is fooled into thinking, "At least I do such-and-such in devotion to God," remembering that there are others who do much less. This is the opposite of the perspective taught in Islam as a way to obtain more gratitude (*shukr*) and contentment (*riḍā'*): "In matters of this world, look to those who have less than you. In your faith, look to those greater than you."

5. NOBLE CHARACTER

Virtuous character, and all of its manifestations, is essential to the full and proper expression of Islam. This is illustrated in the famous narration (*ḥadīth*) in which Prophet Muhammad ﷺ says, "I was sent forth (by God) only to perfect noble character."

Noble character is known to the primary nature (*fiṭrah*) of the soul and is actually an expression of it. For that reason, all people, in all cultures, already know a good deal about what constitutes noble character, and our innate knowledge is enhanced by our religious learning. The following passages highlight a few aspects of virtuous character which are central to Muslims.

COURTEOUS CONDUCT (*ADAB*)

Prophet Muhammad ﷺ said, "My Lord has taught me manners, and thus gave me the best of manners." A litmus test of successfully refining the soul is the attainment of beautiful character, which culminates in what some refer to as **courteous conduct (*adab*)**. The refined person is a beautiful person to interact with. His or her nature is pleasing to be around, and they are a source of ease and comfort to all who know them. This refined manner of interaction is the result of spiritual cultivation and was embodied by Prophet Muhammad ﷺ.

Some scholars state that courteous conduct (*adab*) is a product of combining love with humility. The spiteful or arrogant heart cannot manifest courtesy to others. Such conduct is more than the actions we see; it is an expression of an inner beauty and serenity. This expression in turn fosters love between people. Islam's guidelines about the courteous conduct of daily life are meant to enhance overall social harmony, as a means to a spiritually healthy environment.

A believer should personify any conduct considered good-natured by societal norms. While particular manifestations of good conduct may vary in different cultures, a believer rightfully takes up any form of virtue as his or her own. For example, in most cultures it is considered good etiquette to help a weak or elderly person carry groceries or cross a busy street—and so it is clear that a believer should strive to do such things. The universal call to refined behavior may manifest in different ways for different societies, but all are essentially outward manifestations of an inward beauty.

BENEVOLENCE

The Prophet Muhammad ﷺ said, "None of you [fully] believes until he loves for his brother that which he loves for himself."

This is the golden rule Muslims learn as children but struggle with all their lives. It is the ability to put yourself in another's place so that you may act kindly towards them. The criterion for the treatment of others is that of self-reference: What if others did it to you? How would it make you feel? The answers to these questions will guide a believer towards nobler behavior. The ability to empathize with other people is one of the features of Muhammadan character. Evaluating whether or not we wish another well helps us to identify the influence of the ego (*nafs*) in our thoughts and decisions. This momentous question helps us to gain important self-knowledge in our path of spiritual refinement. It also elevates us to the level of **benevolence,** wishing others well, which in and of itself is a means for the betterment of society.

ALTRUISM

A level beyond treating others as you would like to be treated is to put them before yourself. God describes the Helpers (*Anṣār*) of Medina in the Quran: "those who... have no desire in their hearts for what has been given [to others], preferring them to themselves, even if it means hardship for them" (59:9).

To need something, but to prefer that others in need receive it first, is an even higher level of character than the Golden Rule, and is a quality praised by God Almighty Himself. There are pious people everywhere who, although they live in poverty, when money comes their way, immediately give it to others in need. This should be the ideal we all strive for—we can start by practicing selflessness in regard to wants and luxuries, nurturing the virtue to extend even into our needs. **Altruism** testifies to the suppression of the selfish ego (*nafs*) and is a product of the refinement we all seek.

VIRTUOUS SPEECH

Prophet Muhammad ﷺ gave clear instructions equating **virtuous speech** with faith itself: "Whoever believes in God and the Last Day, he should say something good, or remain silent."

Speech has a most powerful and direct effect on the soul, and the words said may also lead the person being spoken to down a particular path of thought and emotion. The believer's duty is to make sure that everything he or she says is both good and beneficial, not simply that it is the truth. Does it make someone happier? Does it bring two people closer together? Does it remind someone of their duty to God? If so, it is the kind of statement that is positive in its effect. The Muslim is a force of positivity to himself and others around him. Speech is the primary mode of communicating such positivity between people and spreading positive thoughts to others.

At times our egos fool us into thinking that something is worth saying even if it is hurtful, as long as it is true. But our actual motivation may be a desire to inflict pain, and the justification that our statement is "worth saying because it is true" may be pure self-delusion.

This simple yet challenging teaching of Prophet Muhammad ﷺ will improve social relationships between people, while calling us to examine the things we say and the reasons why we say them.

PATIENCE (*ṢABR*)

Patience (*ṣabr*) is the virtue of having grace in adversity, remaining content with the difficulties God ﷻ has decreed. It is to persevere in obedience to God, and to silently endure the trials of life, without complaint or resentment. As one sage put it, "Patience is to make no distinction between ease and adversity, in that in both, the heart of the servant of God is unperturbed." God has promised those of his servants that are patient that He will support them by granting them both the strength to endure—"God does not burden any soul with more than it can bear" (2:286)—and the relief of the burden: "So truly where there is hardship there is also ease; truly where there is hardship there is also ease" (94:5-6).

Prophet Muhammad ﷺ also taught that every difficulty believers endure in this world with patience purifies them from sin and elevates them in rank before God ﷻ. With this prophetic perspective, hardships become divine means by which God tests and refines us and through which we can gain nearness to Him.

HONESTY AND SINCERITY

Speaking the truth is a prerequisite to speaking at all. The character of a believer is always honest, particularly when honesty is difficult. **Honesty** is valued not just as the accurate conveyance of information, but as integrity in all that we say and do. It means that we are who we show ourselves to be.

Sincerity, which is a kind of honesty in dealing with God, is to think and act for God alone, without concern for others or your own self-gratification. It is to act out of the pure intention of worshipping God. This is the noblest motivation for any action and entails the absence of any element of showing off (*riyā'*).

TRUSTWORTHINESS

The product and result of honesty is **trustworthiness**. The Prophet Muhammad ﷺ was known as "The Trustworthy One" before his mission as prophet of God, indicating the dominant characteristic by which he was known to his people. Even when the Meccans fought him, they continued to entrust valuable items to him for safekeeping, for they still considered him the most trustworthy of men.

We know intuitively that trustworthiness is an integral part of moral character and a necessary quality for a believer to possess. It can take the form of performing a task you agreed to, keeping someone's confidence, or fulfilling expectations. Its predominance in a society creates more harmonious living, because people will be more honest vendors, witnesses, friends, and neighbors. As believers, we should all strive to embody trustworthiness by honoring agreements, appointments, and even implicit understandings, even at personal cost.

FORBEARANCE

One of the predominant qualities of Prophet Muhammad ﷺ during his life and mission was his **forbearance**. He had an immense ability not to react to the hostility people directed towards him. The Prophet absorbed such things, always responding with forgiveness and kindness. He was good to those who harmed him personally and fought to defend others who were wronged.

A believer should strive to embody a selfless forbearance and to give up expecting things from others, for such expectations are impulses of the ego (*nafs*). We should instead demand more of ourselves, always asking what we could be doing better and examining where we might be falling short. This moral mindset creates a person who can forgive, forget, and still be good to those who harm him, eventually breaking cycles of negativity and opening up the possibility of winning others over, as Prophet Muhammad ﷺ did.

GENEROSITY

God ﷻ is the Most Generous and has given us all many bounties. In turn, we must show our gratitude by giving to others. Whether with our wealth, time, kindness, or attention, each of us can freely give to others. It is easy to give when you have excess, but **generosity** is simply to give, without regard to what you may or may not have. A narration (*ḥadīth*) from Prophet Muhammad ﷺ states that generosity is a tree from paradise which reaches down to the world, and whoever grabs onto a branch has a means to attaining paradise. At its most basic level, being generous means abandoning pettiness and miserliness and learning to give freely.

A spirit of generosity is essential to Muslim character, whether through giving gifts to others or, particularly, showing gracious hospitality to your guests. Most Muslim cultures have absorbed this into their fabric, and hospitality, sharing, loaning, and giving are all intrinsic to them. A believer understands that all things come from God, and that to be generous with God's creation will engender divine generosity towards you.

JUSTICE

Oppression, in all its various forms, is condemned by God ﷻ repeatedly in the Quran. In turn, He repeatedly praises those who are just and put things as they should be, upholding the balance. To defend and help the weak and oppressed is a moral obligation, but more important is to demand justice not from others, but from one's self. God urges us in the Quran to be just, even if it means we stand against ourselves. He reminds us to avoid letting hatred of others interfere with our obligation towards justice, an error to which humans are easily susceptible.

Pursuing justice for oneself—self-assertion and the securing of one's rights—is part of the virtue of **justice**, but only part; one must pursue the rights of others, as well. To be more concerned with our rights than with our responsibilities is evidence of a selfish pursuit of the desires of the ego (*nafs*), not a dutiful obligation towards balanced justice. God requires us to be just ourselves, but encourages us to not always demand it of others, reminding us that to forgive is best.

We can see that there is a moral imperative common to all the aspects of noble character examined here: to place others before yourself. Prophet Muhammad always forgave personal offences, since they had to do with his personal rights, but he never fell short in his responsibilities towards the rights of others.

The discipline of refining and beautifying the soul (*rūḥ*) is the core of the religion. This brief overview was intended to make the reader aware of this discipline, its centrality, and its immeasurable importance. We share the quality of having physical bodies with other animate creatures God ﷻ has created, but it is the soul that makes us human. Our raw material in the endeavor of growing closer to God is the soul. We must value it and take hold of the chance to refine it, adorning it with virtues and cleansing it of vices in hopes of gaining God's good grace.

CHAPTER 5

The Prophet ﷺ

God said, "My punishment I bring on whomever
I will, but My mercy embraces all things.
I shall ordain My mercy for those who are conscious
of God and pay the prescribed alms; who believe
in Our Revelations; who follow the Messenger—the
unlettered prophet they find described in the
Torah that is with them, and in the Gospel—who
commands them to do right and forbids them to
do wrong, who makes good things lawful to them
and bad things unlawful, and relieves them of their
burdens and the iron collars that were on them.
So it is those who believe him, honour and help him,
and follow the light which has been sent down
with him, who will succeed."

QURAN 7:156–157

The second of the Two Testimonies, "Muhammad is the messenger of God," reminds us that we must live in accordance with the reality of the first Testimony—and that God ﷻ taught us how to do so through the life and teachings of Prophet Muhammad. Here Islam strikes a moderate balance in its view of God's last messenger, neither straying to the extreme of deification like previous prophetic communities, nor relegating God's chosen messenger to the role of a simple mailcarrier, merely receiving and relaying a revelation. For Muslims, Prophet Muhammad ﷺ is a manifestation of divine mercy, God's most central attribute, for the All-Merciful sent His Beloved "as a mercy to all worlds" (21:107). So to more completely know and develop a relationship with Prophet Muhammad ﷺ is to render oneself open to receiving divine grace and spiritual strengthening from God.

It is impossible to do justice to the Chosen One, Muhammad, God bless and grant him peace, in such a short presentation. The aim of this chapter is simply to make you aware of the various fields of study surrounding the Prophet, and the need to further explore them, so as to better know, and thus love, the Beloved of God.

1. THE ROLE OF THE PROPHET ﷺ

The role that Prophet Muhammad ﷺ plays in the lives of Muslims is different from the roles that other prophets or founders of religions may have for their followers. Those who come from a different faith background, with a different frame of reference, may find this somewhat challenging at first. For Muslims, Prophet Muhammad ﷺ plays a dual role that is central to an understanding of our relation with him: *role model* and *lawgiver.*

THE BEST EXAMPLE

"The Messenger of God is an excellent model for those of you who put your hope in God and the Last Day and remember Him often." — Quran 33:21

For Muslims, Prophet Muhammad ﷺ represents the model of a complete human.[1] To understand the best possible way to behave in a particular situation, a believer will always ask, "What did Prophet Muhammad do?" The example and teachings of Prophet Muhammad ﷺ form the basis of his **Prophetic Way** (the ***Sunnah***), or way of life, which is taken as normative for Muslims. An individual act from this Way, particularly if it was his habit to do it, is called a **prophetic practice** (a ***sunnah***). There are many different levels on which Muslims follow the example of Prophet Muhammad ﷺ: in their ritual worship of God ﷻ, in their emulation of his perfect character traits, in their dealings with people, and even in seemingly mundane daily activities, which he taught a unique way of doing. His Way has guided Muslims for centuries, for he not only brought divine guidance, but personified it, standing eternally as a model of human perfection for any to follow.

SPEAKING IN GOD'S NAME

Prophet Muhammad ﷺ is the foremost servant in all of God's creation, spanning the ages. When you read the Quran you can see clearly how often God ﷻ directly addresses Prophet Muhammad ﷺ, guiding his actions and even his thoughts. Receiving revelation, on many levels and in many forms,

1. Absolute perfection belongs to God alone. For finite beings, to be complete means embodying specific attributes whose possession amounts to perfection for those particular beings, reaching its full potential. Therefore, any such perfection is relative.

granted Prophet Muhammad ﷺ access to the knowledge of what God allows and what He prohibits.

"So accept whatever the Messenger gives you, and abstain from whatever he forbids you." — Quran 59:7

For these reasons, the Prophet's words, actions, and tacit approvals and disapprovals are a source of law. He both intimately knew what God ﷻ desires of us all and embodied it completely.

God ﷻ also blessed the Prophet ﷺ with infallibility—God's protection over him which made him incapable of making mistakes in conveying, obeying, and perfectly embodying God's message. For this reason, the companions of the Prophet worked diligently to protect accounts of his words and actions, and countless scholars throughout history have worked to verify them. These treasured accounts, called **narrations (*ḥadīth*)**, are the main source by which the Prophetic Way (Sunnah) is known. Numbering in the hundreds of thousands, these accurately verified narrations teach us about every aspect of the life of God's last prophet ﷺ—both the public aspects and the private and intimate ones.

Through these verified accounts of the infallible Prophet, the guidance he brought was preserved for all time. In them, he warns his followers directly about the pitfalls into which previous religious communities had fallen, those who altered their religion and freely changed its fundamentals. To prevent this, Prophet Muhammad forbade his followers to change the religion through the introduction of what are called "innovations."

A condemnable **innovation (*bidʿah*)** is an attempt to introduce a new teaching or practice into the religion that has no prior basis or foundation in Islam. However, we should not oversimplify this principle, as many do, applying it to every newly initiated act; for the Prophet often allowed new acts that were in conformity with the guidance he brought. Scholars of Islamic law from the beginning concluded that newly initiated acts can fall into any of the five categories of the legal rulings. To come to a conclusion regarding such an act, scholars must examine it closely. They base their legal ruling on the purpose and result of the act, measured against the spirit of the sacred law. The way of moderation is to avoid both an unreasonably inflexible approach to the religion and a leniency that would allow changes to its fundamentals or contradict its teachings.

With respect to innovations, it is important to distinguish between fundamentals and secondary matters. For example, it would be a condemnable innovation (*bidʿah*) to attempt to reduce the number of daily prayers (*ṣalāh*), since this is a fundamental component of the religion. It would be a permissible innovation, on the other hand, for someone to write his own supplications and invocations, since their forms are not essential foundations of the religion, and the acts of supplicating and invoking God have a basis in the sacred law. An innovation is only considered condemnable when it alters a fundamental belief or practice of the religion.

2. AN INTRODUCTION TO THE PROPHET ﷺ

THE PROPHET'S TITLES

Prophet Muhammad ﷺ is also known by other titles, mostly derived from God's descriptions of him in the Quran. There are a good number of them, scholars differing on exactly how many, but we will focus on only a few—for they will highlight aspects of his blessed nature that are essential to know.

The Beloved of God (***Ḥabīb Allāh***)—clearly delineating his most prominent characteristic and the most fundamental aspect of his relationship with God: love.

The Trustworthy One (***al-Amīn***)—a title given to him by his people, the Meccans, in the days before revelation, it refers to his honesty and integrity. Even some who fought him after he proclaimed God's religion would continue to ask "the Trustworthy One," as they called him, to safeguard their valuables.

The Best of Creation—an indication of his status before God ﷻ, this title includes his position not only in relation to all of humanity, but to the entire cosmos.

The Chosen One (***Muṣṭafā***)—a common name used interchangeably with his name Muhammad, this name is indicative of his being selected by God ﷻ for His mission to all of humanity.

The Seal of Prophecy—a title that indicates that he was the last in the succession of God's prophets, and that with the completion of God's message, prophethood came to an end.

The Intercessor (***Shafīʿ***)—a very important title, it refers to the Blessed Prophet's rank and role on the Day of Judgment. In an awesome display of love and compassion, the Prophet ﷺ intercedes with God on behalf of all believers, his followers—for he cannot bear that any believers should be punished. He will plead with his Lord on their behalf, rescuing many wrongdoing believers from the Hellfire.

The Herald of Good and **the Warner**—God has sent Prophet Muhammad ﷺ to bring good news to the believers about what awaits them beyond this life, and to warn those who reject the message about what may await them if they do not accept God's call.

LOVING THE PROPHET ﷺ

For those who know Prophet Muhammad ﷺ well, stating that every Muslim must deeply love him seems unnecessary. God ﷻ has abundantly praised the Prophet ﷺ and called him His Beloved—what then should we say, who are direly in need of his guidance and aid in both worlds? Still, we need to nurture and intensify our love for the Prophet ﷺ by reminding ourselves of this duty and this divine grace, as we will examine below.

In many narrations (*ḥadīths*), Prophet Muhammad ﷺ defines the role of loving him specifically—and not simply loving the religion or his teachings. This spark of personal love within the heart is what prevents a beautiful religion from becoming nothing more than an ideology.

Prophet Muhammad ﷺ himself said, "None of you shall have [complete] faith until I am more beloved to him than his children, parents, and all other people." On another occasion he said the same thing and added, "… than one's own self." Here, we see that the powerful force of love directed toward the Beloved of God is a prerequisite to having complete faith. Fortunately for those seeking divine grace and complete faith, never has God created one so easily loved.

In addition to completing your faith, loving Prophet Muhammad ﷺ affects your destination in the afterlife (*ākhirah*). A man once came to the Prophet ﷺ and asked him when the Day of Judgment will come. Since he was asking about such a momentous event—when we are placed before the Almighty and held to account—the Prophet replied, "What have you done in preparation for it?" The Prophet ﷺ wanted to teach that one should not be concerned about when the Last Day would be, but rather about how to prepare for the momentous meeting with the Almighty Himself. The man replied, "I have not prepared for it with a lot of prayer or fasting or charity, but I love God and His Messenger." The Prophet said, "You will be with the one you love." From this, we learn the immense need to examine the objects of our adoration, as they have other-worldly effects.

How can we tell if a person truly loves Prophet Muhammad ﷺ? Such a person strives to follow his Prophetic Way (*Sunnah*) and to embody all of his teachings, fulfilling his commands and avoiding the things he forbade. God ﷻ says in the Quran, "Say, 'If you love God, follow me, and God will love you and forgive you your sins'" (3:31). So following the Prophet ﷺ is not only a proof of loving God, but a way to ensure divine love—a grace beyond human comprehension. Also, a person who loves the Prophet ﷺ will exhibit the proper respect towards him, feeling a sense of reverence at the very mention of his name. Such a person will be sure to send blessings upon him upon hearing his name.[2]

Loving the Prophet ﷺ also enhances one's motivation to follow him. In this manner, the duty to love and the duty to follow reinforces the other.

Historically, expressions of loving Prophet Muhammad ﷺ took form through the arts, most notably in songs and poetry. Poetry in praise of the Prophet ﷺ has been composed in every language with a significant population of Muslim speakers. From east to west in the Muslim world, for centuries, it has been customary to sing songs praising the fine qualities of Prophet Muhammad ﷺ, filling listeners' hearts with love. Many of these literary masterpieces were composed by the scholars and saints of Islam. To this very day, children across the world learn and sing songs praising him, a fulfillment of God's words, "Did We not... raise high the esteem [in which] you [are held]?" (94:1, 4).

There are many ways of enhancing our love for Prophet Muhammad ﷺ. The most important is to learn about him, his qualities of perfection, the events of his life, details of his characteristics, his miracles, and his unique and special rank with God ﷻ. Additionally, saying plentiful blessings and salutations upon him has the effect of engendering love in the heart. Lastly, we can read the love-inspired poetry of praise of the Beloved of God. Reading or listening to these poems will move the depths of your soul, reminding it of feelings it felt but could not express, and inspiring the kind of deep love the poets felt.

A DESCRIPTION OF PROPHET MUHAMMAD ﷺ

It should now be clear that loving the Prophet is an essential basis of faith. And forming a vivid mental image of the Prophet is one way of reinforcing such love.[3] The more you are aware of who he is, the more you will be motivated to follow him. To transform motivation into behavior, you must know how the Prophet acted towards others, dealt with particular situations, and arranged his priorities.

2. A narration (*ḥadīth*) from Prophet Muhammad describes those who hear his name and do not send blessings (*ṣalawāt*) upon him as the most miserly of people.

3. While there is a general prohibition on the making of images of sentient creatures, it is particularly forbidden (*ḥarām*) in Islamic law to portray Prophet Muhammad in any type of image. When one reflects on the erroneous deification of Prophet Jesus (ʿĪsā), the wisdom in prohibiting the making of images becomes very clear to the believer.

The following excerpt is a brief description of Prophet Muhammad ﷺ by ʿAlī, his son-in-law and cousin. When asked to describe the Prophet, ʿAlī said:

> He was not too tall nor too short. He was medium sized. His hair was not short and curly, nor was it lank, but in-between. His face was not narrow, nor was it fully round, but there was a roundness to it. His skin was white.[4] His eyes were black. He had long eyelashes. He was big-boned and had wide shoulders. He had no body hair except in the middle of his chest. He had thick hands and feet. When he walked, he walked inclined, as if descending a slope. When he looked at someone, he looked at them in full face.
>
> Between his shoulders was the seal of prophecy,[5] the sign that he was the last of the prophets. He was the most generous-hearted of men, the most truthful of them in speech, the most mild-tempered of them, and the noblest of them in lineage. Whoever saw him unexpectedly was in awe of him. And whoever associated with him familiarly loved him. Anyone who would describe him would say, "I never saw, before him or after him, the like of him." Peace be upon him.[6]

Other descriptions of the Prophet tell us more. They mention, among many other details, that his beard was black and profuse, always carefully combed and perfumed. The Prophet's skin was very soft and naturally fragrant. Whenever he shook hands with someone or patted a child on the head, as he often did, the fragrance remained on that person for the rest of the day. Wherever he walked in the alleys of Medina, the same fragrance remained hanging in the air long after he had gone.

The Prophet's speech was uniquely eloquent, profound and concise. People often intentionally insulted, offended, and attacked him, but personal offence never provoked his anger; on the contrary, he invariably remained affable with those who offended him. It was only when divine injunctions

4. Scholars have elaborated on this, describing his skin as not pale, but wheat colored, similar to a full moon on the fourteenth night.

5. In addition to being the actual Seal of Prophecy, sent as God's last emissary, Prophet Muhammad had a physical manifestation of this metaphysical reality. He had a raised area of flesh in between his shoulderblades, with some hairs growing around it, also referred to as "the seal of prophecy." In scriptures of some communities before Islam, the seal of prophecy was included in the description of God's last prophet to all of humanity.

6. Mohamed Zakariya, "The Hilye of the Prophet Muhammad," *Seasons*, Autumn-Winter 2003-4: 16-17.

were defied that he became angry, and then nothing stood before his anger. When he was happy, the Prophet's face lit up like the full moon. He was known for always smiling, but he seldom laughed aloud. The equivalent of hearty laughter for him was to smile so broadly that his molar teeth showed.

Prophet Muhammad ﷺ never allowed himself to be humiliated, but he was always humble. He once said that he was ordered to show such humility that it would be impossible for anyone to justifiably be arrogant towards another. He wore coarse clothes and made do with whatever clothing was available; he liked his clothes to be clean and white in color, and seldom kept more than one of each kind of clothing. Prophet Muhammad ﷺ ate whatever was presented to him and was never picky with his food. He ate from the portion of the dish that was closest to him, instructing others to do so as well. He also drank with his right hand and he usually sat down when he drank; but when he drank water from the well of Zamzam, he drank standing up.

The Prophet often stood in prayer at night for so long that his feet became swollen and painful. When asked why he felt obliged to do this when God ﷻ had already told him in the Quran that He had forgiven him both his past and future sins, the Prophet answered, "Should I not then be a thankful servant?" Being infallible, he committed no "sins" in actuality, but to emphasize the gulf between the Lord and the servant, he thus demonstrated the proper mode of expressing infinite debt.

Whenever he met other people, the Prophet was always the first to give the greeting of peace (*salām*). When he shook hands, he was never the first to pull away, but always let the other person withdraw first. When someone needed to speak to him privately, the Prophet always allowed them to speak without interruption, until they had said all that they needed to say. The Prophet gave his full attention to everyone present in turn, so that each felt he was the most important person in his eyes. He patted children on the head, sat them on his lap, and prayed for them to grow up into pious adults. At home, the Prophet helped his wives do their chores, milked his goat, repaired his sandals, cleaned the house, patched his robes, fed his camel, and helped knead dough, an embodiment of this narration (*ḥadīth*): "The best among you are the best to their wives, and I am the best of you to my wives."

3. BLESSINGS (*ṢALAWĀT*) UPON THE PROPHET ﷺ

"God and His angels bless the Prophet. So, you who believe, bless him too and give him greetings of peace." — Quran 33:56

God ﷻ has given a special gift to the followers of Prophet Muhammad ﷺ in the form of our ability to send blessings (*ṣalawāt*) upon His last prophet. A historical event in the life of the Prophet himself gives us a glimpse of the magnitude of this gift. One day, a companion of the Prophet had followed him into a palm grove where he saw the Prophet prostrate himself for so long a time that the companion feared that God had taken his soul. After coming closer to examine him, and explaining his fear about such a long prostration to God, the companion was told by the Blessed Prophet, "I met Angel Gabriel who said to me, 'I bring you tidings of joy: God, exalted is He, says to you: He who greets you with peace, I shall greet him with peace, and he who sends blessings upon you, I shall send blessings upon him.'" Blessings are invocations in which a believer prays for God to send His grace upon Prophet Muhammad. By blessing the Prophet, we connect ourselves to this guaranteed outpouring of divine grace, exposing ourselves to it and thus partaking in it to some extent.

This doorway to divine peace and blessings, which the Prophet himself rejoiced in for our sake, has been treasured by Muslims for centuries. The number of narrations that detail the virtue, importance, and reward of sending blessings upon the Prophet are many, and entire books have been written explaining each of these facets of *ṣalawāt*. Blessings upon the Prophet are an essential part of a Muslim's life, a vital component of our invocations (*dhikr*), and a means by which many fruits are reaped—the most important of which is love of God, and love of His Beloved, Prophet Muhammad ﷺ.

SENDING BLESSINGS (*ṢALAWĀT*)

The companions (*ṣaḥābah*) of Prophet Muhammad ﷺ asked him about the manner in which they should send blessings (*ṣalawāt*) upon him. In response, he taught them the Abrahamic Prayer (see page 60), which we recite in our daily prayers (*ṣalāh*):

> O God: Send blessings upon Muhammad, and the family of Muhammad, as you sent blessings upon Abraham (Ibrāhīm), and the family

> of Abraham.[7] O God: Bless Muhammad, and the family of Muhammad, as you blessed Abraham, and the family of Abraham. In all the worlds, surely, You are the Praised, the All-Glorious.

This is one way of sending blessings (*ṣalawāt*), and there are countless others. From the beginning of Islamic history, the scholars of Islam have composed innumerable formulae of sending blessings upon Prophet Muhammad ﷺ. Some blessings highlight some of his unique virtues; others are used as a means of supplication (*duʿā'*) to God ﷻ. The simplest blessing which you can easily use for daily invocation (*dhikr*) is:

"*Allāhumma ṣalli wa sallim ʿalā sayyidinā Muḥammad wa ʿalā ālih!*"
(God: Bless and send peace upon our Master, Muhammad and his family!)

SENDING BLESSINGS (*ṢALAWĀT*) ON FRIDAYS

Friday (*Jumuʿah*) is a holy day for Muslims for many reasons. The most obvious is that it is the day of the Friday Congregational Prayer, a very important devotion (see Chapter 7). One of the other reasons is directly related to sending blessings (*ṣalawāt*) upon Prophet Muhammad ﷺ. We learn from the Prophet that sending blessings upon him reaches him by way of the angels who tell him that so-and-so has sent blessings upon him. On Friday, however, things are different, as we see in a narration (*ḥadīth*) where Prophet Muhammad ﷺ says:

> Increase your recitation of blessings (*ṣalawāt*) upon me on Friday, because on this day the angels present themselves to me. There is no servant of God who sends blessings upon me, whose voice fails to reach me from wherever he is.

In response to further questioning by the companions (*ṣaḥābah*), Prophet Muhammad ﷺ taught us that he is still conscious of this presentation of

7. The family of Prophet Muhammad, also given the title "the People of the House," is a special group of people that includes the wives and relatives of Prophet Muhammad (varying definitions exist) and their subsequent descendants, called nobles (*sharīfs*). They have a special status in Islam which makes them ineligible to receive purifying charity (*zakāh*), among other things. What is important for us to know is that both the Quran (see 42:23) and the Prophet Muhammad himself, according to narrations (*hadith*), command us to love the Prophet's family.

our blessings (*ṣalawāt*) upon him even after his bodily death.[8] So on Fridays, we are told, our voices reach the Prophet directly, even now. In turn, he responds to the blessings and salutations himself.

BENEFITS OF SENDING BLESSINGS (*ṢALAWĀT*)

Scholars of Islam have reviewed the many verses (*āyahs*) and narrations (*ḥadīths*) that relate to sending blessings (*ṣalawāt*) upon Prophet Muhammad ﷺ and sifted out many, many benefits of doing so. Here is a small sampling:

- Believers receive ten blessings from God for every blessing (*ṣalawāt*) sent upon the Prophet
- God will raise your spiritual rank ten degrees[9]
- Believers receive the rewards of ten good deeds
- God will erase ten of your sins
- A supplication (*duʿā'*) is more likely to be answered if you close it with a blessing upon the Prophet
- It is a means to being closer to Prophet Muhammad ﷺ on the Day of Resurrection
- It is a means to having God fulfill your needs
- It will help you to remember something you have forgotten
- It can protect you from poverty
- It will lead to better character and manners
- Your love for Prophet Muhammad ﷺ, an essential precondition to true faith, will be sustained and increased.

8. Muslim belief holds that bodily death, particularly for prophets and martyrs in God's way, is a transition to another type of life, which exists in the more powerful "in-between" realm dominated by the nature of the soul. Even physically, there are some, again a special class of people, whose bodies do not decompose after death. Examples of this belief are abundant in Islamic literature: From Prophet Muhammad ﷺ telling us of his seeing Prophet Moses (Mūsā) praying in his grave, to his praying with all of the prophets in Jerusalem, to the Quran's rejection of calling martyrs "dead," declaring their continuing life, we understand that life continues after death in the "in-between" realm of the soul.

9. This spiritual rank is an unseen status based on piety and conscientiousness of God. While the world is consumed with outward appearances of status and who has worldly importance and clout, elevation in spiritual rank is unseen, and represents an all-important standing with God.

These should be more than enough reasons for a wise Muslim to make a regular practice of sending blessings (*ṣalawāt*) upon Prophet Muhammad ﷺ. This is all because God has given us a direct connection to His outpouring of blessings upon Prophet Muhammad ﷺ and his family by sending our blessings upon them.

4. A BRIEF BIOGRAPHY

We will now examine, in brief, the life of the blessed Prophet Muhammad ﷺ. His life can be divided into three main divisions: his early life, the Meccan era after revelation, and the Medinan era after his migration (*hijrah*).

SIXTH CENTURY MECCA

To understand more fully the life and message of Prophet Muhammad ﷺ, one must understand the people and culture within which he appeared. Prophet Muhammad ﷺ was born during the sixth century CE in Mecca, a city founded by Prophet Abraham (Ibrāhīm) and his son, Prophet Ishmael (Ismāʿīl) ﷺ. Although home to the Sacred House (*Kaʿbah*) dedicated to worship of the One God, the Mecca of that era had become overridden with polytheists and their idols. The Sacred House itself had approximately three-hundred and sixty idols within its precincts.

The Arabians were a principled people with a strict code of honor; however, they were mired in cycles of lawless bloodshed, a class-based system of discrimination, blinding tribalism, and idolatrous polytheism. Their culture in many ways paralleled the Mafia culture as depicted in film. Retaliatory killings going back and forth between clans for generations were commonplace. Family and tribe were the institutions to which one gave undying loyalty. Elders were given the highest levels of respect, and they decided the affairs of the family and tribe. Chivalry and bravery were celebrated, and Arabians would quite readily give their lives to keep an oath, believing that integrity and honor were nonnegotiable. The society had and abused the institution of slavery. The weak could easily be oppressed, and the powerful, those from influential tribes, could get away with anything. This period has been called the **Era of Ignorance** (***Jāhilīyyah***). Nonetheless, the Arabian culture was also immensely rich in its poetic and literary heritage. The power of the poet in Arabian society then was tremendous; he could spur entire clans into the heat of battle.

It is important to understand the hallmark values of the sixth century Arabs, because Prophet Muhammad ﷺ came to change some of these values while he reinforced others.

Mecca was the most important city in Arabia. The Sacred House (*Kaʿbah*) was believed, even by idolaters, to be holy, and since it housed idols from many parts of Arabia, people from all over the region would make pilgrimages to Mecca to visit their idols. Arabian custom was built around an understanding to honor Mecca as a holy sanctuary, and the idols were the main source of tourism and income for the city and its people. The Arabian economy was built on trade, and since many caravans would pass through Mecca for pilgrimage, it became included in their trade routes. It was also an oasis, for it was home to the famed endless spring of Zamzam. These factors all made the tribes of Mecca among the most powerful in the Arabian Peninsula.

Figure 16: The Sacred House (*Kaʿbah*) in Mecca

HIS EARLY LIFE

Prophet Muhammad ﷺ was born on the 12th day of the First Spring (*Rabīʿ al-Awwal*), the third Arabian month, in 570 CE. Many miracles took place on the day of his birth, because it marked the coming of God's final message to humanity. His father, **ʿAbd-Allāh bin ʿAbdal-Muṭṭalib**, died before he was born, and his mother, **Āminah bint Wahb**,[10] was told by a voice to give her son the then unknown name of Muhammad, "*the praised one*." It was Arabian custom then to send infants off with desert Bedouins to be raised in the open desert and learn their eloquent Arabic speech. As an infant, Prophet

10. In sixth century Arabia, the naming system was to state the person's given name, then state they are the son (***bin*** or ***ibn***) or daughter (***bint***) of their father. For example, the name of Prophet Muhammad is therefore, Muhammad the son of ʿAbd-Allāh (the name of his father), which would be stated as Muḥammad bin ʿAbd-Allāh. This method preserves the lineage of a person (so-and-so the son of so-and-so the son of so-and-so the son of...). Many Muslim cultures still use this method by making the father's name the middle name, then adding the last name to the end of it: For example, in such a culture, the name "Ali Yusuf Williams" indicates that Ali's father's name is Yusuf Williams.

Muhammad ﷺ was sent with a Bedouin wet-nurse, **Ḥalīmah**. Ḥalimah later recounted the story of the day she found the baby Muhammad. She rode into Mecca upon a weak and emaciated donkey, with no milk in her own breasts. Upon taking in Prophet Muhammad ﷺ, her breasts miraculously filled with milk and her donkey perked up, trotting home.

One day, while under Ḥalimah's care, Prophet Muhammad ﷺ was playing in the desert with Ḥalimah's own son. Two angels, appearing as men dressed all in white, approached the child Muhammad. They laid him down, split open his chest, and placed his heart in a bowl of snow. They washed his heart with Zamzam water, and then returned his blessed heart to its original resting place. Ḥalimah's son witnessed all of this and recounted it in detail to his mother. It was clear to her that the child under her care was far beyond ordinary.

When Prophet Muhammad ﷺ was six years old, his mother passed away and he was placed in the care, first of his grandfather, and then of his paternal uncle **Abū Ṭālib**, an elder of the tribe of **Quraysh**, the most prominent tribe of Mecca. At the age of twelve, Prophet Muhammad ﷺ accompanied his uncle on a journey to Syria for trade. There, a Christian monk named Baḥīrah noticed a cloud hovering over Prophet Muhammad ﷺ, shading him from the sun. Suspecting signs of prophethood, the monk tested Prophet Muhammad ﷺ by asking him for something in the name of an Arabian idol. Prophet Muhammad ﷺ objected to the mention of the very name of the idol. After seeing these signs, the monk told Abū Ṭālib that his nephew had a great future ahead of him but that men would oppose and fight him.

PROPHETHOOD

As he grew older, Prophet Muhammad ﷺ was known as a generous, honest and kind man. He was employed by a wealthy businesswoman named **Khadījah** ؓ. As her most trusted trade representative, he scrupulously carried out business transactions for her. Impressed with the character of Prophet Muhammad ﷺ, she proposed to him, despite being fifteen years his senior—he ﷺ was twenty-five years old and she was forty. They loved one another dearly, and the Lady Khadījah ؓ bore him six children: two sons (Qāsim and ʿAbd-Allāh) and four daughters (Zaynab, Ruqayyah, Umm Kalthūm, and Fāṭimah). All but **Fāṭimah** ؓ, his youngest daughter, would pass away before Prophet Muhammad ﷺ.

One day during this time, the Quraysh were rebuilding the Sacred House (*Kaʿbah*) which had been damaged from flooding. In the eastern corner of the cubic structure rests the sacred **Black Stone**, which descended from heaven white as milk but was then blemished by the sins of men. This heavenly stone was the crown jewel of the Sacred House, and to set it back in its place within the structure was a great honor. The nobles of Quraysh fought over who should have the honor and nearly came to bloodshed over the matter. They agreed that the next person to enter the Meccan Sanctuary would arbitrate for them. Just then, Prophet Muhammad ﷺ entered the Sanctuary. The noblemen were relieved that it would be the Trustworthy One, as they called him, who would judge the matter. Rather than choosing among them, Prophet Muhammad ﷺ called for a large cloth to be brought to him. The Black Stone was placed in its center, and the leaders of each tribe were instructed to grab the edges of the cloth. Together, they carried the stone over to the eastern corner of the structure, with Prophet Muhammad ﷺ placing the stone in its place. Everyone was satisfied, and they celebrated his wisdom.

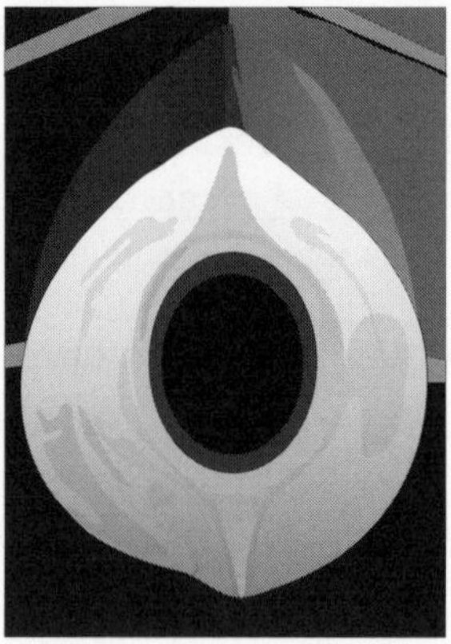

Figure 17: The Black Stone

The city and society of Mecca were overrun with idols, and being adverse to idolatry, Prophet Muhammad ﷺ would regularly retreat to **Ḥirā' Cave** on a mountain outside of Mecca, where he would meditate on the transcendence of God ﷻ for days on end. One night, while he was meditating in the cave, the Archangel Gabriel (Jibrīl) ﷺ appeared to him and proceeded to seize him. "Read!" he commanded. "I cannot read," responded the Prophet. The Archangel Gabriel ﷺ squeezed the Prophet with his wings and repeated his command, which was met with the same reply. This happened three times, after which Archangel Gabriel recited the first verses of the Quran revealed to Prophet Muhammad ﷺ:

> *Read! In the name of your Lord Who created: He created man from a clinging form. Read! Your Lord is the Most Bountiful One who taught by the pen, who taught man what he did not know. — Quran 96:1-5*

Overwhelmed by the sight of the archangel and the experience, Prophet Muhammad ﷺ returned to Lady Khadījah ؓ in a state of shock, unsure of what had just happened. Lady Khadījah ؓ was the first to believe that what had transpired had been no other than revelation from God. She took the Prophet to her cousin Waraqah, a Christian well-versed in their scriptures. When they told him about what happened, he told the Prophet, "You will be called a liar, and ill-treated, and they will cast you out and make war upon you; and if I live to see the day, God knows I will help His cause." Thus, the Lady Khadijah ؓ was the first woman to believe in Prophet Muhammad. The first child to believe in the Prophet's message was **ʿAlī** ؓ, the son of Abū Ṭālib, his first cousin, and the first man was the Prophet's closest friend **Abū Bakr** ؓ, who would become the Prophet's closest companion.

PERSECUTION

Prophet Muhammad ﷺ began to call his people to God's final religion, urging them to accept the two fundamental precepts of Islam: unadulterated monotheism and his prophethood. As Islam began to spread and news of a monotheistic religion reached the leaders of Quraysh, they attempted to bribe Prophet Muhammad ﷺ. He was offered massive amounts of wealth, any of the women of Quraysh of his choosing in marriage, and even kingship. Unwavering in his divine mission, Prophet Muhammad ﷺ replied, "I swear by God, were they to place the sun in my right hand and the moon in my left so that I should abandon this mission before God makes it victorious or I have perished therein, I would not abandon it." Refusing to be bought, the Prophet continued to call people to God. Those who accepted Islam and were not a member of any of the powerful Arabian tribes were persecuted by the Quraysh. The early Muslims would gather in secrecy to learn and practice their faith. As the numbers of Muslims grew, the leaders of the Quraysh began to feel threatened. They increased their mocking of the Prophet and their persecution of the Prophet's companions.[11]

After a few of the early companions (*ṣaḥābah*) were tortured and killed, the first martyrs of Islam, the Prophet gave permission for his followers to emigrate to Abyssinia (modern day Ethiopia). There was a just Christian king, the Negus, who ruled there and would grant them protection from persecution. The Quraysh sent representatives to the Negus asking him to turn back the emigrants, arguing that it was an internal affair of the Meccans. The Negus decided to hear out the Muslims, who pleaded their case, explaining that the Prophet had guided them away from idolatry to monotheism. Their leader, Jaʿfar ﵁, then recited some verses from the Quran, an excerpt from the Chapter of Mary (Maryam). The Negus wept at hearing those verses of the Quran and felt obligated to grant the Muslims refuge in his land. He even privately accepted the distinction that was new to him: that Prophet Jesus (ʿĪsā) ﵇, the Messiah, was born of a virgin birth, but was neither the literal son of God ﷻ nor the embodiment of divinity; rather he was God's servant and distinguished messenger. Many years later when the Negus passed away, Prophet Muhammad ﷺ prayed the Muslim funeral prayer for him in absentia.

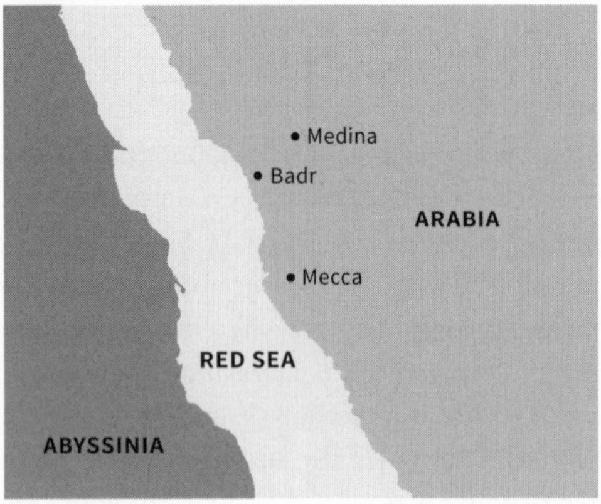

Figure 18: A Map of the Western Arabian Peninsula

11. A **companion** (sing. *ṣaḥābī*, pl. *ṣaḥābah*) is a person who met Prophet Muhammad ﷺ, believed in his message, and died as a believer. A **follower** (***tābiʿī***) is a believer who met a companion of the Prophet. The companions are the best generation of believers overall, while the followers are the second best generation.

A man named **Abū Jahl** was the most vile and vicious of the Prophet's opponents. He became infuriated upon hearing that the convoy from the Quraysh had returned empty-handed from Abyssinia. The attacks upon Muslims in Mecca began to intensify. His nephew was a young man named **ʿUmar bin Khaṭṭāb**, who was known in the city for being big, tough, and fearsome. ʿUmar was also fed up with the problem that Islam began to pose for Mecca's way of life. He resolved to kill Prophet Muhammad ﷺ. He set out to find the Prophet, but was met on the way by a fellow clansman, Nuʿaym, who had kept his Islam secret. Nuʿaym asked him where he was headed. When ʿUmar replied that he was going to kill Prophet Muhammad ﷺ, Nuʿaym knew he had to divert ʿUmar, if only to have time to warn the Prophet. Nuʿaym told ʿUmar that he should worry about his own family first, for his sister and her husband were Muslims. (Nuʿaym knew full well that they would be willing to help him divert ʿUmar's mission.) Enraged at this news, ʿUmar went to his sister's house and confronted her and her husband. In this incident he was first exposed to the Quran, and in a dramatic and fateful turn of events, ʿUmar was so impressed by the Quran, realizing it could not be the speech of any mortal, that he quickly subdued his anger at his sister, as well as at the Prophet. At this fateful moment, he converted immediately.

The leaders of the Quraysh were threatened by the growing body of believers. They made an agreement to boycott the clan of Banū Hāshim, to which Prophet Muhammad ﷺ belonged and within which he found protection. This was an immensely difficult time for Prophet Muhammad ﷺ and those who suffered with him. For a number of reasons, the Quraysh eventually decided to end the boycott. Soon after, weakened by the boycott itself, Lady Khadījah, the wife, friend, and primary supporter of Prophet Muhammad ﷺ, passed away at the age of sixty-five. Shortly afterwards, his uncle and guardian, Abū Ṭālib, fell ill and died. Since both the wife and uncle of Prophet Muhammad ﷺ, his two great supporters, died within the same year, that year is referred to as the Year of Sadness.

With Abū Ṭālib's death, Abū Lahab became the leader of Banū Hāshim. He withdrew the clan's support for Prophet Muhammad ﷺ, which led to the increased persecution of the Muslims in general, and of the Noble Prophet in particular. He was exposed to exceedingly insulting behavior from the Quraysh, and so he chose to seek protection from the people of a nearby city called Ṭā'if. The leaders of Ṭā'if rejected his request for help and insulted the Noble Prophet, sending their children, slaves, and lowly folk to pelt him with stones. Later, the Prophet would recount this moment as the most difficult of his entire mission. Bloodied from the assault, he retreated to a vineyard and prayed a powerful and moving supplication (*duʿā'*):

> O Lord, to You alone I complain of my diminished strength, limited strategy, and insignificance in the eyes of others. Most Merciful of those who show mercy, You are Lord of the downtrodden and my Lord: to whom will You leave me? To those who mistreat me, or to an enemy in whose hands You place my affair? As long as Your wrath is not upon me, it concerns me not, although security is easier for me. I seek refuge in the light of Your Countenance, which illuminates darkness; and the affair of this world and the next is set right, from Your wrath descending upon me, or Your displeasure enveloping me. For You alone have the right to reprimand until You are pleased; and there is no strength, no power, save with You.[12]

In these words he complained to God ﷻ of his situation and expressed that his ultimate concern was God's contentment with him. There in the vineyard, an angel came to Prophet Muhammad ﷺ and offered to punish those who insulted and attacked him, and to destroy the city and its people by smashing them between two mountains. But the Prophet desired guidance for people, not revenge or domination over them. He refused, expressing hope that perhaps their descendants would believe in God.

One night, not long after the incident in Ṭā'if, while sleeping beneath the Sacred House (*Kaʿbah*), the Prophet was awakened by the Archangel Gabriel. Along with him, the Archangel had a white riding beast with wings, named Burāq. Upon this amazing heavenly steed, the Prophet rode alongside the Archangel until they reached Jerusalem. Along the way, he was shown glimpses of the afterlife, including both Paradise and Hell. In Jerusalem, an assemblage of God's prophets awaited him—Noah (Nūḥ), Joseph (Yūsuf), Isaac (Isḥāq), Jacob (Yaʿqūb), Abraham (Ibrāhīm), Moses (Mūsā), Jesus (ʿĪsā), and others ﷵ. They gathered in prayer, with Prophet Muhammad ﷺ leading. Then, with the Archangel Gabriel ﷵ as his guide, Prophet Muhammad ﷺ began a heavenly ascent. As he progressed through the seven heavens,[13] he met again some of the prophets he had prayed with. The Prophet continued to ascend until he reached what the Quran calls "the Lote Tree of the Farthest Limit"—which represents the limit of the knowledge of every knower save God Himself. At this point, this meeting with the Divine, Prophet Muhammad ﷺ was given the command for his followers to institute the daily prayers—fifty of them in one day and one night. On his

12. Hamza Yusuf, *The Prayer of the Oppressed* (USA: Sandala, 2010), 21.

13. In the Quran, God tells us that He created seven heavens - not to be confused with the pardisical Heaven. They are layered in succession, as we see from the account of Prophet Muhammad's incremental ascent through them.

descent, Prophet Muhammad ﷺ was met by Prophet Moses, who advised him to ask his Lord to lighten the command. When the Prophet did so, it was reduced by ten, but Prophet Moses still advised him to return to God ﷻ and ask for it to be further reduced. This happened until it was reduced to its current requirement of five, for which those who perform it will still be rewarded as if they had prayed the fifty. After descending to Jerusalem, the Prophet then returned to Mecca, in time to pray the dawn prayer. This was the **Night Journey and Ascension** of Prophet Muhammad ﷺ.

When he returned, Prophet Muhammad ﷺ began to tell the people of his journey, only to be met by the mockery of his enemies. The people hurried to Abū Bakr ؓ, his closest companion (*ṣaḥābī*), to hear his reaction. He replied, "If he says so, then it is true," for he was the deepest kind of believer: unwavering. He was given the title al-Ṣiddīq, the confirmer of truth.

The Prophet had also described in detail certain caravans he passed on his journey home and stated when they might be expected to arrive. Some of those who found his journey hard to believe had second thoughts when the caravans began to arrive as predicted.

MEDINA

To the north, there was a city called Yathrib that was lost in civil conflict, as its two major clans were locked in endless feuding. There was among them a small group of converts that had pledged their faith to Prophet Muhammad ﷺ while visiting Mecca during the pilgrimage season. The Prophet sent a companion (*ṣaḥābī*) of his to Yathrib to instruct its people in the new faith. As time passed, the followers grew in number and more Muslims pledged their faith to the Prophet. They saw Prophet Muhammad ﷺ as a solution to their civil strife, and so a group of seventy-five converts traveled from Yathrib to the outskirts of Mecca to pledge their allegiance to Prophet Muhammad as their leader, and swore to protect him as their own. This marked the beginning of a number of smaller migrations of Meccan companions to Yathrib. Soon all had left Mecca, save Prophet Muhammad ﷺ, his close friend Abū Bakr, and his cousin ʿAlī ؓ.

During this time period, the Prophet's enemy Abū Jahl wanted to permanently put an end to the religion and contrived a plan to assassinate Prophet Muhammad ﷺ. Each clan would select and send one of their own warriors to simultaneously strike the Prophet in his home. In this manner, blame would not fall on one clan, and Banū Hāshim, the clan of the Prophet, would have to accept blood-money in place of justice. At this time, the Archangel Gabriel came to Prophet Muhammad ﷺ and informed him that God ﷻ had granted him permission to emigrate to Yathrib. He informed Abū Bakr ؓ that it was time to leave, and gave his cloak to ʿAlī, telling him to sleep in his bed, guaranteeing that no harm would come to him. That night, the murderous assassins surrounded the Prophet's house. Prophet Muhammad ﷺ recited some verses of the Quran and walked out right in front of them, miraculously not visible to his assailants. Waiting until morning, the conspirators realized they had been fooled when it was ʿAlī ؓ who awoke and came out of the Prophet's house. Meanwhile, the Prophet, accompanied by Abū Bakr, began his journey to the northerly city of Yathrib by first heading south. With a price on the Prophet's head of one hundred camels, he and Abū Bakr ؓ had many enemies in their pursuit. They headed to Thawr Cave, in which they hid for three days. On the third day, several horsemen searching for Prophet Muhammad ﷺ and Abū Bakr came upon Thawr Cave. When they neared its entrance, they noticed that a spider had woven a web over the mouth of the cave, alongside a dove's nest filled with eggs. They decided it was impossible that anyone could have been around the cave without disturbing the nest and web, so the men quickly left to look elsewhere.

Prophet Muhammad ﷺ and Abū Bakr neared Yathrib fifteen days after leaving Mecca. The believers waited anxiously by the outskirts of the city for any sign of the Beloved and his companion. When they saw them, they welcomed the Prophet with a song of welcome that has been sung by countless children for centuries since:

The white moon rose over us, from Farewell Valley,
And we owe it to show thankfulness, where the call is to God.
Oh you who were raised amongst us, coming with a message to be obeyed,
You have brought to this city nobleness: welcome, best caller to God's way.[14]

Since then, Yathrib has been known as **Medina**, the Prophet's City. When Prophet Muhammad ﷺ entered the city, naturally everyone there pleaded that he should stay as a guest in their home. The Prophet declared that wherever his camel knelt would be the site of his new home. Many waited in anticipation to see where it would stop. Meanwhile, Abū Ayyūb al-Anṣārī, a famous companion, took the Prophet's luggage to his own house, knowing that the Prophet would need a place to stay while his home was built.

14. This translation is taken from Yusuf Islam's rendition of the song, with a slight variation.

Eventually the Prophet's camel stopped at the site of what would be his home in Medina.

This marked the completion of the **Migration** (***Hijrah***) of believers from Mecca to Medina, from which the Muslim calendar begins. Historically, those who left Mecca are known as the **Emigrants** (***Muhājirūn***), and those believers who welcomed them into Medina were known as the **Helpers** (***Anṣār***). The Prophet ordered that each Emigrant should pair up with a Helper, who would share his wealth and home with his brother in faith. Also, the Prophet immediately began building the mosque, to be called the Prophet's Mosque forever more, next to the site of his new home. Thus the new community of believers began to grow in relative peace and freedom.

With the move to Medina and the new sovereignty the Prophet had over its citizens, a new spiritual phenomenon arose. In Mecca, with its harsh persecution, there was no incentive to convert to Islam other than true faith. Now, in Medina, a group of people called the **hypocrites** outwardly embraced Islam—usually for political gain—while secretly disbelieving. These people were insincere in their commitment to the Prophet and the religion, and they would work to undermine his mission at pivotal moments in the years to come. Their leader was a man who was the frontrunner to be king of Medina before the Prophet was made the city's ruler. He continuously looked for an opportunity to undermine the Prophet and reassert his claim to Medina's throne.

Prior to the Migration (*Hijrah*), Prophet Muhammad ﷺ received inspiration from God ﷻ that he was to marry the daughter of Abū Bakr, **ʿĀ'ishah**, who was a young girl at the time. Early in the Medinan period, she entered his home, beginning their new life together. Some scholars place her age at that time at twelve, or possibly eighteen years of age, and the Prophet was fifty-three. Although such a practice might be taboo in modern cultures, it was considered socially acceptable in medieval societies, even Western ones. This may be partly due to the relatively greater psychological maturity of young ladies of that era. History proved Lady ʿĀ'ishah to be a brilliant and intelligent wife, the perfect guardian of prophetic guidance, who gave us unparalleled access to the private life of the Prophet—a source of even more guidance. Over time, Prophet Muhammad ﷺ would marry other wives. These women, who would be designated by God as the "**Mothers of the Believers**," enjoyed a privilege second to none—proximity to the Beloved of God—along with which came a unique status and responsibility. They would collectively serve to show us the love and mercy the Prophet showed towards his wives in particular and women in general.

As the political leader of a sovereign city, Prophet Muhammad ﷺ now played the dual roles of spiritual and political leader, and thus was now granted permission by God ﷻ to lead his followers in battle to defend themselves against those who had expelled them from their homes. Some companions had wanted this permission while in Mecca, but there they were ordered to patiently endure. To have fought in self-defense while in Mecca would have amounted to causing civil strife within a relatively stable society, uprooting that stability and causing anarchy. At the same time, in their new status as a sovereign community, the Muslims of Medina entered into a peaceful alliance with the city's Jewish population, agreeing that they would jointly defend their city from foreign threats. With the ceasefire between the two warring clans of Medina, the city enjoyed newfound social harmony, and under this security the religion of Islam began to spread more easily amongst the people.

The first battle against the Meccans, who had continued to persecute the Muslims, was the **Battle of Badr**, named after a region about halfway between the two cities. On Friday, the 17th of Ramaḍān, during the second year of the migration (*hijrah*) of the Prophet, the Muslim army of just over three hundred believers met the Quraysh army, which numbered approximately one thousand. Many in Mecca were sure this would result in a massacre of the Muslims, which would rid them of Islam once and for all.

It was the Arabian custom of battle that the best warriors from each side would duel in the open arena between the two armies. The Prophet sent forth his uncle, the mighty and fearsome **Ḥamza** ؓ, and his cousin ʿAlī, a skillful warrior, as well as a third companion, ʿUbaydah. The Muslims decisively won all the duels. Then the battle began and was filled with numerous miracles witnessed by both the Muslims and the disbelieving polytheists of Mecca. The Archangel Gabriel and an army of angels descended to take part in the battle. By the battle's end, the Muslims had miraculously defeated the much larger army. A great victory in the battle was the fall of Abū Jahl, the great enemy of the Prophet, who had instigated much of the violent aggression against the Muslims, both while they lived in Mecca and even now that they lived in Medina. Humiliated by their defeat, the Quraysh vowed revenge against the Muslims.

Around this period, other great events were also taking place in Medina—the Prophet's cousin ʿAlī married the daughter of the Prophet, Fāṭimah ؓ, in a simple but blessed wedding ceremony. They lived simply and in poverty, united in faith, and were soon blessed with their first son, whom the Prophet named al-Ḥasan ؓ.

Less than a year later, the Quraysh raised an army of three thousand, led by one of their leaders, Abū Sufyān, in an attempt to decisively defeat the Muslims and subdue the message of Islam. Abū Sufyān's wife Hind, an elite woman of Quraysh, vowed to avenge the killing of her father, uncle, and brother, who had fallen at the hands of the mighty Ḥamza at Badr. She offered freedom and wealth to an Abyssinian slave, Waḥshī, an expert spearman, in return for killing only one person: Ḥamza.

The armies faced off just outside of Medina, to the north, at **Mount Uḥud**, a sacred mountain which the Prophet said is a "mountain that loves us." The Muslims already knew that the Quraysh were three thousand in number, and they were marching to Mount Uḥud with only one thousand men. On the way there, the leader of the hypocrites and his battalion of three hundred men deserted the Muslims. The Muslims were now seven hundred. They arrived at Mount Uḥud before the Quraysh and quickly took the strategic high ground. The Prophet stationed the army with their backs to the mountain. Off to the side, on a small hill, called the Archers' Hill, the Prophet placed fifty archers and gave them explicit instructions not to leave their post without a direct order from him. They would serve to protect the Muslim army from being flanked by a group of the Quraysh. At the outset of the battle, the Muslims took an early lead, striking down prominent leaders of the opposing army. Volleys of arrows held off a Qurayshite battalion of horses led by the master war-strategist Khālid bin Walīd.

In the heat of battle, Waḥshī, focused on his sole mission, found Ḥamza ؓ, "the Lion of God," as the Prophet called him, fighting fiercely. With one spear throw he felled the beloved uncle of the Prophet, and one of the greatest warriors of Islam fell to the ground. But even with Ḥamza's death and martyrdom, the Quraysh knew well they had been defeated and stood little chance of victory against the Muslims, so they began to retreat. Some of the archers saw this, and with the battle seemingly over, they wanted to run down to gather some of the war spoils. The leader of the group reminded them of the Prophet's instructions, but still they went. Watching patiently, Khālid bin Walīd saw this opening and led his battalion of one hundred horses to flank the Muslims. Suddenly, the tide of the battle had turned, and the Quraysh rallied against the cornered Muslims. They pushed a small group of them, who fought fervently to protect the Prophet, deeper into the mountains. The Prophet himself was struck and knocked down in the fighting. His face was wounded, bleeding profusely, and his front tooth was broken. Some announced that the Prophet had been killed, and the Quraysh rejoiced at their apparent victory, while the Muslims hurriedly moved the Prophet to a cove behind the mountain. His companions, hurt and angry at seeing the Prophet of God injured so, asked him to invoke God's wrath against their enemies, but he answered, "I was not sent as one who curses but as a summoner and a mercy. O God, guide my people, for they do not know!"

Abū Sufyān's wife Hind, in an act of bitter vengeance, sought out the body of Ḥamza ؓ and cut out his liver, chewed it, and spit it out. She then mutilated the rest of his body, cutting off his nose, ears, and other body parts. The Prophet ﷺ was very close to Ḥamza, and this pained him deeply. He buried his uncle, along with the rest of those martyred, at the foot of the mountain, and would visit them regularly in the years to come.

Abū Sufyān, excited by the Meccan victory, began to taunt the Muslims. He yelled out that wars take turns, a day of victory for a day of defeat, referring to Badr. ʿUmar ؓ was told to respond, "We are not equal: Our slain are in Paradise, yours are in the Fire." The Meccans challenged the Muslims to meet them in battle again after one year's time. The Muslims accepted the challenge.

The next time the Muslims would face the Quraysh, the Meccans would not be alone. Creating a coalition of allies, the Quraysh led an army of over nine thousand upon the city of Medina itself. A prominent companion, Salmān ؓ, suggested that the Muslims use a tactic used by his people, the Persians. His suggestion was to dig, at the passage-way into Medina, a wide trench that could not be crossed by man or horse. The Muslims worked around the clock, taking shifts digging, and so the battle is known as the **Battle of the Trench**. The trench surprised the invading coalition, and their only hope of taking the city became treachery: Unbeknownst to the Muslims, the Quraysh entered into a deal with a tribe of Jews that lived on the outskirts of Medina. In an act of treason, the Jewish tribe agreed to allow the Quraysh to enter into the city, ensuring the defeat of the vastly outnumbered Muslims. Eventually, however, the Prophet caught wind of this and strategically worked with a secret convert to prolong the negotiations between the Meccans and the Jewish tribe. Seeds of mistrust were sown between them, and after days of being held at bay by the trench in the harsh desert, the invaders began to show signs of fatigue. Then, in response to the Prophet's supplication (*duʿā'*), divine aid came. God ﷻ sent a great and torrential windstorm which sent the invaders scattering, giving up on any hope of taking Medina. God saved the Muslims and gave them victory. Later, the Jewish tribe was held accountable for the treason of working with foreign invaders against the citizens of their own city. The decision was made for them to be judged by the law of the Torah, which holds such treason to be a capital offense.

VICTORIOUS

Through divine inspiration, the Prophet had a dream in which he saw himself and his companions entering the Sacred House (*Kaʿbah*) and shaving their heads—the ritual after completion of a pilgrimage to the Holy Sanctuary. Inspired by this sign of divine permission, the Muslims set out to make the pilgrimage to Mecca. They made the journey with no weapons to protect themselves—during the sacred months of pilgrimage all were granted safe passage into Mecca. The Quraysh did not want to let the Muslims enter Mecca—for it would be a symbolic defeat for them—but they could not violate the laws of the sacred months upon which their status as governors of the Holy Sanctuary depended. En route to Mecca, the Muslims set up camp in a region outside of the city called Hudaybiyyah. The Quraysh sent a delegation to negotiate with the Muslims, working to strike a deal in which they would not enter Mecca. Eventually they signed the Treaty of Hudaybiyyah, an agreement that the Muslims felt was unfair and one-sided. The terms stated that the Muslims could not enter Mecca this year, but could make the pilgrimage next year; that any Muslim fleeing Mecca had to be sent back there, but that anyone defecting from Medina would be allowed to leave for Mecca; and that there would be no conflicts between the two parties and their respective allies for a duration of ten years.

The Prophet then moved to fulfill the sacred rituals that normally mark the successful completion of the Pilgrimage (Ḥajj)—he shaved his head and sacrificed an animal. The companions were frozen in bewilderment and disappointment; they had been turned back from the Holy Sanctuary in a seeming defeat! But they eventually followed the lead of the Prophet, and revelation descended, showing believers a different perspective on what had just taken place.

> *Truly We have opened up a path to clear triumph for you. — Quran 48:1*

There was a temporary peace, and indeed, the Muslims did return the following year to perform a lesser pilgrimage (*ʿumrah*) at the Holy Sanctuary of Mecca.

After some time, however, the Quraysh and their allies violated the treaty, dissolving it altogether. The Prophet ﷺ then began preparations for war, amassing an army of over ten thousand men of the Muslims and their allies. This army, the largest in Arabian history, marched for Mecca. The Meccan leaders grew distraught, contemplating the inevitable outcome. As the massive army entered the city, Abū Sufyān watched. Some of the Muslims began to exclaim that it was a day of revenge, the day that the Quraysh were to be abased. The Prophet responded to the contrary: that it was a day of mercy, a day that the Quraysh were to be exalted. The Prophet offered sanctuary to anyone who desired it—they needed only remain in their homes, or go to the home of Abū Sufyān. As Abū Sufyān was a Quraysh nobleman, the Prophet maintained his dignity and honor by making his home the safe haven. Unlike arrogant conquerors motivated by self-glory, the Prophet's head was bowed in humility and gratitude to God Almighty. In this, the Prophet showed that already he was living according to a new way, not according to the old rules of Ignorance (*Jāhilīyyah*).

Interestingly, the "conquest" of Mecca, in 630 CE, was actually a turning point towards peace in Arabian history. Prophet Muhammad ﷺ prayed in the Holy Sanctuary in front of the Sacred House (*Kaʿbah*). He then circled the Sacred House and pointed with his staff to each idol in the Holy Sanctuary declaring, "The truth has come, and falsehood has perished; for falsehood is bound to perish" (17:81). Each idol fell onto its face. Next, he turned to address the Meccans. The Prophet ﷺ asked them what they thought he would do with them. It was customary in Arabia at that time that the conqueror of a land, particularly one who had suffered at the hands of those conquered, would take revenge and decimate its people. Instead, to the astonishment of everyone, he quoted a verse from the Quran spoken on the tongue of Prophet Joseph ﵇, "There is to be no blame on you today" (12:92). And thus, just as Prophet Joseph ﵇ forgave his family, Prophet Muhammad ﷺ forgave his people and, in that one act, ended the violent feudal cycle of revenge that had plagued Arabia for centuries.

After conquering Mecca and other nearby regions, Prophet Muhammad ﷺ began to distribute the massive spoils of war to prominent members of the Quraysh and other tribes who were, until that time, resistant to the message of Islam. Most of the recipients were prominent tribesmen who were already wealthy. Some of the Helpers (*Anṣār*), who had been living in poverty for years, began to worry that Prophet Muhammad ﷺ had forgotten them, and that he was showing favoritism to his tribesmen, when actually he was simply trying to strengthen the bond between those shaky believers and their new faith. In a famous and moving speech he addressed their concerns:

> "Men of the Helpers, word has come to me that you are deeply moved against me in your souls. Did I not find you erring, and God

guided you; poor, and God enriched you; enemies of each other, and God reconciled your hearts?"

"Yes indeed," they answered. "God and His Messenger are most bountiful and most gracious."

"Will you not rebut me?" the Prophet said.

"How would we rebut you?" they asked, perplexed.

"If you wished," he answered, "you could say to me, and say rightfully, and be believed: 'You came to us discredited, and we believed you; desperate, and we helped you; an outcast, and we took you in; destitute, and we comforted you.' O Helpers, are you stirred in your souls about the things of this world wherewith I have reconciled men's hearts that they may submit unto God, when unto you yourselves I have entrusted your Islam? Are you not well content, O Helpers, that these people take with them their sheep and their camels, and that you take with you the Messenger of God unto your homes? If all men but the Helpers went one way, and the Helpers another, I would go the way of the Helpers. God have mercy upon the Helpers, and on their sons, and their sons' sons."

They wept until their beards were wet with their tears, and responded in one voice, "We are well content with the Messenger of God as our portion and our lot."

THE LATTER DAYS

Every Ramaḍān, the Archangel Gabriel (Jibrīl) ﷺ would have Prophet Muhammad ﷺ review the entire Quran from memory with him. Then in 632 CE, he had the Prophet review it twice. This was a sign of the Prophet's imminent transition to God ﷻ and the death of his temporal body. He announced that he would lead the Muslims in Pilgrimage (*Ḥajj*) to Mecca. Over thirty thousand believers left Medina with the Prophet. It was on this Pilgrimage that he delivered the famous Farewell Sermon:

> "O people: Lend me an attentive ear, for I know not whether I will ever meet you again after this year in this setting.
>
> "O people: The life and property of every Muslim are forever as inviolable as the sanctity of this month, this day, and this city. Have I not conveyed the message? O God, be my witness! Whosoever has goods entrusted to them should [be sure] to return them to their rightful owners.

"All usurious obligations from the Era of Ignorance (*Jāhilīyyah*) are nullified, but your capital is yours to keep. You will neither inflict nor suffer any inequity. God has decreed that there shall be no usury, and I begin with the usury due to my uncle ʿAbbās bin ʿAbd al-Muṭṭalib: It is waived. All blood-vengeance from the Era of Ignorance has been cast away, and the first blood-vengeance we will start with is that of [my kinsman] ʿĀmir bin Rabīʿah bin al-Ḥārith bin ʿAbdal-Muṭṭalib... Have I not conveyed the message? O God, be my witness!

"O people: Beware of Satan, for the safety of your religion. He has lost all hope that you will follow him completely, but he would be happy to have you follow him in small things... Have I not conveyed the message? O God, be my witness!

"O people: You have responsibilities towards your women, and they have responsibilities towards you. Their responsibilities towards you are to not lay with another man in your beds, nor to let anyone whom you dislike into your home without your permission, and to not commit indecencies. If they fulfill their responsibilities, then to them belongs the right to be fed and clothed in kindness. Treat your women well and be kind to them, for they have trusted you and relied on you to manage their affairs. Remember that you have taken them as your wives only under God's trust and with His permission. So be conscientious towards God in your treatment of women, and treat them well. Have I not conveyed the message? O God, be my witness!

"O people: All believers are brothers, and nothing which belongs to a Muslim shall be legitimately taken by a fellow Muslim unless it was given freely and willingly. Have I not conveyed the message? O God, be my witness! So do not go back to the ways of disbelief by fighting and killing one another after I have gone. For I have left you with two things, the Quran and my Prophetic Way (*Sunnah*), and if you follow these you will never go astray. Have I not conveyed the message? O God, be my witness!

"O people: You all have the same Lord, and you all have the same father. All of mankind is from Adam, and Adam was made from earth. The most noble among you is the most pious and conscientious towards God. An Arab has no superiority over a non-Arab except by [the measure of] piety and conscientiousness towards God. Have I not conveyed the message? O God, be my witness!"

And they replied, "Yes, O God!"

He said, "And let those who witness this pass on my words to those who did not...".

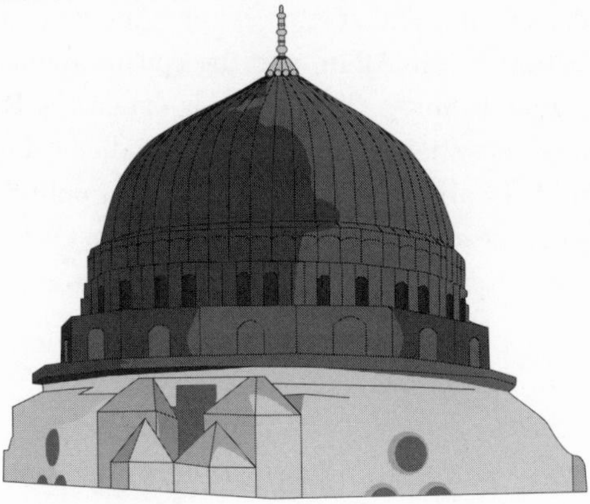

Figure 19: The Green Dome of the Prophet's ﷺ Mosque in Medina

Soon afterwards, the Prophet addressed the Muslims gathered in his mosque: "There is a servant among God's servants to whom God ﷻ has offered the choice between this world and that which is with Him, and the slave has chosen that which is with God." The Archangel Gabriel ﷺ presented Prophet Muhammad ﷺ with a choice: He could have the world, with all of the riches and splendors it had to offer, and live its entire duration, or he could pass on in transition to his Lord. He chose what he called "the most supreme companion." His health worsened and he fell very ill. In his last days, the Prophet gave his community parting advice, focusing primarily on guarding the prayer and taking good care of the weak and the womenfolk of the community. This advice indicated that, as he was on his way to meet his Lord ﷻ, it was his concern for the believers that was foremost on his mind.

On the 12th day of the Arabian month of the First Spring (*Rabīʿ al-Awwal*), at the age of sixty-three, the blessed Prophet Muhammad ﷺ passed away. The companions wept and grieved, for their beloved Prophet, the Beloved of God ﷺ, could no longer look at them, smile, touch their hands, listen to their troubles, and comfort them in the ways he had done ceaselessly for so many years.

After the death of the Prophet, Abū Bakr ؓ, his closest friend and companion, was named as his successor or **caliph (*khalīfah*)**. The caliph stands in the place of the Prophet as the political leader of the nation (*ummah*) of believers. The majority of scholars of normative Islam have held that the first four caliphs, who were the four closest companions of the Prophet, represent the order of the four best Muslims after Prophet Muhammad ﷺ. They are, listed in order of rank and rule as caliph: Abū Bakr as-Ṣiddīq, ʿUmar bin al-Khaṭṭāb, ʿUthmān bin ʿAffān, and the cousin and son-in-law of the Prophet, ʿAlī bin Abū Ṭālib ؓ. This group is called the **Rightly Guided Caliphs**, whereas rulers after them were simply called caliphs.[15] The period of the Rightly Guided Caliphs was one of righteous political rule after the end of prophethood, the end of direct revelation from God.

15. After these four of the most noble companions, scholars include a short period of time ruled by the grandson of Prophet Muhammad ﷺ (and son of ʿAlī) al-Ḥasan, as well as the period ruled by the righteous caliph ʿUmar bin ʿAbd al-ʿAzīz (d. 101AH/720CE), as part of the period of the Rightly Guided Caliphs.

5. HIS MIRACLES

Miracles, by definition, are the suspension of conventional norms by God ﷻ via a prophet, as a sign of the prophet's truthfulness in claiming to have been sent by God. The grandest and most lasting of the miracles of Prophet Muhammad ﷺ is unequivocally the Noble Quran. Much of this is discussed in the section dedicated to the last divine revelation (Chapter 6). Still, Prophet Muhammad ﷺ performed many other miracles throughout his life, although he seemed to be quite reserved in performing them, saving them for only specific situations.

Perhaps the best known of these lesser miracles occurred when a group of Qurayshi leaders challenged him to perform a miracle. The masses were gathered near the mountains, just outside of Mecca. Prophet Muhammad ﷺ then split a full moon into two halves before everyone's eyes. The believers rejoiced and were increased in faith, but many of the disbelievers simply accused Prophet Muhammad ﷺ of sorcery.

Another incident, which was witnessed by so many of his companions that its authenticity is of the highest caliber,[16] happened one day in Medina. Prophet Muhammad ﷺ used to deliver the Friday Sermon while leaning on a particular date-palm tree. Later, when a pulpit was built and the Prophet began to deliver the sermon from there, the date-palm was heard audibly moaning and weeping. The Prophet of Mercy went over to the date-palm, and gently rubbed it with his hand, soothing it. He then offered it to join him as a tree in paradise, which it accepted. Such a miracle teaches us many things. It reminds us of the love a tree felt for the Prophet and calls us to examine our own. It also indicates to us that there are levels of consciousness other than the kinds we are used to experiencing, which are beyond our perception.

There are many other miracles which are recorded in various accounts: the Prophet prayed for rain during a drought, and the clouds came forth immediately from the clear sky and rain poured for seven days; on many an occasion, the food the Prophet ate could be heard invoking and praising God ﷻ while in his blessed hands; he caused water to pour forth from his fingers, giving drink to many thirsty companions; and the Prophet also

16. Narrations and historical events are assigned various levels of authentication based on a number of elements, including the veracity of the reporters, the reputation of their memories, and the number of corroborating reports. Some reach the level of being considered undeniable. This is based on there being such a multitude of corroborating reports that it becomes impossible to believe that the report could be an agreed-upon fabrication.

took a meal for two and fed with it hundreds of hungry companions after a long day of labor.

Each of these incidents was a proof of the authentic claim of Prophet Muhammad ﷺ, like other prophets with miracles, of having being sent by God Almighty. They also remind us that there are powers that supersede the way of the world in which we live. Miracles are an essential part of Muslim belief; they are a much needed door to the optimism of unlimited possibilities.

صلى الله عليه وسلم

May God bless him and grant him peace!

Although one can never fully bring to light the beauty that is Prophet Muhammad ﷺ, hopefully these brief overviews provide a glimpse of that beauty. A famous poet, Ḥassān ibn Thābit رضي الله عنه, succinctly summed up the situation of anyone who attempts to discuss or explain the virtues of the Prophet:

I have not honored Muhammad with my words;
Rather, it is my words that have been honored with Muhammad.

CHAPTER 6

The Quran

God has sent down the most beautiful of all teachings: a Scripture that is consistent and draws comparisons; that causes the skin of those in awe of their Lord to shiver. Then their skin and heart become soothed at the mention of God: such is God's guidance. He guides with it whomever He will; no one can guide those God leaves to stray.

QURAN 39:23

We have sent the Scripture to you only to make clear to them what they differ about, and as guidance and mercy to those who believe.

QURAN 16:64

At the beginning of the human story, when God expelled Adam and Eve from the Garden, He gave them the following promise as consolation:

But when guidance comes from Me, as it certainly will, there will be no fear for those who follow My guidance, nor will they grieve. — Quran 2:38

And so it was the will of God to send to mankind guidance from another realm, from beyond creation. As it is, God's final revelation, the Quran[1]—which in Arabic means *the recitation*—is not of this world, but of the divine. That becomes apparent very early to the reader—the Quran is unlike anything you will have ever encountered before. It is at once engaging and challenging, enveloping the reader, taking him on a journey of eloquence, beauty, and soul-altering perspectives.

It serves primarily, as God ﷻ describes it, as "...a reminder for all worlds" (38:87), for the human is a most forgetful creature. We forget where we came from, where we are going, why we are here, and how we should live. The Quran answers clearly all of these essential questions of our existence, providing us with the deep insights necessary for knowing our Creator, our species, and our world. And so the Quran is not a book of information, although it definitely contains information, but a book of guidance, showing us how to fulfill our purpose: to know and serve God ﷻ.

1. The Arabic word *Quran* has been transliterated in many different ways over history. Some of these include: Quran, Qur'an, Koran, and Alcoran, among others. These are all attempts at conveying the sounds of the Arabic word, the first letter of which does not have an exact English equivalent. The proper transliteration is *Qur'ān*, but in this book we'll use the word as it has entered into the English language: *Quran*. There is no difference in meaning—all refer to the same book, the last revelation of God to humanity via Prophet Muhammad ﷺ.

1. THE NATURE OF THE QURAN

THE WORD OF GOD

While many other religious scriptures are said to have been authored by men inspired by God ﷻ, the Quran is the direct word of God Himself, verbatim. Every syllable and inflection is based on the transmission of God's own speech, by way of the Archangel Gabriel (Jibrīl), to Prophet Muhammad ﷺ. More than once, God ﷻ reminds us in the Quran that the Prophet plays no role in its composition and that he dutifully relays the scripture with the utmost integrity. Even the language of the Quran reflects this: Most verbs are in the second person, directly addressing the Prophet, telling him to say or do certain things.

The revelation of the Quran began in the month of Ramadan when the Prophet was forty years old. He was meditating on the oneness of God ﷻ in Ḥirā' Cave. During this meditation, Gabriel (Jibrīl) came with the first revelation. From then on, the revelation would come down, part by part, over a period of twenty-three years. Some verses would be revealed to answer questions believers and non-believers posed to the Prophet. Others were revealed in response to historical events during the prophetic mission—an indication that the divine revelation and the circumstances of the Prophet's life were inseparable.

Being the Word of God, the Quran is a manifestation of the divine attribute of speech in the form of scripture. It is God's message to humanity, in which He tells us of Himself. It is therefore accessible to all people everywhere for all time. To recite and act upon it is to partake in the divine grace of God's revealing the Quran.

THE ARRANGEMENT OF THE QURAN

As a book, the Quran is divided into 114 **chapters (*sūrahs*)**, each with its own title and content. Each chapter is comprised of **verses (*āyahs*)**. Some verses are long, others are single sentences, some are phrases, and others still are only letters. A collection of verses makes up a chapter, and the different chapters vary in length. After the first chapter, "The Opening (*al-Fātiḥah*)," the chapters are arranged more or less in order of length, from longest to shortest.

Chapters (*sūrahs*) are classified into two main categories, *Meccan* and *Medinan*, depending on whether they were revealed before or after the migration of Prophet Muhammad ﷺ to Medina. Each category is characterized by particular themes. The Meccan chapters present aspects of belief: primarily, the oneness (*tawḥīd*) of God ﷻ, prophethood, the resurrection of the dead, and the Day of Judgment. These chapters also concern ethical and moral behavior, calling people to act with justice and social consciousness. After the migration, when the community had progressed from a collection of individuals to an actual political entity, the Medinan revelations addressed laws governing communal life, including laws of marriage and divorce, criminal law, treaties of peace, rules of engagement for war, and commercial contracts. Still, both the Meccan and Medinan chapters are primarily a call to ethical and moral behavior—even legal edicts are clothed in moral language that appeals to the psyche of a believer.

From this description, it should be apparent that the Quran is not arranged according to neatly designated topics, nor is it a story that follows a linear timeline. At first, when reading it, one can feel surprised by the constant changes of subject and verb tense. But it soon becomes clear to the attentive reader that the Quran is a book that must be accepted on its own terms. Only when you let go of your preconceived notions about what a divine book should contain are you taken on a journey through the shimmering, guiding lights of the Quran. This unique quality of the Quran is a reminder of its divine source: that it comes from beyond the created world, that it is Divine Speech, here for all to engage with and experience. As mentioned, its purpose is not simply to relay information, but rather to guide humanity.

"AN ARABIC QURAN"

The Quran is only considered to be the actual Quran, that is, the Speech of God ﷻ, when it is in its original Arabic. Because divine wisdom chose Arabic to be the vehicle to manifest God's word in the world, some scholars have held that Arabic is not a man-made language, but rather a language revealed by God ﷻ.

Attempts to convey the meaning of the Quran in other languages can only be considered interpretations, so the text in another language would not be the actual Quran. It can be be a means to further develop your relationship with the Quran, but it could not, for example, replace the Arabic Quran for devotional use in prayer. When reciting the Quran in Arabic, all

Muslims, from Japan to California, are uttering the exact words God revealed to Prophet Muhammad ﷺ, as relayed through the Archangel Gabriel ﷺ.

THE MIRACULOUS NATURE OF THE QURAN

The Quran was revealed to the people of 7th century Arabia. They were a desert people with a rich oral tradition of poetry and story. On a social level, nothing had a greater impact on the people of the Arabian peninsula than poetry. Everyone listened to it and was moved by it. Poetry appealed to the very core of the Arab and stirred him to action. For that reason, the poet was an influential member of society, who could rally entire tribes to a cause by composing one simple poem. To the Arabs, poetry was almost sacred; the most celebrated poems were so esteemed that they were posted on the Sacred House (*Kaʿbah*) in Mecca.

The Quran is, quite simply put, a literary masterpiece beyond human capability. It is inherently inimitable—no human effort could compare. This was a challenge put forth by God ﷻ: to compose a book like it. When no one could, God then challenged deniers to compose ten chapters that could compare with it, and finally challenged all of Arabia to produce even one chapter comparable to it.

Even the disbelieving Arabs who opposed Prophet Muhammad were awestruck by its recitation. They used to claim that it had magical powers over those who heard it. Many were so moved by it that they yearned to hear more. When a leader of the Meccan disbelievers was caught eavesdropping on a recitation of the Quran, it was embarrassing proof that even those who opposed its message were in awe of it and drawn towards it.

The Quran is rhythmic in nature, and that also exerts an effect on the soul of whoever hears or recites it. It is enchanting and captivating. It is also inexhaustible. Volumes could be written expounding each verse. The meanings found within it are limitless, because it is the Speech of God, the Infinite. Each word is used and placed with divine wisdom.

Each of these facets is enough to make the Quran inimitable. Together, all of them are a reminder of its divine origin. Because of this, the Quran is considered the greatest miracle of God ﷻ, brought to all of humanity by Prophet Muhammad ﷺ.

In the Quran itself, God ﷻ calls the Quran by other names as well, to reveal to us some of its other dimensions. One group of names indicates the knowledge the Quran contains: the Guidance, the Truth, the Wisdom, the Judgment, the Light, the Proof, and the Reminder, among others. Another group of names indicates reasons for its revelation by God: Mercy, Healing, Generous, and Blessed. Each of these qualities exists for our benefit, and each contributes to the miraculous nature of the Quran.

DIVINE PRESERVATION

Over time, as the human story progressed, God ﷻ sent messengers to people to remind them of where they came from and why they were here. Part of the message He sent took the form of scripture. Divine decree and the acts of men caused previous scriptures to be either lost or altered, losing their authentic, original form. But God promised that the Quran would not suffer the same fate. He oversees its preservation, guaranteeing what is a verifiable historical fact: The Quran we possess today is the same text that was present during the life of Prophet Muhammad ﷺ.

THE QURAN IN OUR LIVES

One of the names of the Quran, given by God ﷻ in the Quran itself, is "The Reminder." We humans are, by our very nature, neglectful and forgetful of our duty to God. The world pulls us towards egotism: we become lost in self-adoration, deluded into thinking we are self-sufficient. The Quran serves to remind us of the answers to our most important questions. It reminds us repeatedly where we came from, why we are here, where we are going, and what is expected of us. Instead of presenting a concise list of these teachings, the Quran brings them to life with examples, parables, historical accounts, and more. Through a daily engagement with the Quran, a believer develops an internal sense of these realities. Much like physical fitness, in which a lifestyle of regular physical activity changes the very makeup of your body, a lifestyle that includes a daily, deep relationship with the Quran alters the very composition of your soul.

To achieve this kind of relationship with the Quran requires two types of reading. The first is a consistent devotional recitation of the Quran in its original Arabic, even if you don't understand the language. The Quran is the Speech of God and has metaphysical power that affects both the soul and the physical world. God ﷻ describes the Quran as a "healing," and Prophet Muhammad ﷺ even used it to heal physical ailments. Prophet Muhammad ﷺ related to us that those who struggle to recite it will be rewarded doubly for their effort. The term "Quran" means "often recited," and it should be recited in a measured melodic manner, not read in the way you might read an Arabic newspaper. The sounds and rhythms affect the reader. They transform the spirit in ways beyond our understanding.

The second type of reading is for reflection and study. God ﷻ asks the question, "Will they not contemplate the Quran?" (47:24). To read a translation of the Quran in your native tongue will allow you to more deeply appreciate its meanings, which in turn lend themselves to reflection.

Each of us should read the Quran as if it were speaking directly to us. Each injunction, reminder, or moral challenge that it calls to, we should take on personally. Believers should reflect upon God's statements and examine how their lives match up to them. In this way, our lives can become Quranic, and eventually we will be transformed into people who resemble the qualities of the recipient of the Quran, the Beloved Prophet Muhammad ﷺ.

CHALLENGES IN INTERPRETATION

Religious scripture in Islam can contain both unequivocal and ambiguous statements. Naturally, the ambiguous statements require deeper examination. To aid in the study of the meanings and message of the Quran, a discipline of Muslim scholarship was developed. **Quranic exegesis** is the specialized discipline of scholarly interpretation of the meanings of Quranic verses. It requires an in-depth knowledge of many fields, including the Arabic language, its grammar, the Prophet's biography, and more. Some works of Quranic exegesis have been translated into English and other languages. To read from these works will give you context and ensure a proper understanding of the text, which may differ from what a cursory literal reading might lead you to think. It will also help you to more deeply understand the divine message of guidance contained in the various chapters and passages of the Quran. It is an endless ocean that is constantly revisited by scholars from every generation, including our own.

Like all religious texts, the Quran can be misinterpreted. The reasons for erroneous, as well as simply differing, interpretations are many. For one thing, the language of the Quran is highly concise. Pronouns are used frequently, and it often requires an in-depth analysis to determine exactly what they are referencing. Also, in Arabic a word can have different meanings based on the context of its use. Determining its meaning in a particular verse requires both a deep knowledge of the many meanings of the word and an understanding of that particular context. There are also phrases and statements in the Quran which have become proverbial in nature, and which are sometimes quoted in isolation, without the parts of the verse that come before and after, leading to a misunderstanding of the intended meaning. For all of these reasons, interpreting the Quran can be quite complex, and there is a dangerous potential of misunderstanding the divine guidance.

A notorious example of gross misinterpretation is the use of Chapter 2, verse 191, to justify killing non-Muslims. The verse states, "kill them wherever you encounter them", and taken without any regard for context, it can appear as license to take the life of any non-Muslim anywhere. But a deeper examination reveals that this is not the case at all—this verse concerns a specific historical situation and is not to be applied categorically.

The verse that precedes this excerpt (2:190) defines "them" as "those who attack you." Historical context shows us that the Muslims at the time of this revelation were in conflict with the polytheists of Quraysh, who attacked them and forcibly expelled them from their homes. The Muslims were also concerned about what to do if they were attacked in the Holy Sanctuary, where violence was forbidden. So this verse informs believers that they are to fight against this specific group, in this specific situation, even if it means fighting in the Sanctuary itself. Verse 2:190, setting further context and regulation, also stipulates, "do not overstep the limits"—the limits had been detailed by Prophet Muhammad ﷺ as not attacking non-combatants, women, children, and the like.

It becomes evident how quoting a Quranic excerpt out of context—ignoring the verses before and after, and quoting it without regard to its historical setting—can lead to gross misinterpretation and misapplication. In this case, the disparity between the accurate meaning and the misinterpretation, as well as the drastic inherent consequences of such a misinterpretation, highlights the need for highly qualified scholarship to guide our reading of the Holy Quran.

MEMORIZATION OF THE QURAN

God ﷻ, in His divine wisdom, revealed the Quran to a people with an oral tradition. The Arabians of that period preserved knowledge primarily through memorization, and relied on writing things down only as a safeguard. And so the primary means of learning the Quran was, and still is, to internalize its words through verbatim memorization. From a very young age, Muslims strive to memorize parts of the Quran, in part for use in devotions like prayer (*ṣalāh*).

You should work to commit the divine words of the Quran to memory. Start with what you will need for your daily prayers (*ṣalāh*), and gradually expand the number of verses you can recite by heart. Divine speech is illuminating, and learning the Quran "by heart" will illuminate both your heart and your soul. A very special status in both this life and the next is given to a person who commits the entire Quran to memory and embodies it in his or her life.

2. MAJOR THEMES IN THE QURAN

The Quran is God's last call to humanity. It contains 114 chapters and more than 6000 verses. To help you in grasping its essential message, the Quran's seven major themes,[2] as outlined by scholars, are presented below. These themes recur often and are reexamined multiple times throughout the scripture. Together, they make up the central message of the Quran and tell us about God ﷻ, unseen realities ***(ghayb)***, the afterlife, virtue and vice, and other qualities needed for our salvation.

1. THE LORDSHIP OF GOD

The bedrock of our faith is belief in God ﷻ. We believe that He is pre-existent, all-powerful, and that He created us. The sum of all of these beliefs defines our relationship with respect to God: He is our Lord and we are His servants, subject to His will. We were made to worship Him, and He is intrinsically deserving of worship. All of creation, the sun, moon, stars, and every snowflake, moves as God commands. It is up to us whether or not we want to willingly fall in line with the rest of His creation.

In the Quran, God ﷻ reminds us of His supreme authority over us and teaches us that an understanding of His absolute authority and supremacy is essential for true faith. Our relationship with Him is not one of negotiation, but one of submission. It is important to bear this in mind at all times. As we live our lives with the unique backgrounds that God has given us, we may at times come across a commandment of His that we, His servants, will find challenging to fulfill. We must take these times as opportunities to subject our own whims to the command of God and to reaffirm our response, "Yea, indeed, we testify... You are our Lord!"

2. PROPHETHOOD

When Adam and Eve were ordered to leave Paradise, God ﷻ promised to send them guidance about how to return to Him. This guidance came in the form of revelation, delivered through people selected by God for the task of prophethood. This phenomenon existed from the very beginning

2. These seven themes were identified by the great exegete of the Quran, Imam Ibn Juzayy al-Kalbī in the introduction to his exegesis of the Quran.

and continued up until the last prophet, the Seal of the Prophets, Prophet Muhammad ﷺ. All the prophets brought essentially the same message, which differed only in details. All of them ultimately called their people to submission (*islām*) to God, and they were themselves in a state of submission, and thus could be called *muslims*.

In the Quran, God ﷻ tells us that He sent a prophet to every people. Of these prophets, we know twenty-five by name and were told by Prophet Muhammad ﷺ that there were thousands of others throughout history. The Quran provides many accounts of the lives of different prophets, all of which collectively provide a more complete picture of God's guidance and of the qualities of believers and deniers.

3. DAY OF JUDGMENT

One of the major themes of the Quran is the reminder that we will all be brought back to life after we have died, so that we may be judged by God ﷻ. The Quraysh believed that our existence ended completely with death. They found it very hard to accept the concepts of resurrection and the afterlife. Many of them would ask mockingly if the believers actually thought that God would be able to reconstruct them after they had decayed. The Quran responds to these questions with clear arguments against denials of the resurrection.

The resurrection and judgment, central tenets of faith, are essential to the concept of our accountability before God. The Quran provides details about the momentous Day of Judgment, when we are presented with scrolls that tally our recorded deeds, and we are placed before the Scales which weigh our good deeds against our misdeeds to see which are greater. All of these details provide the believer with a clearer picture of what each of us must work to prepare for.

4. LEGAL RULINGS

All of creation is subject to the Lordship of God ﷻ. Those who willingly accept this reality strive to live their lives in accordance with His will. Of the over six thousand verses in the Quran, only about three hundred relate to matters of law. These verses delineate the divine commands with respect to various situations; the sum of these commands is the basis of Islamic law (*sharīʿah*). For each legal matter, Islamic jurists examine the relevant commands, and from comparing and analyzing them, develop them into one of the five possible rulings. Overall, this relatively modest proportion of the Quran includes guidance about aspects of devotional worship, property law, inheritance law, and spiritual states of the heart.

As we can see, although it contains divine commands with legal implications, the Quran is much more than a set of laws. Legal rulings, though essential, are only a small part of the guidance provided us by God in the Quran.

5. PROMISE OF REWARD

Present within the Quran are a multitude of verses that tell us that those who strive to walk the straight path and obey God will be rewarded both in this life and the next. The Quran clearly affirms the existence of Paradise in the afterlife, and gives descriptions of it to encourage the believer to toil in the way of God ﷻ. It also provides reminders that God blesses and graces those who do good deeds here during our present life.

6. THREAT OF PUNISHMENT

To aid us to be spiritually balanced, with both hope for mercy and fear of punishment, God ﷻ provides descriptions of the torments of the afterlife for the wicked. The Quran describes Hellfire and its inhabitants, and the terrors of the Day of Judgment. These all motivate us to protect ourselves from the wrath of God, working to avoid what He has forbidden and to do what he has commanded.

Taken together, the promise of reward and the threat of punishment present a part of what some Muslim scholars call the **metaphysical laws of the Quran**. God ﷻ tells us what actions bring forth His blessing (*barakah*) and what actions may incur His wrath or curse. These guidelines begin to show us patterns that reflect metaphysical laws of how things work in the world. For example, we know from the Quran that God will provide for those who are pious and conscious of Him. From studying these patterns, we learn how to make use of metaphysical cause and effect in our own lives.

7. HISTORICAL ACCOUNTS

In certain chapters of the Quran, God ﷾ tells us of the lives of prophets who were sent to different peoples and the resulting fates of their people. We are given detailed reports of many prophets, among them Noah, Moses, David, Joseph, Abraham, and Isaac.

The stories of God's prophets contain many lessons for believers. The prophets typically endure hardship in conveying God's message; they meet resistance from their people; they usually suffer great personal loss; and they are granted victory by God in the end.

One aspect that deserves closer examination is that God ﷾ grants his prophets the ability to perform miracles. Miracles, by definition, are the suspension by God of conventional norms. In the case of a prophet, a miracle serves as a sign of the truthfulness of his claim to have been sent by God. Many miracles are documented by God in the Quran, including accounts of Prophet Noah and his ark, Prophet Abraham and the cooling of the fire, Prophet Moses and the splitting of the Red Sea, Prophet Jesus and the healing of the blind, and many more.

Scholars tend to use different terminology for miracles performed by prophets for the purpose of verifying their claims to prophethood, and "lesser miracles" performed by others, sometimes righteous saints, which play no role in verifying prophethood, since those who perform them do not claim to be prophets or to receive revelation from God ﷾. Nonetheless, both types of miracle are still, in effect, the same thing: the suspension of conventional norms by God via a particular person.

In the modern era, with its overemphasis on scientific measurement as the only means of ascertaining truth, miracles serve as a reminder of God's supreme control over the universe. We should remember that even the most basic "laws of physics" are only consistent because God ﷾ has made them so, and that He can reverse them at His will. Belief in miracles can serve as a means to strengthen our faith overall. Moreover, our affirmation of miracles serves as a much needed door to optimism, allowing believers to see a world with unlimited possibilities.

CHAPTER 7

Islamic Holy Days

So We sent Moses with Our signs: 'Bring out your people from the depths of darkness into light. Remind them of the Day of God: there truly are signs in this for every steadfast, thankful person.'

QURAN 14:5

1. THE ISLAMIC YEAR

God سبحانه وتعالى created the entire universe with all of its intrinsic patterns. He set the orbit of the Earth and moon, and revolution of the Earth upon its axis. Islam teaches us that the calendar is decreed by God. It is He that decreed there to be seven days in one week and twelve months in a year, as reaffirmed in the Quran.

Within this calendar are days that God سبحانه وتعالى has made sacred, ennobling them above other days. Each ennobled unit of time has an act of devotional worship associated with it. Our daily devotion is the ritual prayer (*ṣalāh*); our weekly devotion is the Friday congregational prayer; our annual devotion is fasting (*ṣawm*) the month of Ramaḍān; and the devotion of a lifetime is the Pilgrimage (*Ḥajj*).

The days of the week are the same in Islam as in the common calendar. The holy day for Muslims is Friday, with a special congregational prayer service and sermon. The months, however, are based on the lunar calendar, which is founded upon the moon's orbit around the Earth and is designated for devotional use.

LUNAR MONTHS

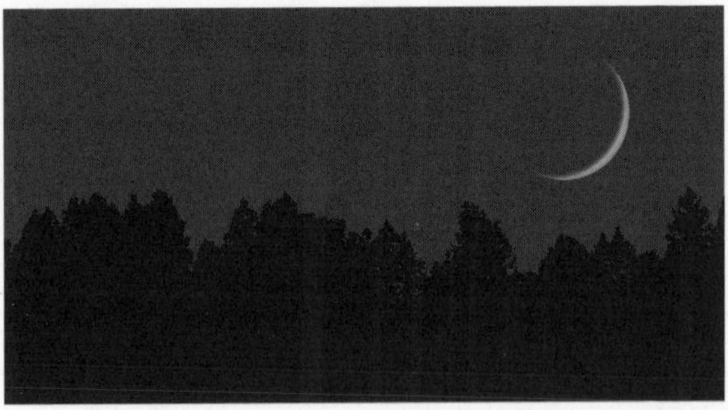

Figure 20: A New Crescent Moon

Some Muslim scholars have elaborated on the distinction between the two calendars God سبحانه وتعالى has placed at our disposal, the solar and the lunar. The solar calendar, based on the Earth's orbit around the sun, is for non-devo tional use. The sun represents the daytime, the time of work and employment, seeking out the bounties and provisions of God.

In contrast, the lunar calendar, which is based on the moon's orbit around the Earth, is for devotional use. All Islamic months and dates—whether Ramaḍān, the Pilgrimage (*Ḥajj*), or the New Year—are based on the lunar calendar. The moon represents the night, the time of intense worship in which servants draw nearer to their Lord, seeking provisions for the next life.

Because the world of business and trade requires exact predictability, God ﷻ, in His wisdom, decreed that the solar calendar be always predictable and calculable. But the lunar calendar, the basis of our acts of surrender to God, includes an element of irregularity. As a natural phenomenon, lunar months vary in length between twenty-nine and thirty days. The start of each month is based on the sighting of the new crescent, an event whose occurrence can vary based on the age of the new moon, the prevailing atmospheric conditions, and a number of other factors. This element of unpredictability reminds us that our duty to God is a matter of surrender, not convenience.

THE ISLAMIC DAY AND NIGHT

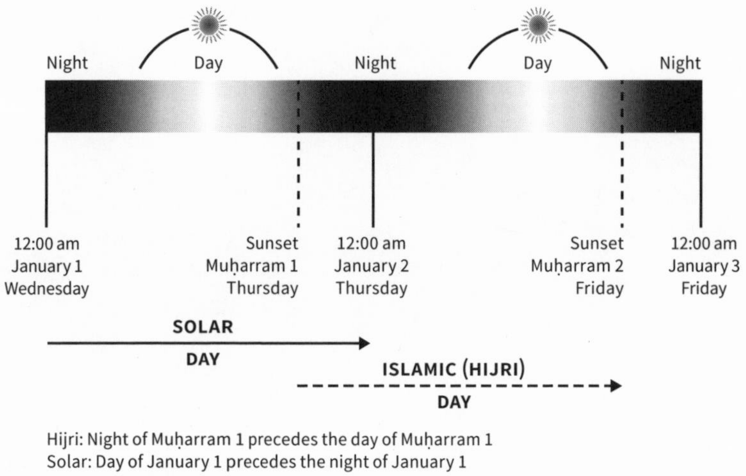

Figure 21: A Comparison of the Lunar Hijri Day and the Solar Day

For the Muslim calendar, a day starts at sunset and ends with the next sunset; thus Friday begins with the sunset on Thursday, and "Friday night" comes before the daytime portion of Friday. This is a concept we have in English: "the eve of" a particular day is the evening before it. So in the Muslim calendar, the change of date (e.g., from the 11th to the 12th of a lunar month) happens at sunset, not at midnight, as in the solar calendar we all use.

2. THE FRIDAY CONGREGATIONAL PRAYER (*ṢALĀT AL-JUMUʿAH*)

Believers! When the call to pray is made on the day of congregation [Friday], hurry towards the reminder of God and leave off your trading—that is better for you, if only you knew. — Quran 62:9

God ﷻ has decreed that Friday is the holy day for Muslims and that on Friday a special congregation is to be held. The Friday Congregational Prayer (*Ṣalāt al-Jumuʿah*) consists of two main parts: a sermon (*khuṭbah*) and the Friday prayer (*ṣalāh*) that takes place at midday. As its name indicates, the Friday Congregational Prayer is prayed in congregation and cannot be prayed alone. Friday is thus celebrated by the community as a time of special devotions that grant us the opportunity to grow in piety and nearness to God. Note that, unlike the Jewish and Christian Sabbaths, the holy day of Muslims is not a day of required rest or abstention from work.

THE MOSQUE (*MASJID*)

The mosque (*masjid*) is a sacred space, a House of God, and a special set of etiquettes is associated with visiting it. Prophet Muhammad ﷺ taught us to pray a voluntary prayer called the Mosque Salutation upon entering the prayer area of a mosque.[1] Also, because the mosque is a place of reflection and worship, we should contribute to an environment conducive to those practices by, for example, keeping our voices lowered.

Mosques (*masjids*) are very simple buildings. The main part of every mosque is the prayer area, a large carpeted area with no furniture, where believers congregate and pray. The carpet is ritually clean, and great care is taken to maintain this cleanliness. For this reason, no shoes are worn inside the prayer area, since they may track in filth (*najāsah*). When entering the mosque, therefore, you should remove your shoes and place them on the shoe racks that are usually located near the entrance of the mosque. Most mosques also have a *wuḍū'* (ritual washing) area, with a number of faucets where people can perform their ritual wash before entering the prayer area.

At the front of the prayer area, on the side towards the prayer-direction (*qiblah*), you will usually see a large cove indented into the wall. This

1. This prayer (*ṣalāh*) is prayed silently and is two prayer-units (*rakʿahs*) in length.

is called a prayer niche. Here the prayer leader (*imām*) stands to lead the congregation. Next to the prayer niche is a structure, usually with steps and a podium of sorts, where the prayer leader delivers the sermon during the Friday Congregational Prayer (*Ṣalāt al-Jumuʿah*).

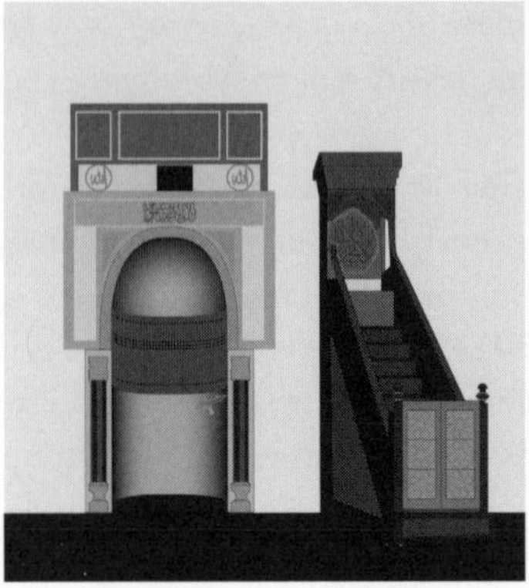

Figure 22: The Prayer Niche (left) and Pulpit (right) at the Front of a Mosque's Prayer Area

In the prayer area, men and women are separated by the standard formation of the prayer congregation: the prayer leader in front, followed by the men, with the women behind them, as taught by Prophet Muhammad ﷺ. Some mosques have a wall separating the genders, although this was not practiced by the Prophet ﷺ himself.

Although you may enter the mosque in a state of minor ritual impurity (which can be lifted with *wuḍūʾ* (ritual washing)), remember that, if you are in a state of major ritual impurity, entering the prayer area is forbidden (*ḥarām*) altogether. In this case, it is important to distinguish between the building of the mosque, which might include things like offices and libraries, and the actual prayer area of the mosque. For although it is a house of worship, a mosque is also a place of gathering, learning, and celebration, unlike some temples which are reserved for worship alone.

WHO IS REQUIRED TO ATTEND

To attend the Friday prayer is a requirement (*farḍ*) upon every Muslim male who fulfills the following conditions:

1. He resides in the vicinity of the Friday Congregational Prayer (*Ṣalāt al-Jumuʿah*)[2]
2. He does not have a valid excuse for not attending, such as being ill or quite elderly

s the Holy Quran (62:9) indicates, a Muslim male who fulfills these condi-ons has a religious duty to leave work, school, or other such obligations to ttend the Friday Congregational Prayer (*Ṣalāt al-Jumuʿah*). Many Muslims n the West work out various arrangements with their employers or teach-rs in order to facilitate this obligation. You should hope for reward from od ﷻ for any hardship involved.

For those for whom the Friday Congregational Prayer (*Ṣalāt al-Jumuʿah*) s not required (*farḍ*) (for example, women), it is nevertheless commendable *nustaḥab*) that they attend. Those who do not attend are still obligated to erform the *Ẓuhr* (Midday) prayer.

THE SERMON (*KHUṬBAH*)

he Friday Congregational Prayer (*Ṣalāt al-Jumuʿah*) is unique in that it has wo Prayer Calls (*Adhāns*) as opposed to just one, as in regular daily prayers. he first is generally called when the *Ẓuhr* (Midday) prayer time enters. Then ne prayer leader (*imām*) who will give the sermon (*khuṭbah*) ascends the ulpit and greets the congregation with peace, saying "*as-Salāmu ʿAlaykum.*" his marks the beginning of the sermon. Then, the *muezzin*, or prayer caller, ecites the second Prayer Call.

The prayer leader (*imām*) then delivers the sermon. The **sermon (*khuṭ-ah*)** is usually brief, lasting approximately fifteen to thirty minutes. In it, the rayer leader reminds the faithful of their duties to God ﷻ, usually select-ng a topic of religious life to highlight. The sermon is meant to inspire the ongregation to grow in conscientiousness (*taqwā*) and piety. After speak-ng for some time, the prayer leader will pause and sit down. During this ntermission, petitions to God for His forgiveness are particularly accepted, nd so the congregation all silently ask for forgiveness. Then the prayer eader stands and completes the sermon. Next, the prayer caller announces ne Call to Rise (*Iqāmah*), to commence the prayer portion of the Friday *Jumuʿah*) Congregational Prayer.

That is, he is not in a state of travel, or has been at his travel destination for a period long nough to lose the legal status of a traveler (four or more days).

THE PRAYER

The prayer (*ṣalāh*) of the Friday (*Jumuʿah*) Congregational Prayer is tw prayer-units (*rakʿah*) in length. The prayer leader (*imām*) recites the Qura aloud in both of them. The Friday Congregational Prayer replaces the *Ẓuh* (Midday) Prayer for those who attend.

SPECIAL CONSIDERATIONS FOR THE FRIDAY CONGREGATIONAL PRAYER

There are certain rulings specific to the Friday Congregational Prayer (*Ṣal al-Jumuʿah*), some of which concern requirements (*farḍ*), some of whic concern prophetic practices (*sunnah*), and others which concern forbidde (*ḥarām*) actions. We will briefly cover the most pertinent of these rulings.

It is forbidden (*ḥarām*) to speak, even in a whisper or in reply to a gree ing, during the sermon.[3] One is to sit attentively and face the prayer lead (*imām*) who is delivering the sermon. Also, it is recommended that you li ten to the sermon as if it were directed towards you, personally, so as t maximize your benefit from hearing its counsel.

On the other hand, there are a number of commendable (*mustaḥab*) act some of which are even prophetic practices (*sunnah*). It is commendable t groom yourself on Friday before the prayer by clipping your nails, trimmin your mustache, and taking a ritual bath (*ghusl*). It is also commendable f men to scent themselves beautifully. You should wear your best clothin white in color if possible.

SENDING BLESSINGS (*ṢALAWĀT*) UPON THE PROPHET

Friday (*Jumuʿah*) is a holy day for Muslims for many reasons. One of the is related to sending blessings (*ṣalawāt*) upon Prophet Muhammad ﷺ. W learn from the Prophet that sending blessings upon him reaches him by wa of the angels, who tell him that so-and-so has sent blessings upon him. O Friday however, the situation is different, as we see in a narration (*hadit* from Prophet Muhammad ﷺ:

3. Glorifications, praise, or salutations upon the Prophet said quietly to yourself in respons to the content of the sermon (*khuṭbah*), however, are allowed.

> Increase your recitation of blessings (*ṣalawāt*) upon me on Friday, because on this day the angels present themselves to me. Any servant of God who sends blessings upon me, his voice will reach me, no matter where he is.

In response to further questioning by the companions (*ṣaḥābah*), Prophet Muhammad ﷺ taught them that he is still conscious of this presentation of our blessings (*ṣalawāt*) upon him even after his bodily death. So on Fridays, we are told, our voices reach the Prophet directly, even now. In turn, he responds to the blessings and salutations himself.

3. RAMAḌĀN & THE FESTIVAL OF COMPLETING THE FAST (*ʿĪD AL-FIṬR*)

Ramaḍān, the ninth month of the Islamic lunar calendar, is the month of required fasting, special devotions, and intensified study of the Quran. We emerge from Ramaḍān renewed, with a sense of our moral responsibility to change ourselves, and the world around us, into that which is more righteous and more pleasing to God.

GENEROSITY IN CHARITY

A time of self-deprivation and abstaining, Ramaḍān reminds us what the less fortunate experience, and we are consequently even more compelled to come to their aid for the sake of God. The Prophet Muhammad ﷺ was described as the most generous person, whose generosity was further amplified during Ramaḍān. It is the month of charity (*ṣadaqah*) with a particular emphasis on feeding the poor.

INTENSIFIED WORSHIP

During Ramaḍān, every commendable (*mustaḥab*) act is given the reward of a required (*farḍ*) act, and for every required act, the reward is multiplied seventyfold. Night vigil prayers are especially encouraged, and rewarded, during this month. For these reasons, it is called the Month of Worship.

THE NIGHT OF GLORY (*LAYLAT AL-QADR*)

Ramaḍān contains one special night, called the Night of Glory (*Laylat al-Qadr*), on which a devotional act is rewarded more greatly than the same act performed for a thousand months of ordinary time. Interestingly, the exact date of the Night of Glory is not known to us with certainty. Prophet Muhammad ﷺ taught us that it falls within the last ten nights of Ramaḍān on an odd-numbered date. Most Muslims, and much of Islamic scholarship believe it to most likely be the night of the 27th. Those who most earnestly seek God ﷻ intensify their devotional worship for the entire ten days and nights.

The Night of Glory (*Laylat al-Qadr*) is the night when the Prophet Muhammad ﷺ first received the revelation of the Quran from the Archangel Gabriel. A chapter (*sūrah*) of the Quran is named after the night and describes it:

> *We have sent it down on the Night of Glory. What will explain to you what that Night of Glory is? The Night of Glory is better than a thousand months; on that night the angels and the Spirit descend again and again with their Lord's permission on every task. Peace it is until the rising of the dawn. — Quran 97:1-5*

RAMAḌĀN

28	29	30	1	2	3	4
5	6	7	8	9	10	11
12	13	14	15	16	17	18
19	20	21	22	23	24	25
26	27	28	29	30		1

Figure 23: A Calendar of Ramadan Highlighting the Last Ten Odd-Nights. Note: The odd numbered nights precede the odd number days (e.g. the night of the 21st of Ramaḍān begins after sunset of the 20th day of Ramaḍān)

THE QURAN

The month of Ramaḍān is also called the month of the Quran. This is partly because the revelation of the Quran began in Ramaḍān, but also because Ramaḍān is a time of study, recitation, and reflection upon the Quran. Muslims attempt to complete one entire devotional recitation of the Quran (i.e., reciting it in Arabic) on their own during the month. This intense focus on the word of God provides Muslims with renewed clarity with which to guide their hearts and affairs throughout the year.

TARAWĪḤ PRAYERS

A special form of voluntary prayer (*ṣalāh*) takes place during the month of Ramaḍān. The Tarawīḥ Prayers are congregational ritual prayers that take place every night during Ramaḍān. Because the new day begins with sunset, the first night of Tarawīḥ Prayers is on the first night of Ramaḍān, which is the evening that comes before (i.e., the eve of) the first day. There are varying opinions among Islamic jurists regarding the number of prayer-units (*rakʿahs*) that can be prayed in Tarawīḥ. The most dominant opinion, which you will most likely encounter, is that it is composed of twenty prayer-units prayed as ten sets of two each. Another opinion holds it to be eight prayer-units. Each of these is a legally valid opinion. Also, during Ramadan, a community usually attempts to recite the entire Quran within the aggregate of the month's Tarawīḥ prayers.

THE ALMS FOR COMPLETING THE FAST (*ZAKĀT AL-FIṬR*)

An act of charity helps bring Ramaḍān to a close. It is an obligation (*farḍ*), for those who are financially able, to donate the value equivalent of one Arabian *ṣaʿ* (approximately 2.3 kilograms) of foodstuff. This amount should be donated by the head of a household for each of his dependents, no matter how young. This amount may be given to those in need up to two days before the Festival of Completing the Fast (*ʿĪd al-Fiṭr*) and should be given before the Festival Prayer (*Ṣalāt al-ʿĪd*). In Muslim communities, mosques (*masjids*) and charitable organizations tend to facilitate this process by collecting the money and distributing it to those in need.

THE FESTIVAL OF COMPLETING THE FAST (*ʿĪD AL-FIṬR*)

After the completion of Ramaḍān, the next Islamic month, Shawwal, begins with either the sighting of the new crescent moon, or the completion of thirty days of fasting, whichever comes first. The first day of Shawwal is a holiday called the Festival of Completing the Fast (*ʿĪd al-Fiṭr*).[4] It is a day celebrating a month filled with devotion to God ﷻ. There is truly no greater reason to celebrate than gaining nearness to God.

---

4. While the proper transliteration, *ʿĪd*, is used throughout this book, it is more common to see the word transliterated as *Eid* in many Muslim settings.

The Festival of Completing the Fast (*ʿĪd al-Fiṭr*) is a day of joy and festivities, and is usually a time of visiting to share the occasion with relatives, community elders, and other loved ones. Parents also usually give children gifts or money to celebrate the joyous occasion.

After praying the *Fajr* (Dawn) Prayer of the day of the Festival (*ʿĪd*), you should perform a ritual bath (*ghusl*) and wear new clothes, or the best clothes you have. Before leaving for the Festival Prayer (*Ṣalāt al-ʿĪd*), a special prayer for this day, you should have a small bite to eat, such as a few dates.[5] On the way to the prayer service, you should invoke God repeatedly by saying *Allāhu Akbar* (God is greater!). Enhanced variations of this invocation can be used, but in general, this is the glorification you should recite until you reach the place of the prayer service and the prayer leader (*imām*) arrives.

THE FESTIVAL PRAYER (*ṢALĀT AL-ʿĪD*)

Typically, the community holds a large prayer service on the day of the Festival (*ʿĪd*), and everyone attends. Its format is similar to the Friday Congregational Prayer in that it contains a sermon (*khuṭbah*) and prayer (*ṣalāh*), but in the Festival Prayer service, the prayer takes place *before* the sermon.

Although it resembles the Friday Congregational (*Jumuʿah*) Prayer in that Quran is recited aloud, the format of the Festival Prayer (*Ṣalāt al-ʿĪd*) has a unique feature: Each prayer-unit begins with the proclamation Allāhu Akbar (God is even greater!), repeated multiple times. It is said seven times in the first prayer-unit (in addition to the opening proclamation) and five times in the second prayer-unit (in addition to the proclamation to rise from the first prayer-unit). The format of the Festival Prayer is the same for both Festivals (i.e. that of Completing the Fast and that of the Sacrifice).

5. You should not be in a state of fasting when you go to the congregational prayer for the Festival of Completing the Fast. In contrast, before the congregational prayer for the Festival of Sacrifice (discussed below), you *should* be in a state of fasting—i.e., you should *not* eat anything.

4. THE FESTIVAL OF SACRIFICE (*ʿĪD AL-AḌḤĀ*)

The **Festival of Sacrifice** (***ʿĪd al-Aḍḥā***) is celebrated on the tenth day of the Month of Pilgrimage (*Dhul Ḥijjah*), the twelfth month of the Islamic lunar calendar. The timing coincides with the performance of the pilgrimage (*Ḥajj*) by pilgrims from all over the world. For believers who are not performing the pilgrimage, it is commendable (*mustaḥab*) to fast the nine days before the Festival, with a particular emphasis on the *ninth* day of the month—the day when the pilgrims are standing on Mount ʿArafah.

On the morning of the Festival (***ʿĪd***), after praying the *Fajr* (Dawn) Prayer, you should perform a ritual bath (*ghusl*) and wear new clothes, or the best clothes you have. Before leaving for the Festival Prayer (*Ṣalāt al-ʿĪd*), you should be in a state of fasting and not eat anything. As on the Festival of Completing the Fast, on the way to the prayer service, you should invoke God repeatedly by saying *Allāhu Akbar* (God is greater!), or a variation of this invocation, until you reach the place of the prayer service and the prayer leader (*imām*) arrives. Also, during the Festival of Sacrifice (*ʿĪd al-Aḍḥā*) and for three full days afterwards, you should recite this invocation after each daily prayer (*ṣalāh*), ending with the *Fajr* (Dawn) Prayer of the fourth day.

Just as on the Festival of Completing the Fast (*ʿĪd al-Fiṭr*), the community holds a large prayer service (see above) for the Festival of Sacrifice (*ʿĪd al-Aḍḥā*), and everyone attends. It, too, is a day of joy and festivities, and is usually a time of visiting to share the occasion with relatives, community elders, and other loved ones.

THE SACRIFICE

After the prayer, in commemoration of the faith and perseverance of the Prophet Abraham (Ibrāhīm) ﷺ and his son, it is a prophetic practice (*sunnah*) for Muslims to sacrifice a lamb or similar animal. The meat of the lamb is usually divided among needy families and loved ones, with some kept for oneself. Some Muslims pay a charitable organization to sacrifice a lamb or similar animal on their behalf.

Each of these festivals and calendar-related devotions reminds us to be aware that there are months, days, and hours that God ﷻ has made especially sacred, ennobling them above others. We should sense this ennoblement, become connected to the passage of time in our lives, and take full advantage of these unique acts of devotional worship associated with the passing of time. Time is the capital with which we make investments for the afterlife (*ākhirah*). For each person, time will eventually end, all too soon, and the wisest among us are those that make the most of their time to draw closer to God.

CHAPTER 8

Lifestyle

He said,

"Our Lord is He who gave everything its form,

then gave it guidance."

QURAN 20:50

As mentioned in Chapter 3, Islamic law (*sharīʿah*) has two divisions: the devotional, which is concerned with ritual acts of worshipping God ﷾, and the social, which is concerned with the mundane aspects of daily living and interacting with others. Thus, Islamic law deals with every sphere of life, by virtue of the comprehensive nature of the guidance sent to us through Prophet Muhammad ﷺ. Because God knows best the nature of the world, He has guided us to the ways that are best for us, both in this transient world (*dunyā*) and in the afterlife (*ākhirah*).

For many rulings pertaining to social life, we may have some insight into the reason God ﷾ has decreed something. This is either because God or the Prophet ﷺ has explicitly stated the reason, or because scholars have been able to deduce the rationale behind God's ruling. For a number of rulings, however, this is not the case. These rulings can serve as tests of faith that, if we pass them, are a testament to our belief that God is the ultimate authority and that we should obey Him even if we do not completely comprehend the wisdom behind His commands. Through obeying God's decrees, we affirm God's right to dictate whatever He wills for us, confident in our knowledge that He is the All-Merciful and the All-Knowing.

In the legal rulings of Muslim social life we are provided with a clear proclamation of the scope of the religion: life itself. For every element and every aspect of our lives Islam provides guidance, for those who seek it. This is what makes Islam more than just "a religion," which for some means only a set of beliefs. Islam is a lifestyle that illuminates every aspect of the otherwise mundane enterprise of life.

1. LIVING ISLAMIC LAW

OBJECTIVES OF ISLAMIC LAW

By reviewing the entire body of Islamic law (*sharīʿah*), scholars were able to identify five main values that its rulings, taken as a whole, aim to preserve. These are called the **Objectives of Islamic Law**; they are those elements without which both worldly and religious life would become disordered and incomplete. They are, in order of priority:

1. **Religion**
2. **Life**
3. **Intellect**
4. **Family**[1]
5. **Wealth (or Property)**

Islamic law, both as a whole and in individual rulings, supports and protects, first and foremost, our relationship with our Creator. Its next priority is to support and nurture conditions conducive to life, and to protect life from harm and senseless loss. The third objective is to create an environment conducive to the use and development of the intellect, which results from protecting the mind from harm, whether material or psychological. After that, the preservation of the family unit is prioritized as the fourth essential component of the vision of Islamic law. The last objective is to protect people's personal assets, for such protection is necessary for a healthy society.

Understanding this framework may be helpful in seeing how individual rulings fit into the larger picture.[2]

THE LAW, SIN, AND FAITH

An important theological debate in Islamic history took place several hundred years ago over the question: Does committing a major sin equate to an open rejection of God's authority over us, and thus invalidate one's status

1. Some scholars also included under the preservation of family and lineage a sixth objective of Islamic law: the preservation of people's honor.

2. For additional information about the Objectives of Islamic Law, and more, see "Living Islam with Purpose," by Dr. Umar Faruq Abd-Allah (http://www.nawawi.org/wp-content/uploads/2013/01/Article6.pdf)

as a believer? The orthodox position won this debate with a resounding "no." This should serve as a reassurance that, although each of us will fall short in our duties to God, we will nonetheless, God willing, owing to His vast mercy, be counted among the believers.

So if a believer struggles with living up to one aspect of God's law, that does not take him or her outside the pale of the faith. Indeed, the only thing related to Islamic law that can take one outside the fold of the religion is to deny the authority of Islamic law or a **necessarily evident ruling**.[3] It is one thing to fall short of our duties to God ﷻ and to feel remorse and shame before Him. It is quite another—it is rebellion—to say to the Lord of the Universe that He cannot command us to do something. As believers, we know that it is His right to command us as He wills, and our duty to strive to obey.

EXCEPTIONS

Most rules have an exception, and the same applies to the legal rulings about social and daily life. It is important to understand that temporary exceptions can be made for legal rulings in situations where a person's life or health is threatened. These situations are relatively rare, and you will likely never encounter them, but to be aware of these exceptions will provide you with a deeper understanding of the spirit of Islamic law, and thus of God's expectations. Although it is important not to abuse these exceptions, it also important to keep in mind that Islamic law was sent for our benefit, and that we should not foolishly cast aside God's mercy in an attempt to express what we think may be piety.

3. A necessarily evident ruling is one which is stated in proof-texts in unequivocal terms, leading the jurists of Islam to reach a unanimous consensus about it. As for issues over which they differed, those should be viewed as a source of mercy for us, and we should refrain from condemning valid opinions that conflict with our own.

2. DAILY LIFE

FOOD & DRINK

When God ﷻ created the world, He filled it with plentiful bounties for His creation. He also set limits, through His messengers, as to what believers were to consume and what they were to avoid. Earlier faith traditions, for example, Judaism, had specific dietary laws. Some of these continue to be observed in Islam, while others are specific only to their original community.

Pork Products

God ﷻ explicitly forbids the consumption of pork and its related byproducts (e.g., pork-based gelatin). This prohibition extends to all parts of the animal regardless of the method of preparation or slaughter. Some scholars speculate that one possible reason why God forbade this is that what we consume affects our spiritual composition: The Quran commands us to eat what is not only lawful, but also "good," teaching us to be mindful of the nature of what we consume. Swine, in particular, embody greed, a spiritual vice, and are scavengers, and thus physically filthy animals.

Some speculate that a connection between spiritual composition and food may also explain why carnivorous animals (e.g., lions) are also forbidden to eat, although no one can say with certainty what wisdom lies behind the divine injunction.

Intoxicants

Certain substances cause an alteration of human consciousness such that the faculty of reason is subdued and the animalistic tendencies (rage, lust, sloth, etc.) are intensified. These substances are called intoxicants. Because one of the objectives of Islamic law (*sharīʿah*) is to preserve the intellect consuming such substances is forbidden (*ḥarām*).

Although some people may be able to consume small amounts of intoxicating substances without reaching the point of intoxication, the consumption of *any* amount of intoxicant is forbidden. In the Quran, God ﷻ states that wine actually has some benefit, but that since the benefit is far outweighed by the harm it brings, it is forbidden altogether. The harm to society at large is quite clear; even a cursory examination of the proportion of incarcerated violent offenders who were intoxicated at the time of their crime will indicate how much societal harm flows from the "personal choice" to consume intoxicants.

The spectrum of forbidden intoxicants includes anything from alcoholic beverages sold at restaurants to hard narcotics banned by most governments. Humans may change their minds about what is good or bad for society (alcohol was once illegal in the United States), but God has gifted us with a timeless sacred law that provides divine insight into the realities of things as they truly are.

Meat

Certain animals are categorized as permissible (*mubāḥ*)—we may eat their products—while others are forbidden (*ḥarām*) to eat.[4] Even for animals that are permissible to eat, there are preconditions. One must not eat any of the following:

1. The carcass of a dead animal (carrion)
2. Animals sacrificed to anything other than God
3. Animals inhumanely killed, or not properly slaughtered

So in order to be permissible (*mubāḥ*) to eat, an animal (e.g., a lamb) should be alive and then slaughtered humanely and in the name of God ﷻ. To slaughter an animal humanely means to kill it with a sharp blade—not to strangle or bludgeon the animal—and to slaughter it in a place that is not stained with other animal blood (as this will frighten the animal in its last moments). The slaughtering should begin with invoking the name of God and should be quick and thorough, so that the animal dies quickly and its suffering is minimized. Meat produced from this process is called **ḥalāl meat**.[5] While some assume that one can only consume meats prepared by Muslims, one can also eat meat prepared by Jews or Christians that also fulfills these requirements (e.g., Kosher meat).[6]

---

4. Although there are varying opinions with respect to the details, animals that are generally considered either forbidden or disliked to eat include carnivorous animals, birds of prey, mules and donkeys, most reptiles, pests, and insects. Animals that are generally considered permissible to eat include cattle, poultry, sheep and goats, deer (venison), camels, rabbits, and all types of seafood. However, the blood of any animal is forbidden to consume, even if its meat is permissible to eat.

5. Common Muslim parlance will sometimes use the term *dhabīḥah* (Arabic for "slaughtered"), sometimes pronounced *zabihah*, to denote the same concept.

6. A segment of the Muslim community holds that any meat (from permissible animals) prepared by a Jew or Christian is permissible to eat, even if it does not fulfill the above requirements.

CLOTHING

The limits set by God ﷻ pertaining to clothing are generally associated with two areas: the materials one wears, and the parts of the body that are covered or left bare.

Materials of Clothing

The rulings of Islamic law regarding clothing materials are gender-specific. Women are subject to no restrictions on what materials they may wear. For men, on the other hand, it is forbidden (*ḥarām*) to wear gold (as jewelry or otherwise) and natural silk (whether in clothes or accessories).

Modest Clothing

Every society draws arbitrary lines as to the minimum a person must wear in public. Most societies also vary the minimum based on the situation (e.g., a beach and a restaurant may have different dress codes). Fortunately, God, through Islamic law has provided us with a divinely guided definition of human nakedness to guide us in our daily lives.

For a man, it is required (*farḍ*) to cover the area of the body from the navel to just above the knees when in front of others. This requirement is the same whether in public or private, and regardless of whom he is with.

For women, the limits of what should be covered vary by situation. In public, the entire body, except the face and hands, should be covered.[7] This means that it is required (*farḍ*) for women to cover their hair completely. Traditionally Muslim women wear the **headscarf** (***ḥijāb***), a simple cloth wrapped around the head, to cover their hair and neck. The requirement of what must be covered is reduced when a woman is in two settings: when she is surrounded only by other women, or when she is with unmarriageable kin.[8] When only surrounded by other women, a woman must cover at least the area between her navel and her knees (although this varies somewhat by legal school). When with unmarriageable male kin, she may show her

7. In the Hanafi school of law (*madhhab*), the woman covers the body except for the face, hands, and feet. If a woman chooses to expose the feet, she should still cover the tops of her feet when performing the prayer (*ṣalāh*), even if she does so by wearing a dress that covers them.

8. These are defined in the Quran (24:31) to include a woman's father, brother, son, grandson, uncle, and nephew. After a woman marries, her father-in-law, son-in-law, stepfather, and stepson also become permanently unmarriageable to her.

arms from the shoulders down, neck, head and feet. She must cover her torso—both chest and back—and legs up to her ankles.

There is no minimum area that must be covered between spouses, although modesty is a virtue that is always encouraged.

FINANCIAL MATTERS

As we have previously discussed, one pillar of the practice of Islam, the Purifying Alms (*zakāh*), is related to a believer's finances. Several other issues concerning financial transactions and contracts are also subject to regulations revealed by God ﷻ to Prophet Muhammad ﷺ. We will examine two in particular: inheritance and usury.

Inheritance

It is common in many societies that when people die, their wealth is distributed either to a person (or institution) of their choice or to relatives. In the Quran, God ﷻ has provided clear instructions for how believers should divide a deceased person's estate.

The details are numerous, with specific fixed ratios of the deceased person's estate allotted to particular family members. On a basic level, what is important to understand is that the system exists, and that a person's relatives have a right to their inheritance. In this, Islamic law (*sharīʿah*) is somewhat different from other systems of law, which allow the entire estate to be distributed at the discretion of the deceased, with no limitations. In Islamic law, you can assign up to one-third of your wealth however you desire (usually for charitable purposes), but the remainder must be distributed to the relatives who are considered the rightful inheritors.

Usury

One financial restriction, laid out by God ﷻ in very strong terms, is the forbidding of **usury (*ribā*)**. Usury is defined as a financial transaction (trade or loan) that dictates an increase in the amount or value of an exchange (e.g., currency, goods, etc.) between two parties. For example, if a person were to loan you one hundred dollars and demand that you repay him or her one hundred and ten dollars (i.e., charging ten percent interest), that would constitute usury. Such transactions can lead to the wealthy unjustly exploiting the poor, leading to a further disproportionate distribution of wealth.

To engage in usury, as either the recipient or the payer of the increase, is explicitly forbidden (*ḥarām*). This prohibition has led to two phenomena you will see in the Muslim community. The first is the establishment of charitable organizations for small, interest-free loans, since a loan is seen as a form of charity rewarded by God. The second is the establishment of alternative financing models in which a co-operative or bank finances larger purchases through co-ownership and the like. In these scenarios, money is not made into a commodity to be sold.

PERSONAL HYGIENE

Prophet Muhammad ﷺ taught Muslims that personal cleanliness and hygiene are signs of true faith. Since they are essential parts of a Muslim's lifestyle, some aspects of personal hygiene are discussed below. The Prophet also taught us that hygiene has both practical and spiritual implications. On a practical level, it is conducive to bringing about harmonious social interaction, because everyone's primary nature (*fiṭrah*) is attracted to beauty. Spiritually, the state of the body affects the psyche and soul, and cleanliness opens one to inviting the company of angels. We are taught that angels inhabit places of cleanliness and good scents, while devils are drawn to places of filth and vile odors.

Beards

Many ancient cultures and religions hold male facial hair to be a sign of nobility, wisdom, and healthy masculinity, itself a celebration of the division of gender as God ﷻ created it. It is well known that the Prophets of old grew beards, and Prophet Muhammad ﷺ instructed his male followers to grow their facial hair. He also taught that they should groom it and keep it neatly combed. Men should trim their mustaches, never allowing the hair to grow over the lips. Generally speaking, a man should trim and groom the beard to look neat and clean, for it is considered an emblem of handsome masculinity, and it should not become straggly or unkempt.

Hair Removal

In contrast to male facial hair, which is beautiful when grown and groomed, the hair of the armpits and pubic region of both men and women is considered unclean, and so it should be removed by trimming, shaving, plucking, waxing, or some other means. This should be done at least once every forty days. It makes one cleaner and less prone to developing body odor.

Scents

Prophet Muhammad ﷺ loved beautiful scents and encouraged the men of his community to wear them in public. Women may do so in private spaces with other women, but they should not wear them publicly, out of modesty and to avoid attracting unwanted attention. Good scents are pleasing to those around you and are a sign of cleanliness. It is considered a form of charity to others when one wears a beautiful scent, perhaps because our sense of smell can provoke strong psychological reactions.

In addition to wearing beautiful scents, Prophet Muhammad ﷺ strongly encouraged believers to practice good oral hygiene. He would always carry a toothstick with him,[9] and encouraged others to use it often—especially before the ritual prayer (*ṣalāh*) and when in a gathering. A person's oral hygiene (or lack thereof) affects their psychological and spiritual state, as well as that of the people around them.

Using the Restroom

In the discussion of preparation for prayer we learned that the bodily excrements, urine and feces, are both filth (*najāsah*) according to sacred law. Great care must be taken to ensure the proper removal of such filth from our bodies after using the restroom. This ensures the ritual purity of our bodies and the clothes in which we pray.

The preferred method to remove filth (*najāsah*) from the body is to wipe the opening (either urethra or anus) with a clean and dry substance, such as toilet paper, until it is clean. Use your left hand to do so.[10] Next, use water to wash the body part (either urethra or anus), again using the left hand to wipe the area clean. When finished, you should dry the area, if possible. You should then wash your hands to make sure they are clean.

If you are unable to clean the impurities in the above manner, then washing with water alone is the next best means, and if not that, then wip-

9. The toothstick is a brush, usually made from a branch of the Arak tree, used to clean the teeth.

10. In Islamic etiquette, Prophet Muhammad taught us to use our left hand to carry out less refined actions, and to use the right hand for other activities, including those that entail interaction with others (e.g., shaking hands). This applies regardless of whether or not a person is right or left-handed when writing or performing other tasks requiring fine motor skills.

ing with a clean, dry substance until nothing remains. (For a more detailed discussion, see Chapter 3.)

Another etiquette of using a restroom is the manner in which you enter and exit, since it a place of filth (*najāsah*). You should enter a restroom using your left foot and leave it using your right, as taught and modeled by Prophet Muhammad ﷺ. While in any area dominated by filth, such as a restroom, you should refrain from sacred speech, including pronouncing the name of God ﷻ, saying invocations, reciting verses of the Quran, and so on; and while using the toilet, one should not speak at all.

MISCELLANEOUS ISSUES

Legal rulings are associated with many issues of everyday life, further illustrating the comprehensiveness and completeness of the guidance brought by Prophet Muhammad ﷺ. The following are a few issues about which questions frequently arise.

Dogs

Prophet Muhammad ﷺ taught a specific way of cleaning the saliva of a dog from a bowl that it has licked. He instructed his followers to cleanse the vessel seven times—to wash it six times with water, and then to rub it once with earth. This very specific instruction led scholars to examine the legal status of dog saliva, and thus of dogs themselves.

Some scholars deemed the saliva to be filth (*najāsah*), while other scholars held that the Prophet's instructions were of a hygienic nature, not related to ritual law, and that the saliva was not filth. One could therefore use water that a dog drank from for devotional use, such as making *wuḍū'* (ritual washing) or taking a ritual bath (*ghusl*), and being licked by a dog would not require one to wash the licked area before praying. This difference of scholarly opinions, each opinion valid, provides a religiously sound option for those who need to interact with dogs, such as at a relative's house. It is important to understand that there is some valid leeway regarding this issue for those who may need it.

Some scholars deemed keeping a dog forbidden (*ḥarām*) if done without a need, such as a seeing-eye dog or a guard dog, while others hold that it is disliked (*makrūh*) and strongly discouraged, but not forbidden.

Gambling

Gambling is the act of wagering something of value on an event of chance, in order to win another thing of value. In the Quran, God ﷻ forbids gambling. This is because of the intrinsic evil associated with gambling, and not just because it is almost always associated with other immoral acts. Anyone who studies gambling, its addictiveness, and its impact on society will clearly understand the immediate benefits of God's categorically forbidding it.

Tattoos

Permanent alteration of the body as God ﷻ created it is considered forbidden (*ḥarām*) by Islamic law. Tattoos and similar body modifications may fall under this category. In our age these practices are becoming more common as ways to express one's individuality. In Islam, the natural human form, as God created it, is what is celebrated.

3. COMMUNAL LIFE

Complementary to the rulings about personal daily life are those related to interactions among people. Below we will examine the guidance of Islamic law (*sharīʿah*) about several of the essential components of our social lives.

THE ETIQUETTE (*ADAB*) OF CUSTOMARY ACTS

Because of the symbiotic relationship between actions and spiritual constitution, a focal point of spiritual cultivation is developing a refined character and behavior. Since Prophet Muhammad ﷺ modeled human perfection, his actions are thus the model of perfect behavior.

Part of that prophetic behavior included a particular way of performing actions which might, to the unaware, seem mundane. In reality, nothing is mundane: Every action can be infused with a righteous intention and the proper manner of performance, and every action we perform can thus enhance our spiritual constitution. The appropriate manner of performing an action is called its **etiquette (*adab*)**.

Greeting

Prophet Muhammad ﷺ taught us the way to greet one another when we meet or begin a conversation. The first statement exchanged in an encounter is the **greeting of peace (*salām*)**, "*as-Salāmu ʿAlaykum*," which means, "May peace be upon you." The response is "*wa ʿAlaykum as-Salām*," which means, "And peace be upon you, too." We are encouraged to be the first to pray for peace by saying the greeting when meeting another Muslim. Beyond this general rule, there are a few other protocols that relate to greeting other Muslims.

Prophet Muhammad ﷺ taught that whoever has entered upon an assembled group of people should be the one to initiate greetings with them. Also, a younger person should initiate greetings with an older one. It is required (*farḍ*) to return a greeting, with an equal or better greeting.[11] You should greet even those Muslims whom you don't already know personally.

11. There are three greetings (listed in ascending order of reward and virtue): *as-Salāmu ʿAlaykum* ("may peace be upon you"), *as-Salāmu ʿAlaykum wa Raḥmat-Allāh* ("may peace and God's mercy be upon you"), and *as-Salāmu ʿAlaykum wa Raḥmat-Allāh wa Barakātuh* ("may peace and God's mercy and blessings be upon you").

The greeting of peace (*salām*) is also the manner in which conversations and encounters are concluded. Muslims thus wish peace, mercy, and blessings upon all whom we meet and converse with.

Eating & Drinking

Food and drink are two bounties of God ﷻ through which we find enjoyment and nourishment and which all people need. The Prophet ﷺ taught a specific way to partake in these bounties. When we reflect on the multitude of people around the world who are in a state of starvation, being able to eat and drink clearly becomes one of the greatest bounties we enjoy. This brings to light the importance of infusing these actions with prophetic etiquette in service of God.

Before a meal, you should wash your hands first, as Prophet Muhammad ﷺ taught. He also taught us that we should always commence eating or drinking by saying ***Bismillāh*** (in God's name). If you forget to say it at the beginning of a meal, you should say it at the end, because it is a prophetic practice (*sunnah*) and thus highly commendable (*mustaḥab*). It is also commendable to eat and drink with our right hands, no matter what our dominant handedness may be. The Prophet taught us that the devil consumes food and drink with the left. He also taught that if you are taking food from a shared platter, you should only take from the food directly in front of you, and you should offer to share your food with those around you, regardless of how little you may seem to have. God ﷻ will send blessings upon the shared food to give it the effect of more food. In the end, when you finish a meal or a drink, you should express gratitude for the bounties by saying, ***Alḥamdulillāh*** (Praise belongs to God).

Dressing

A Muslim should always be well-dressed, looking clean and presentable, as well as modest. Beyond the rulings of Islamic law pertaining to what materials may be worn and what parts must be covered, there is a particular manner, an etiquette, when dressing yourself.

When you put on a garment, you should begin with the right limb first, and then the left. When removing a garment, you should remove the left limb first, and then the right. This method was taught to us by Prophet Muhammad ﷺ himself. The same etiquette applies to footwear and other garments associated with limbs.

Speaking

Speaking creates a connection between people, and therefore between their hearts. Words are powerful, as most evident in the greatest miracle God has given to us, the Quran. It should come as no surprise, then, that Islam has provided guidance on an action that has such a powerful influence on our hearts and relationships.

The etiquette of speaking has several rules, the most significant of which is to *speak the truth* always. Prophet Muhammad ﷺ hated lying, so much so that he stated that being a habitual liar is incompatible with true faith.

Other rules of etiquette include not whispering when there are only three people in a group. This is to ensure that the third person does not feel excluded, or wonder whether he or she was the subject of what was whispered. It is also bad manners and a breach of etiquette to interrupt someone speaking, or to correct them, if what they are saying is something mundane and not a matter of belief or religion. If someone is telling you something you already know or have heard, it is best not to tell them so, but just to listen politely. Also, you should always speak in a moderate tone, not raising your voice or showing disrespect towards others, even if there is a disagreement.

Islam places great emphasis on courteous speech. It is very important to keep in mind how much trouble the tongue can cause. We are taught to say something good, or to remain silent; to avoid backbiting;[12] and to say things that engender love and harmony. All of these teachings should be kept in mind before you speak—for each word is recorded for the Day when we will all be called to account for our actions.

Elders

Bestowing a special status to elders is not unique to Islam. Most cultures over history have afforded elders an enhanced level of respect on the basis of their age alone. An elder does not need to be a wise, learned, or pious person to deserve this enhanced respect. Wisdom, knowledge, and piety are reasons for further respect, not prerequisites for the respect due to an elder.

It is customary to offer elders spaces in the first row of the prayer assembly, seats at gatherings, the first turn to eat, and other such signs of deference. Whatever behavior our culture or society considers respectful

12. Backbiting is defined as saying anything about a person who is not present that would make them unhappy, had he or she been present to hear it.

and well-mannered, that is the behavior we should show to the older members of our community.

SUPPLICATIONS (*DUʿĀ'S*) FOR PARTICULAR CIRCUMSTANCES

God's grace and mercy in this world take many forms. One such manifestation of His divine grace is the placing of **blessing** (***barakah***) in our lives. A blessing, in the simplest sense, is a grace sent by God ﷻ which enhances the bounties of God. Blessing makes us able to do many things in a short amount of time; it makes a small amount of something sufficient for a large group; it makes the money that we receive from God enough for our needs. There are particular times, places, and objects that contain especially great blessing. And there are ways of increasing the blessings in our lives—the simplest of which is to call upon God in supplication (*duʿā'*).

Prophet Muhammad ﷺ taught various supplications (*duʿā*) to be said in association with particular acts. These are many in number and important to read and learn. There are supplications (*duʿā's*) for acts such as waking up, going to bed, leaving the house, returning home, riding in a vehicle, traveling, visiting a sick person, eating, parting with loved ones, and many more. These special prescriptions allow you to receive and increase the blessing (*barakah*) that God ﷻ sends down upon you and upon whatever or whomever you interact with.

GENDER RELATIONS

God ﷻ created the human race with two genders, each different and unique. Islam teaches that they have different natures, tendencies, and needs. The difference between genders, like the differences among races and ethnicities, is to be celebrated as a sign of God's greatness.

Regarding status before God ﷻ, Islam openly proclaims equality of the sexes. There are no implications of inferiority, such as one gender being the cause of expulsion from the Garden, nor does Islam hold the belief that sexual relations are inherently immoral, or other historical misconceptions related to gender.

In one sense, Islam considers women to have a religious advantage over men: their spiritual composition has a greater tendency towards mercy, forgiveness, and compassion. On the other hand, in Islam, men are assigned roles with a higher level of worldly responsibility than women. For example, the responsibility of a family's financial needs falls on the husband and is not shared equally between the spouses. Each of these points should be taken as an affirmation that God made the two genders inherently different—physically, psychologically, and spiritually—and that it is healthy to recognize and honor their differences. While certain religions and cultures have allowed an unhealthy imbalance between genders, or conversely have attempted to obliterate the distinction between them, Islam holds that each gender has unique qualities vital to a balanced society.

In addition to acknowledging and reaffirming the different natures of the genders with gender-specific rulings, Islam also provides guidelines that govern the interaction between the two genders. Some of them are discussed below.

Seclusion

Part of the wisdom of sacred law (*sharīʿah*) is that it not only protects us from actions that are directly harmful to us, in both this world and the next, but also from actions that are likely to lead to harm. One example of this wisdom is the ruling that forbids two marriageable persons of the opposite gender to be in a state of **seclusion**—alone together where no one can directly see them. They are, however, permitted to converse out of earshot of others, or in a room with large windows with others just outside, where they can carry on a private conversation but still be seen—these situations do not constitute seclusion and thus are not forbidden. The kind of situation that would be forbidden is one that could allow physical touching without anyone seeing.

This is an example of a ruling set forth by God and His messenger to prevent acts that might not seem serious in themselves but which could lead to serious harm. Since seclusion could tempt persons of opposite gender to engage in sensual activity some of the time, it is forbidden all the time.

To Look and Touch

In the Quran, God ﷻ commands the believers to lower their gazes, out of modesty, so as not to allow sensually stimulating images to enter a heart striving to concern itself with God. As a general rule, whatever body part would be forbidden (*ḥarām*) for a person to expose would be forbidden for another to look at without a reason. The faculty of sight is considered the most direct inroad to the heart, and any images we see have an immediate spiritual impact. This may be realized by considering the extreme use of visually stimulating images in modern marketing.

For reasons similar to the prohibition of seclusion, it is also forbidden (*ḥarām*) to touch a marriageable person of the opposite gender. Since such touching can be a precursor to illicit sensual activity, Islam, as a preventative measure, forbids it in and of itself.

Through these guidelines, God ﷻ has regulated the powerful force of sensual stimulation in public spaces while providing an appropriate environment for its expression and enjoyment in a private space.

Marriage

The family is the foundational unit of society, and its preservation and enhancement is central to a harmonious society that facilitates service of God ﷻ and service of humanity. As part of this vision for life, God has provided us with a set of guidelines to preserve the institution of family. Among them are those related to the institution of marriage.

In Islamic law, marriage is a contract entered into by a man and a woman willingly, with the intention of establishing a permanent relationship. The contract can be verbal or written, and it must be witnessed by at least two Muslim men of integrity, besides the bridegroom. After the contract has been witnessed, it is a prophetic practice (*sunnah*) to announce the marriage and to hold a wedding feast for loved ones and family. A few features of the Islamic concept of marriage are worth reviewing here.

First, as already mentioned, marriage is intended as a permanent agreement between two members of the opposite gender, so that they may start a family. Also, although it is initiated with the intention of being permanent, the relationship can be terminated through the process of divorce. Divorce is considered the most disliked (*makrūh*) of acts, although it is not forbidden (*ḥarām*). This ruling highlights Islam's emphasis on the preservation of marriage. Its overall permissibility shows that the Islamic worldview acknowledges that some relationships do more harm than good, both to the individuals and to society at large.

Another feature is the ruling about who can marry whom: It is permissible (*mubāḥ*) for a Muslim man to marry either a Muslim, Christian, or Jewish woman, but not a woman from another religion or one with no religion at all. For a Muslim woman, on the other hand, it is only permissible to marry a Muslim man.[13] Part of the reason for this is that children

13. Historically, Muslim jurists held that if a woman converts to Islam while she is married to a non-Muslim male, she must divorce her husband if he refuses to accept the religion as

predominantly take on the religion of their father, and it is a condition of Islamic marriage that the children be raised as Muslims. Additionally, in this world, children take after their father in lineage (i.e., their last/family name). The preservation of lineage, the ability to know one's ancestry, is an important goal of Islamic law.

Within the institution of marriage, God ﷻ has placed the responsibility of a family's upkeep on the man. Whereas a wife may do with her wealth as she personally desires, the same is not true for a husband or father. His wife and children have a right to access and use his wealth for their basic needs. The responsibility of upkeep falls first upon him. Islam also recognizes that a family, like all institutions, requires defined leadership to achieve internal harmony. The vast majority of societies over history have followed this arrangement, but Islam defines the role of family leader not in terms of power and authority to be used for male domination, but in terms of a higher degree of responsibility and accountability before God. Prophet Muhammad ﷺ placed much emphasis on this, perhaps as a warning to men, when he said: "The best of you is the one who is best to his wife, and I am the best to my wives."

Although this is different from the cultural norms we may be used to, it is worth mentioning that Islam allows for men to marry multiple wives (up to a maximum of four) under particular circumstances. There are many preconditions to such an arrangement, the most important of which is a fair and just treatment of the wives, financially and otherwise. This illustrates Islam's acknowledgement of the complexities and diversity of human society, for particular societies may find this permissibility useful in preserving social harmony, while others may prefer not to utilize it.

Before Marriage

One of the means through which God ﷻ has guided us to righteousness, which also preserves the institution of the family, is by regulating gender interaction outside of marriage. Some aspects of this were touched upon in the discussions of seclusion, looking, and touching. What each of these limitations emphasizes is that there really is only one relationship of significance between a man and a woman: marriage. Nothing else officially changes the legal status between two people. So for the phases of a relationship that precede marriage, such as courting and engagement, the same

---

well. For Muslims living as a religious minority in a predominantly non-Muslim land, there are some valid legal opinions that allow for a woman in that situation to give her husband some time to consider the matter.

restrictions apply regarding touching, seclusion, and the like that exist for any marriageable persons of opposite genders.[14] These rulings only change when marriage takes place.

There are honorable ways to pursue marriage which are accepted by many cultures across the world. Parental and family involvement is a good early step in the courting process. In some cultures with Muslim influence, it is customary that the prospective couple interact while in the presence of family or friends. It is important that they be allowed to get to know one another well enough to make such an important decision, within the limits set for all unmarried persons of opposite genders.

Prophet Muhammad ﷺ gave guidance for those in search of a spouse. For men he advised that, when considering all the reasons to marry a woman, her dedication to her religion should be the weightiest criterion.[15] For women, he advised marrying men of good character and temperament. Each of these recommendations contains an indication of what each gender needs for a successful marriage.

While religion works to preserve marriage, it has unfortunately become more acceptable in our time to engage in premarital sexual relations. Any such activity outside of marriage is a most grave sin, explicitly forbidden (*ḥarām*) in the Quran. Even if a couple is engaged to marry, pre-marital sexual relations still constitute fornication. It is important to hold tight to these values, resisting temptation, and to reserve acts of intimacy for the domain of marriage, where they are cherished and sacred.

Homosexuality

Islam has defined the basis and manner for romantic and sexual relationships as being between a married couple, a man and a woman. Islamic law (*sharīʿah*) is concerned with actions, and sexual acts between members of the same gender (e.g., sodomy) are explicitly forbidden (*ḥarām*). There are discussions among the scholars regarding whether or not some people have a natural disposition to be attracted to members of their own gender, but any such discussion is always coupled with an emphasis on the need to

---

14. These restrictions apply to actions a person may perform, not feelings a person may experience. Considering the restrictions Islamic law puts forth, it might be unwise to cultivate intense feelings for a person to whom you are not yet married, although it is not forbidden to *have* such feelings.

15. In the full narration (*ḥadīth*), Prophet Muhammad ﷺ states that a woman is married for four things: her beauty, her lineage (if she were related to a prominent historic figure), her wealth, and her religious commitment. He then says that whoever holds onto a woman with a strong commitment to her faith will be successful.

resist sinful behavior. A person is not blameworthy for having the desire to sin (this also applies to heterosexual desires), but is held accountable for whether or not he or she acts on that desire.

There is a modern movement that has defined an entire subset of the population based on sexual desire alone. People with homosexual tendencies have been made to feel that acting upon these feelings freely is essential to their identity and that resisting them would equate to hypocrisy. This has caused a push for the entire society not just to protect the legal rights of such individuals, but also to declare homosexual acts morally acceptable. This is in complete contradiction to what God and Prophet Muhammad ﷺ have brought us and can be a challenge for the modern believer. We are taught to reach beyond our time to find guidance in the timeless: our universal religion brought by the Prophet for all times, Muhammad ﷺ.

Aside from understanding the ruling of Islamic law concerning these acts, it is also important to remember the status of those that sin. People can be weak, and we all have fallen short of our duty to God ﷻ. It is the responsibility of fellow believers to be there to strengthen and support one another in our path of abandoning disobedience and fulfilling our duties—the fundamental task of life. This applies to any number of sins a fellow believer may fall into. Supporting a fellow believer through a struggle is not the same as implicitly condoning his or her actions; it is partaking in that person's process of turning to God in repentance.

FAMILY LIFE

The family is the building block of society. When families, and thus societies, function harmoniously, life becomes conducive to spiritual growth. In fact, working towards familial harmony directly enhances your spiritual refinement. While protecting the institution of marriage is essential, creating and maintaining healthy families requires much more than that. Relations with family members are often challenging, and that is why Islam places so much emphasis on expressing love of God ﷻ through kind treatment towards others. Below are several other elements needed to live a harmonious family life.

The Spouse

In the Quran, God ﷻ illustrates the relationship between spouses through the metaphor of garments to be worn. Each spouse is the garment of the other—a source of protection, comfort, and shared intimacy. God also uses specific terms when describing a healthy marriage: *love*, *tenderness*, and *serenity*. To be blessed with these in your marriage is truly a gift from God, for which we should be very grateful..

What we learn from examining God's words is that, although love is essential to any relationship, love is incomplete without *tenderness*—a mildness of character even during the difficult times of a marriage. Tenderness means mercifully letting things pass even when you could justifiably take your spouse to task. To put forth both love and tenderness selflessly is the formula for attaining serenity in the home. Both love and tenderness require serious spiritual refinement, because the ego (*nafs*) can easily disrupt a relationship, as it is always lashing out at others, fighting for its own rights. Rising above these tendencies and loving another person, so that you may even put your own personal interests second to theirs, is easier for a refined soul. And so, you need a refined soul to put your best into a marriage, and working to put your best into a marriage purifies your soul.

Far from indulging in visions of utopian family life, the Quran acknowledges the intrinsic difficulty in marriage. God's message repeatedly calls us to be patient, to forgive, and to suppress our ego (*nafs*) as we work to preserve and honor this sacred institution.

Righteousness Towards Parents

Every one of us has parents through whom we were brought into this world. In the Quran, God ﷻ grants parents certain rights to which they are inherently entitled with no preconditions. The sum of these rights amounts to righteous behavior towards them, a concept which can be termed **filial piety**.

Righteous behavior towards your parents means that you obey their wishes, tend to their needs, and always show them the utmost respect. You should address your parents in a mild tone that always reminds them of the esteem in which you hold them. This applies particularly to mothers: While Prophet Muhammad ﷺ emphasized filial piety to both parents, he placed added emphasis on the respect and honor showed to mothers.

It is also important to appreciate the impact of filial piety on your relationship with God Himself. We know that the only sin that is unforgivable (if you do not repent) is *shirk* (associating partners with God). To show the emphasis He places on filial piety, good behavior towards parents is the only act God ﷻ conjoins with the command to not associate partners with Him

Your Lord has commanded that you should worship none but Him, and that you be kind to your parents. If either or both of them reach old age with you, say no word that shows impatience with them, and do not be harsh with them, but speak to them respectfully and lower your wing in humility towards them in kindness and say, "Lord, have mercy on them, just as they cared for me when I was little." — Quran 17:23-24

Filial piety is simply a right of parents. Even if God ﷻ tests us with challenging or difficult parents, or parents who did not play a role in our lives, we still owe them filial piety.

Oftentimes those new to Islam find a conflict between their new convictions and the lives their parents are living, particularly if they are not Muslim. Differences in religion should not be an obstacle to filial piety. Some scholars of Islam state that if a person's mother is Christian and elderly, it is that person's obligation to help take her to church. It is well known that Prophet Muhammad ﷺ taught his companions (*ṣaḥābah*) to remain kind and respectful towards their disbelieving parents, even those who opposed them most offensively. Keep in mind that for some parents, seeing their child convert to a new religion can be difficult. Some will adjust well, and others will work to change their child's mind. In all cases, patiently show your parents the filial piety they are due. Work to develop a strong relationship with them whether or not they are supportive of your choice.

Like all the rights afforded to people, parental rights have limits. Prophet Muhammad ﷺ taught us, "There can be no obeying a creature by disobeying the Creator." If your parents ask you to do something forbidden (*ḥarām*), you should politely refuse, explaining kindly to them why you will not do it. Beware of the tendency to allow differences in beliefs to create a rift between you and your parents—Islam should only enhance your relationship with them. It is important that you obey God ﷻ in both ways: by staying away from what He has forbidden and by showing your parents filial piety.

Keeping Ties with Kin

Another category of people with a special status from God ﷻ is those to whom you are related by blood. You owe these people a constant relationship on good terms: You should keep in touch with them, visit them, and ask about those things that are important to them. The Arabic term for this obligation literally means "to keep the wombs connected." It is a reminder to us that healthy families are essential to societies conducive to spiritual growth.

We also know very well that we had no part in deciding who our relatives are. Regardless of how difficult it may be to maintain a constant relationship with them on good terms, it is an obligation of the highest order. The opposite of keeping ties with kin is to sever ties with them. The punishment that befalls someone who severs ties with kin is extraordinary—they will be deprived of divine mercy. The word for mercy in Arabic is "*raḥmah*" and it shares its root with the word for womb which is "*raḥm*." In a narration (*ḥadīth*) from Prophet Muhammad ﷺ, we see the inseparable relationship between the two. He recounts a statement from God ﷻ which says:

> I am God and I am the Merciful (*al-Raḥmān*). I created the womb (*raḥm*) and derived its name from My own. If someone connects the [ties of the] womb, I will connect him with Me, but if someone severs the [ties of the] womb, I will cut him off from Me.

Therefore, a believer should work to keep connected with extended family members, hoping for divine mercy. You should make family functions a priority in your life and put forth an effort to attend such events. Whether they are family reunions, holidays, or simple get-togethers, you can attend these functions with the intention of keeping ties with kin. While you cannot partake in the religious rituals of other religions' holidays, you may still visit and buy gifts on non-Muslim holidays in order to keep ties with kin, and in turn, with God's mercy. The key lies in your intentions.

Neighbors and Guests

There are two more groups who are afforded certain rights and duties: neighbors and guests. A believer has duties towards anyone who lives near his or her home. This means that a believer has to make sure that his or her neighbors are keeping well overall. If any of them need anything, they should feel comfortable approaching their Muslim neighbor for help. In most societies today, people don't even know their neighbors' names. As Muslims, we should strive to get to know our neighbors and to keep channels of communication open, so that if a need arises, we will know about it.

People who visit you in your home also enjoy a special status. To host guests is an honor that comes with accompanying duties. Prophet Muhammad ﷺ highly emphasized the importance of generously honoring your guests. This means working to put the best that you have before them ensuring their comfort and joy during their visit.

Although it is important to give food and drink, and to share whatever you have, the hospitality we should offer guests should not be just material. It also includes giving your guests a sense of security and mental comfort, while removing any feeling of being a burden. These duties, and those towards kin and parents, illustrate the centrality of concern for others to the character of a believer. We should be hospitable, displaying care for the comfort and ease of others. When we nobly embody these virtues, putting others before self, God ﷻ will in turn grace us with divine comfort and ease in our lives.

THE MUSLIM COMMUNITY

Before Islam, Arabia was a collection of tribes. What defined one's relationship to others was lineage alone, and people gave unyielding allegiance to the tribe above all else. Prophet Muhammad ﷺ eradicated such backward tribalism, which refused to be subjected to any higher order or law. He did not replace it with another form of tribalism (e.g., religion); instead he put forth a new paradigm.

The Prophet taught that complete allegiance is to God ﷻ alone, and in turn, to truth and justice. This could make one stand against kin and potentially against anyone, in order to stand with justice before God. A Muslim was to maintain familial and tribal affiliations and not to reject them or attempt to suppress their influence. Instead, they were to be complemented with a brotherhood in faith proclaimed by God, which supersedes, but does not negate, all other types of associations.

Brotherhood in Faith

We share a form of brotherhood with our countrymen,[16] our race or ethnicity, and our fellow humans. And there is a special form of brotherhood which is based on faith. In the Quran, God ﷻ reminds us that this brotherhood in faith is a bounty from Him which He has bestowed upon us. This brotherhood supersedes other associations and is the basis for overcoming racism, classism, sexism, and other divisive human constructs. With an outlook based on faith, one can find a connection with others, and a reason for valuing them, which society may not provide. A pious poor man is mightier in the sight of God, and thus in the sight of the Muslim, than a wealthy or

16. Due to the limits of the English language, the term brotherhood will be used to denote a relationship akin to siblings that binds people together and transcends gender altogether.

powerful immoral person. A righteous person of another race is better than a corrupt person of our race, regardless of social norms of a particular time or place.

By simply being a Muslim, a person becomes your brother or sister in the faith—a member of the **Nation of Believers** (***Ummah***). Prophet Muhammad ﷺ instilled a unified consciousness in the Nation of Believers, instructing us to have mutual concern for each other's welfare and guidance. We have many duties towards other believers simply because of their faith, because it is a bond we share. We are united in our commitment to God ﷻ and our reaffirmation of the Grand Covenant. Prophet Muhammad ﷺ likened this mutual connection and concern to that of a physical body—if one part is ailing, the entire body is deeply affected by that pain.

This brotherhood must be understood within the backdrop of our allegiance to God ﷻ alone, and His command that we always side with truth and justice. Our duty to our brothers and sisters in faith who err, is to remind them of the moral character that God commands. This is in stark contrast to the tribalism of the Age of Ignorance (*Jāhilīyyah*) in Arabia before Islam, when people would commit errors in order to display solidarity with their erring tribe. By his teachings, Prophet Muhammad ﷺ eradicated this type of loyalty—loyalty at the cost of justice—from Arabia.

The dynamics of the relationship between brethren in faith is captured in this famous narration (*ḥadīth*) of Prophet Muhammad ﷺ:

> None of you [fully] believes until he loves for his brother that which he loves for himself.

Scholars of Islam have elaborated on the implications of our brotherhood in faith. Our duties to a brother or sister in faith include providing material assistance, caring for their needs as you would your own, making sure their hearts are at ease, and speaking to them with warmth and concern, avoiding hurtful comments and petty criticism. This does not mean you should avoid sincere advice; indeed, sincere advice is a central pillar of brotherly interaction. You are obliged to advise your brothers and sisters to fulfill their obligations and to desist from obvious errors or sins. Such brotherly intervention must be done in a kindly manner, so as not to cause a worse situation than the one being addressed. Also, you should be careful not to intervene in matters about which scholars have multiple opinions, because your brother or sister might simply be following an opinion other than the one you follow.

Other duties include forgiving mistakes and shortcomings, giving the benefit of the doubt whenever possible, remembering your brothers and sisters in faith in your prayers, and being a loyal and sincere friend even after their death. Holding these bonds as sacred and keeping up with the relevant duties will create strong communities and healthy societies where we are there for each other. These are the kinds of communities and relationships that are conducive to cultivating the spirit and strengthening our relationship with God ﷻ.

Variety of Understandings

Today, Muslims number well over one billion people and are part of every culture on Earth. Naturally, many Muslims understand Islam through their own cultures and experiences, while still sharing the core beliefs and practices of the religion. As you navigate the Muslim community, you will undoubtedly encounter various perspectives that inform how different Muslims understand their religion.

To outline each of these perspectives would be beyond the scope of this presentation, but it is important to understand that they exist, and to have some understanding of their origin and dynamics. This is not to encourage you to waste time in analyzing particular claims, but rather to help you navigate the differences you might encounter.

As the previous sections have made clear, Islam provides guidance for all spheres of life, for all peoples, and for all times. What tends to develop into a particular group's perspective is an emphasis on one aspect or teaching of Islam that stems from their particular set of historical and cultural experiences. Very few groups introduce absolutely foreign elements into the religion—that would constitute plain opposition to orthodoxy. Instead, they tend to use one element from within the Islamic tradition itself as the lens through which they view the world and the rest of Islam. For this reason, you could potentially agree with most of the ideas any Muslim puts forth, at least on the surface, even if their perspective differs from yours in certain ways.

These differences are simply a reminder to us that we should strive for a balanced approach to the complete guidance of our religion. There is something to be learned from each of these groups, even if what we learn is simply what *not* to do. Just be aware that you shouldn't spend too much energy oscillating between different perspectives. Prioritize the issues before you, and strive to incorporate elements from each facet of Islam into your life.

Islam and the Muslims

Although Islam is a perfect religion from God ﷻ, it is practiced by imperfect people. We may tend to expect that Muslims must necessarily live a life consistent with the standards of Islam. But Prophet Muhammad ﷺ taught us that, as time elapses from the time of divine intervention in the world, the state of the practice of religion diminishes. The best generation of Muslims was the one that sat with the Prophet and learned from him—the companions (*ṣaḥābah*). We know that near the end of time, corruption will begin to spread on earth. This should help us set realistic expectations about the overall state of the Muslim Nation (*Ummah*), while still holding our fellow Muslims in high esteem.

Converts and those newly returning to Islam tend to be graced by God ﷻ with an enthusiastic earnestness in learning and practicing their religion. It may therefore seem odd to them when they see others, especially those born as Muslims, being less earnest in their practice. Some Muslims may even harbor bad habits that stem not from their faith but from their cultures and backgrounds. For some newer believers, these negligent birth-Muslims may seem like spoiled children who take their riches for granted, becoming wasteful and ungrateful, whereas the newer Muslims feel like people who have lived in poverty and never known wealth: They tend to be very aware of the bounties they live in once they find Islam.

You should expect to encounter this, and it should not distract you from your path of furthering your relationship with God ﷻ. You should simply strive to fulfill your duties to God and thank Him for the perfect guidance He has sent us. We should always overlook the weaknesses and faults of our fellow believers, and hold ourselves to the higher standard.

Military Force

History over millennia testifies to the fact that war and conflict are simply a part of human nature. This presents a challenge to both those involved and those who witness it. To understand the Islamic values related to the use of military force, one must understand the depth and complexity of our moral obligation to struggle for the preservation of truth and justice.

The Islamic concept of **struggle** (***jihād***) is of two main types: internal, also termed the greater struggle, and external, known as the lesser struggle. The objective of both is to facilitate the recognition and preservation of truth by removing obstacles. The internal struggle (*jihād*) is against one's own ego (*nafs*), passions, and weaknesses. This is the greater of the two. It requires struggling against Satanic insinuations and the destructive vices towards which our egos tend. The internal struggle can be thought of as a prerequisite to the external, or lesser, struggle. Only a serene soul purified of destructive vices can be trusted to use military force without going to excess.

The external form of struggle (*jihād*) refers to the use of armed force either for self-defense or to remove oppression. It is the use of state-sanctioned martial force to restore harmony and equilibrium to society because, as the Quran tells us, "persecution is worse than killing" (2:217).[17] It is not vengeful vigilantism, but a regulated use of force by which states can remove agents of belligerence and tyranny. It is a matter of necessity by which persistent violence and oppression is prevented and eliminated.

Prophet Muhammad ﷺ also established many guidelines to regulate the use of such force. Civilians and non-combatants are never to be attacked. Prophet Muhammad ﷺ strictly forbade the killing of women and children. Islam forbids the destruction of the environment in war, as well as the use of fire as a weapon, which some scholars say would render the use of nuclear weapons forbidden (*ḥarām*). Monasteries and other places of worship should not be attacked. Such restrictions, forbidding indiscriminate killing and the destruction of the land, were unprecedented in their time and speak to the spirit, method, and purpose of the regulated use of violence in Islam.

It is important to maintain balance in understanding these guidelines. Many have attempted to use them to justify blood-lust and revenge, while others have erred on the other side in neglecting to intervene against oppression. We should struggle on all levels against oppression while following the guidelines set by God and staying mindful of the ego's ability to lead us astray. We should conquer our own ego (*nafs*) before presuming to answer the call of sacrifice and service in defense of others. Noble warriors who are selfless and fight valiantly in defense of the weak are celebrated in every culture and society—Islam is no exception.

ISLAM & CULTURE

While Islam is a universal and timeless religion, it is expressed and practiced by people who are products of their environments, and who are very much of this world. As a result the practice of Islam has taken on many different cultural expressions of the universal elements it contains. For exam-

---

17. It is important to note that God gave the Muslims permission to defend themselves only after they had migrated to Medina and were considered an independent polity; He did not grant that permission before the transition.

ple, modesty is a universal value that has a minimum defined by Islamic law (*sharīʿah*), but modesty is expressed differently in the cultural norms of different societies. For another example, customs related to hospitality may differ in different Muslim cultures. Within the boundaries dictated by Islamic law, many such variations can exist; they are a sign of the complexity and intricacy of God's creation.

It has been said that Islam itself is like a clean and pure stream of water. It runs over bright rocks of different colors—the cultures of the Muslims. The purity of the water allows the color to still be seen. It is not opaque; it does not prevent or obstruct the expression of the culture. Instead, it refines and enhances it. Mosques (*masjids*) in sub-Saharan Africa are African in architecture and different than mosques in Asia. Islam encourages us to be ourselves, removing the cultural customs that contradict the teachings of Islam and enhancing the ones that don't.

Many cultures have had Muslim influences for generations, and as a result, Islam has become nearly inseparable from their cultural customs. This does not mean that each of their cultural customs is an accurate expression of Islamic principles, although some may assume so. But such cultures, where many customs are indeed founded in Islamic principles, are fortunate in that people can subtly absorb the teachings of Islam without needing to learn them explicitly.

No Muslim should be made to feel as if their native culture as a whole is antithetical to Islam. Some elements within it will no doubt be so, while others will be in perfect synchrony with the religion. Your criterion in these issues should be Islamic law, which will guide you in finding your place of comfort in your culture as a person, and in your faith as a believer. The production of cultural norms that are both genuinely native and genuinely Islamic takes time, sometimes generations, and if your native culture is not predominantly Muslim, you should proudly contribute to this process.

If you have read this far, you have taken in a huge amount of information about a broad spectrum of topics. Remember to keep in mind that, as mentioned previously, you are in this for the long run, and you need to pace yourself. It is quite an accomplishment to have finished the material, but don't fret if you find it difficult to remember it all. Use this book as a reference guide to the basics of Muslim belief and practice, and refer to it as often as you need. As you grow into your practice of Islam, take things in gradually and internalize them at a pace that is appropriate for you, while, on the other hand, pushing yourself to ever higher levels of understanding and practice, and avoiding complacency.

Regularly revisit your reasons for all your actions, including learning and worship. Remember, Prophet Muhammad ﷺ taught us that "actions are [judged] according to intentions." Keep in mind that while you must grow, growth is a gradual process. Although it will take some time to internalize the material in this book, you will spend the rest of your life perfecting what it teaches. You'll likely have good days and bad ones. Be patient and perseverant, and rely on God to take care of the rest.

Lastly, push yourself to be spiritually ambitious, aiming high, always seeking to draw nearer to God. After learning well the contents of this book, move on and learn more, for knowledge is the foundation of our religion.

Alḥamdu lillāhi Rabbil-ʿālamīn
All praise is for God, Lord of the Worlds!

wa ṣall-Allāhu ʿalā sayyidinā Muḥammadin
wa ʿalā ālihi wa ṣaḥbihi wa sallim.
May peace and blessings be upon our master Muhammad,
his family, and companions.

APPENDIX I

Selections from the Quran

This appendix will introduce you to some of the shorter chapters (sūrahs) from the Quran. A transliteration is provided for each chapter to help you on your way to memorizing Quran for devotional recitation in prayer (ṣalāh). For pronunciation, please refer to the transliteration chart at the beginning of the book.

CHAPTER 1: THE OPENING (AL-FĀTIḤAH)	
Bismil-lāhir -Raḥmānir-Raḥīm	*In the name of God, the Lord of Mercy, the Giver of Mercy*
Alḥamdu lillāhi Rabbil-ʿālamīn	Praise belongs to God, Lord of the Worlds,
Arraḥmānir-Raḥīm	the Lord of Mercy, the Giver of Mercy,
Māliki Yawmid-Dīn	Master of the Day of Judgment.
Iyyāka naʿbudu wa 'Iyyāka nastaʿīn	It is You we worship; it is You we ask for Help.
Ihdinaṣ-ṣirāṭal-mustaqīm	Guide us to the straight path:
Ṣirāṭal-ladhīna 'anʿamta ʿalayhim ghayril-maghḍūbi ʿalayhim wa laḍ-ḍāallīn.	the path of those You have blessed, those who incur no anger and who have not gone astray.
(Āmīn)	Amen

CHAPTER 114: PEOPLE (AL-NĀS)	
Bismil-lāhir -Raḥmānir-Raḥīm	*In the name of God, the Lord of Mercy, the Giver of Mercy*
Qul 'aʿūdhu bi-Rabbin-nās	Say, "I seek refuge with the Lord of people,
Malikin-nās	the Controller of people,
Ilāhin-nās	the God of people,
Min-sharril-waswāsil-khannās	against the harm of the slinking whisperer–
Alladhi yuwaswisu fi ṣudūrin-nās	who whispers into the hearts of people–
Minal-jinnati wan-nās	whether they be jinn or people."

CHAPTER 113: DAYBREAK (AL-FALAQ)	
Bismil-lāhir -Raḥmānir-Raḥīm	*In the name of God, the Lord of Mercy, the Giver of Mercy*
Qul 'aʿūdhu bi-Rabbil-falaq	Say, [Prophet], "I seek refuge in the Lord of daybreak
Min-sharri mā khalaq	against the harm of what He has created,
Wa min-sharri ghāsiqin idhā waqab	the harm of the night when darkness gathers,
Wa min-sharrin-naffāthāti fil-ʿuqad	the harm of witches when they blow on knots,
Wa min-sharri ḥāsidin idhā ḥasad	the harm of the envier when he envies."

CHAPTER 112: PURITY OF FAITH (AL-IKHLĀṢ)	
Bismil-lāhir -Raḥmānir-Raḥīm	*In the name of God, the Lord of Mercy, the Giver of Mercy*
Qul Huwal-lāhu Aḥad	Say, "He is God the One,
Allāhuṣ-Ṣamad	God the eternal.
Lam yalid wa lam yūlad	He begot no one nor was He begotten.
Wa lam yakul-lahū kufuwan aḥad	No one is comparable to Him."

CHAPTER 109: THE DISBELIEVERS (AL-KĀFIRŪN)	
Bismil-lāhir -Raḥmānir-Raḥīm	*In the name of God, the Lord of Mercy, the Giver of Mercy*
Qul yā 'ayyuhal-kāfirūn	Say, [Prophet], "Disbelievers:
Lā 'aʿbudu mā taʿbudūn	I do not worship what you worship,
Wa lā 'antum ʿābidūna mā 'aʿbud	you do not worship what I worship,
Wa lā 'ana ʿābidum-mā ʿabattum	I will never worship what you worship,
Wa lā 'antum ʿābiduna mā 'aʿbud	you will never worship what I worship:
Lakum dīnukum wa liya dīn	you have your religion and I have mine."

CHAPTER 108: ABUNDANCE (AL-KAWTHAR)	
Bismil-lāhir -Raḥmānir-Raḥīm	*In the name of God, the Lord of Mercy, the Giver of Mercy*
Innā 'aʿṭaynākal-kawthar	We have truly given abundance to you, [Prophet]–
Fa-ṣalli li-Rabbika wan-ḥar	so pray to your Lord and make your sacrifice to Him alone–
'Inna shāni'aka huwal-'abtar	it is the one who hates you who has been cut off.

CHAPTER 107: COMMON KINDNESS (AL-MĀʿŪN)	
Bismil-lāhir -Raḥmānir-Raḥīm	*In the name of God, the Lord of Mercy, the Giver of Mercy*
Ara 'aytal-ladhī yukadh-dhibu biddīn	[Prophet], have you considered the person who denies the Judgment?
Fadhālikal-ladhī yaduʿ-ʿul-yatīm	It is he who pushes aside the orphan
Wa la yaḥuḍḍu ʿalā ṭaʿāmil-miskīn	and does not urge others to feed the needy.
Fawaylul-lilmuṣallīn	So woe to those who pray
Alladhīna hum ʿan ṣalātihim sāhūn	but are heedless of their prayer:
Alladhīna hum yurā'-ūn	those who are all show
Wa yamnaʿūnal-māʿūn	and forbid common kindnesses.

CHAPTER 103: THE FADING DAY (AL-ʿASR)	
Bismil-lāhir -Raḥmānir-Raḥīm	*In the name of God, the Lord of Mercy, the Giver of Mercy*
Wal-ʿAsr	By the fading day,[1]
Innal-'Insāna la fi khusr	man is [deep] in loss,
'Illal-ladhīna ʿāmanū wa ʿamiluṣ-ṣāliḥāti	except for those who believe, do good deeds,
wa tawāṣaw bil-ḥaqqi wa tawāṣaw biṣ-ṣabr	urge one another to the truth, and urge one another to steadfastness.

1. The Arabic construction here is an oath in which God swears by the passing of time.

CHAPTER 102: COMPETING FOR MORE (AL-TAKĀTHUR)	
Bismil-lāhir -Raḥmānir-Raḥīm	*In the name of God, the Lord of Mercy, the Giver of Mercy*
Alhākumut-takāthur	Competing for more distracts you
Ḥattā zurtumul-maqābir	until you go into your graves.
Kallā sawfa taʿlamūn	No indeed! You will come to know.
Thumma kallā sawfa taʿlamūn	No indeed! In the end you will come to know.
Kallā law taʿlamūna ʿilmal-yaqīn	No indeed! If only you knew for certain!
Latarawunnal-jaḥīm	You will most definitely see Hellfire.
Thumma latarawunnahā ʿaynal-yaqīn	Then you will see it with the eye of certainty.
Thumma latus'alunna yawma 'idhin ʿanin-naʿīm	On that Day, you will be asked about your pleasures.

CHAPTER 101: THE CRASHING BLOW (AL-QĀRIʿAH)	
Bismil-lāhir -Raḥmānir-Raḥīm	*In the name of God, the Lord of Mercy, the Giver of Mercy*
Al-qāriʿatu	The Crashing Blow!
Mal-qāriʿah	What is the Crashing Blow?
Wa ma adrāka mal-qāriʿah	What will explain to you what the Crashing Blow is?
Yawma yakūnun-nāsu kalfarāshil-mabthūth	On a day when people will be like scattered moths
wa takūnul-jibālu kalʿihnil-manfūsh	and the mountains like tufts of wool,
Fa 'ammā man-thaqulat mawāzīnuhū	the ones whose good deeds are heavy on the scales
fa huwa fi ʿīshatir-rāḍiyah	will have a pleasing life,
Wa 'amma man khaffat mawāzīnuhū	but the one whose good deeds are light
fa 'ummuhu hāwiyah	will have the Bottomless Pit for his home—
Wa mā 'adrāka mā hiyah	what will explain to you what that is?—
Nārun ḥāmiyah	a blazing fire.

CHAPTER 100: THE CHARGING STEEDS (AL-ʿĀDIYĀT)	
Bismil-lāhir -Raḥmānir-Raḥīm	*In the name of God, the Lord of Mercy, the Giver of Mercy*
Wal-ʿādiyāti ḍabḥā	By the charging steeds that pant,
fal-mūriyāti qadḥā	and strike sparks with their hooves,
fal-mughīrāti ṣubḥa	who make dawn raids,
fa 'atharna bihī naqʿā	raising a cloud of dust,
fa wasaṭna bihī jamʿā	and plunging into the midst of the enemy,
'Innal-'insāna li-Rabbihī lakanūd	man is ungrateful to his Lord–
wa 'innahū ʿalā dhālika lashahīd	and he is witness to this–
wa 'innahū liḥubbil-khayri lashadīd	he is truly excessive in his love of wealth.
'Afalā yaʿlamu 'idha buʿthira mā fil-qubūr	Does he not know that when the contents of graves are thrown out,
wa ḥuṣṣila mā fiṣ-ṣudūr	when the secrets of hearts are uncovered,
'Inna Rabbahum bihim yawma'idhil-lakhabīr	on that Day, their Lord will be fully aware of them all?

CHAPTER 99: THE EARTHQUAKE (AL-ZALZALAH)

Bismil-lāhir -Raḥmānir-Raḥīm	*In the name of God, the Lord of Mercy, the Giver of Mercy*
'Idha zulzilatal-arḍu zilzālahā	When the earth is shaken violently in its [last] quaking,
wa akhrajatil-'arḍu athqālahā	when the earth casts out its burdens,
wa qālal-'insānu mā lahā	when man cries, "What is happening to it?"–
Yawma 'idhin tuḥaddithu 'akhbārahā	on that Day, it will tell all,
bi 'anna Rabbaka 'awḥā lahā	because your Lord will inspire it.
Yawma 'idhiy-yaṣdurun-nāsu 'ashtatal-liyuraw 'aʿmalahum	On that Day, people will come forward in separate groups to be shown their deeds:
Fa may-yaʿmal mithqāla dharratin khayray-yarah	Whoever has done an atom's-weight of good will see it,
wa may-yaʿmal mithqāla dharratin sharray-yarah	but whoever has done an atom's-weight of evil will see that.

CHAPTER 95: THE FIG (AL-TĪN)

Bismil-lāhir -Raḥmānir-Raḥīm	*In the name of God, the Lord of Mercy, the Giver of Mercy*
Wat-tīni waz-zaytūn	By the fig, by the olive,
wa ṭūri sīnīn	by Mount Sinai,
wa hādhal-baladil-'amīn	by this safe city,
Laqad khalaqnal-'insāna fi aḥsani taqwīm	We have created man in the finest state,
thumma radadnāhu asfala sāfilīn	then reduced him to the lowest of the low,
'Illal-ladhīna 'āmanū wa ʿamiluṣ-ṣāliḥāti	but those who believe and do good deeds
falahum 'ajrun ghayru mamnūn	will have an unfailing reward.
fa mā yukhadh-dhibuka baʿdu bid-dīn	After this, what makes you [man] deny the Judgment?
Alays-Allāhu bi'aḥkamil-ḥākimīn	Is God not the fairest of judges?

CHAPTER 94: RELIEF (AL-INSHIRĀḤ)	
Bismil-lāhir -Raḥmānir-Raḥīm	*In the name of God, the Lord of Mercy, the Giver of Mercy*
'Alam nashraḥ laka ṣadrak	Did We not relieve your heart for you,
wa waḍaʿnā ʿanka wizrak	and remove the burden
'Alladhi 'anqaḍa ẓahrak	that weighed so heavily on your back,
Wa rafaʿnā laka dhikrak	and raise your reputation high?
Fa 'inna maʿal-ʿusri yusrā	So truly, where there is hardship there is also ease;
'Inna maʿal-ʿusri yusrā	truly, where there is hardship there is also ease.
Fa 'idhā faraghta fanṣab	So when you are free, work on,
wa 'ilā Rabbika farghab	and direct your requests to your Lord.

CHAPTER 93: THE MORNING BRIGHTNESS (AL-ḌUḤĀ)	
Bismil-lāhir -Raḥmānir-Raḥīm	*In the name of God, the Lord of Mercy, the Giver of Mercy*
Waḍ-ḍuḥā	By the morning brightness
Wal-layli 'idha sajā	and by the night when it grows still,
Mā waddaʿaka Rabbuka wa mā qalā	your Lord has not forsaken you, [Prophet], nor does He hate you,
Wa lal-'Ākhiratu khayrul-laka minal-'ūlā	and the future will be better for you than the past;
Wa lasawfa yuʿṭīka Rabbuka fatarḍā	your Lord is sure to give you [so much] that you will be well pleased.
'Alam yajidka yatīman-fa-'āwā	Did He not find you orphaned and shelter you,
Wa wajadaka ḍāallan-fahadā	find you lost and guide you,
Wa wajadaka ʿā'ilan fa-'aghnā	find you in need and satisfy your need?
Fa'ammal-yatīma falā taqhar	So do not be harsh with the orphan
Wa 'ammas-sā'ila falā tanhar	and do not chide the one who asks for help;
Wa 'ammā biniʿmati Rabbika faḥaddith	talk about the blessings of your Lord.

APPENDIX II

Recommended Readings

GENERAL BOOKS ON ISLAM

SHALABI, ABDUL WADOD

Islam: Religion of Life

Edited by Abdul Hakim Murad. Starlatch Press, 2001.

A short book that introduces Islam by focusing on the tenets of faith, practice, and an introduction to Muslim life.

LUMBARD, JOSEPH

Submission, Faith & Beauty: The Religion of Islam

Edited by Hamza Yusuf, Zaid Shakir. Fons Vitae/Zaytuna, 2009.

A great introduction to Islam that clearly elucidates the four dimensions of the religion.

MURATA, SACHIKO; CHITTICK, WILLIAM

Vision of Islam

Paragon House, 2008

More in-depth than *Submission, Faith & Beauty*, this book explores the fundamental beliefs of Islam, covering practice, faith, spirituality, and the Islamic view of history. It interweaves teachings from the Quran, the sayings of the Prophet ﷺ, and the great authorities of Islam.

ISLAMIC BELIEF

AL-TAHAWI, ABU JA'FAR

The Creed of Imam al-Tahawi

Translated and annotated by Hamza Yusuf. Sandala, 2009.

Of the many Islamic creedal texts, *The Creed of Imam al-Tahawi* is the simplest, most effective, and the least controversial. It avoids complex theological points and systematically presents a clear foundational dogmatic theology. Historically, this text has seen a wide degree of acceptance by Muslim scholars across the centuries.

ISLAMIC LAW

Maliki School of Law

IBN 'ASHIR, ABD AL-WAHID

The Helping Guide

Translated and annotated by Hamza Yusuf. Sandala (forthcoming).

This didactic poem, one of the most widely studied in Africa, covers the disciplines of theology, devotional law, and spirituality. The poem clearly and succinctly encapsulates the fundamental aspects of the three central tenets of *iman* (faith), *islam* (practice) and *ihsan* (spiritual excellence).

Hanafi School of Law

AL-SHURUNBULALI, ABU 'L-IKHLAS

Ascent to Felicity: A Manual on Islamic Creed and Hanafi Jurisprudence

Translated and annotated by Faraz Khan. White Thread Press, 2010.

This primer covers basic creed in addition to basic Hanafi jurisprudence. It covers all five pillars of Islam, as well as the topics of slaughtering, ritual sacrifice, and hunting. It also contains well-researched explanatory notes.

Shafi'i School of Law

AL-NAWAWI, YAHYA

Al-Maqasid: Nawawi's Manual of Islam

Translated by Nuh Ha Mim Keller. Amana Publications, 2003.

A very good medium-size handbook available in English for teaching the basic Shafi'i devotional law. It includes supplemental notes and three essays that are helpful in understanding various developments in Islamic scholarship.

LIFE OF THE PROPHET MUHAMMAD ﷺ

LINGS, MARTIN

Muhammad ﷺ: His Life Based on the Earliest Sources

Inner Traditions, 2006.

A book of moderate length and detail, this is an internationally acclaimed comprehensive and authoritative account of the life of the Prophet ﷺ. It is based on eighth- and ninth-century Arabic biographies that recount numerous events in the Prophet's life, and it contains original English translations of many important passages.

THE QURAN

The Qur'an: A New Translation (Oxford Classics)

Translated by M.A.S. Abdel Haleem. Oxford University Press, 2008.

This translation of the Quran, by a classically trained scholar, is written in contemporary language that is easy to read and follow. It places the separate passages into paragraphs, instead of verses, in order to help a reader grasp the main themes.

The Qur'an: A New Translation

Translated by Thomas Cleary. Starlatch, 2004.

Another translation into clear and contemporary language which has been appreciated by many scholars and readers.

SELLS, MICHAEL

Approaching the Qur'an: The Early Revelations

White Cloud Press, 2007.

The book, which focuses on the earlier Meccan chapters, includes an introduction to the Quran, commentaries on the chapters, and a glossary of technical terms related to the study of the Quran.

AL-NAWAWI, YAHYA

Etiquette with the Quran

Translated by Musa Furber. Islamosaic, 2013.

Written by one of the greatest scholars in Islamic history, this classic is a guide for those who wish to engage with the Quran. It covers topics related to ritual cleanliness, the best times for recitation, the etiquette of students with their teachers, and other topics related to study of the Quran.

AL-MAHALLI, JALALU'D-DIN; AL-SUYUTI, JALALU'D-DIN

Tafsir al-Jalalayn

Dar al-Taqwa, 2012.

Tafsir al-Jalalayn, meaning "The Commentary of the Two Jalals," named after its two authors, is considered one of the best short and simple, complete commentaries on the Quran.

HADITHS (NARRATIONS) OF THE PROPHET ﷺ

AL-NAWAWI, YAHYA

A Treasury of Hadith: A Commentary on Nawawi's Selection of Prophetic Traditions

Commentary by Ibn Daqiq al-'Id, translated by Mokrane Guezzou. Kube Publishing, 2014.

This collection of forty-two narrations by one of the most famous compilers of hadith is generally regarded as the most popular anthology. It is a collection of hadiths that summarizes the spirit and vision of the entire religion. This book includes a commentary on the hadiths by the great 14th century master Ibn Daqiq al-'Id.

The Content of Character: Ethical Sayings of the Prophet Muhammad

Translated by Hamza Yusuf. Sandala, 2005.

This is a remarkable collection of the sayings of the Prophet Muhammad. It illustrates the concise, yet comprehensive, wisdom contained in his speech. The content of the hadiths focuses on character-building, morals, good manners, and ethics. A very accurate and accessible translation brings the hadiths to life. It is also greatly enhanced by scholarly appendices on the hadith sciences.

ISLAMIC SPIRITUALITY

AL-MAWLUD, MUHAMMAD

Purification of the Heart: Signs, Symptoms and Cures of the Spiritual Diseases of the Heart

Translated and with a commentary by Hamza Yusuf. Sandala, 2012.

This modern classic of Islamic spirituality examines the spiritual and psychological diseases of the heart. A work that everyone can benefit from, this book offers an analysis of the root causes of, and treatments for, all human problems.

AL-GHAZALI, ABU HAMID

The Beginning of Guidance

Translated by Mashhad al-Allaf. White Thread Press, 2010.

This work, by one of the greatest scholars in Islamic history, is a widely studied introduction to the fundamentals of Muslim piety and etiquette.

AL-HADDAD, ABDALLAH IBN 'ALAWI

The Book of Assistance

Translated by Mostafa Badawi. Fons Vitae, 2003.

This short classic manual presents some of the essential aspects of religious development in thirty-two chapters, each essential to developing spiritually.

AL-HARITH AL-MUHASIBI

Treatise for the Seekers of Guidance

Translated by Zaid Shakir. New Islamic Direction, 2008.

This book includes a translation, notes, and commentary on Imam al-Muhasibi's famous text. It is intended to serve as a layman's guide to Islamic spirituality.

Glossary of Commonly Used Terms

This Glossary contains definitions of specialized terms used in this book, as well as a selection of other terms commonly used by Muslims. It also includes the names of important figures in the early history of Islam.

A

ʿĀ'ishah bint Abū Bakr: Lady ʿĀ'ishah ؓ was the daughter of Abū Bakr ؓ and the wife of Prophet Muhammad ﷺ. She was a young woman known for her intelligence and strength. After the death of Prophet Muhammad ﷺ, she was able to provide believers with unparalleled access to details of the domestic life of the Prophet, thus giving us many insights into the standard we should emulate.

ʿAbdAllāh bin ʿAbdal-Muṭṭalib: The father of Prophet Muhammad ﷺ, who passed away in Medina before his only child was born. He was the tenth son of his father, ʿAbdal-Muṭṭalib, and was a man of nobility and beauty. He was of the clan of Banū Hāshim, an important part of the tribe of Quraysh.

Abū Bakr as-Ṣiddīq: The first of the Rightly Guided Caliphs, he was the first adult male to accept the message of Prophet Muhammad ﷺ and was the closest and most loyal of his Companions (*Ṣaḥābah*). He was the only one who accompanied Prophet Muhammad for the migration to Medina, and as the father of Lady ʿĀ'ishah ؓ he would eventually become the father-in-law of the Prophet. He was well known for his humility and unwavering commitment to Prophet Muhammad ﷺ.

Abū Jahl: One of the most vile and vicious of the Prophet's opponents, his title means "the owner of ignorance." He constantly fueled the flames of animosity towards the Prophet and worked to assassinate him. He also personally led much of the persecution of Muslims in Mecca.

Abū Ṭālib bin ʿAbdal-Muṭṭalib: The paternal uncle of Prophet Muhammad ﷺ, he was his loyal supporter and protector from the Prophet's childhood onward. He became his guardian after his parents and grandfather passed away. He protected Prophet Muhammad ﷺ from the Quraysh's oppression and violence during his life. Abū Ṭālib is also the father of ʿAli, the cousin and son-in-law of Prophet Muhammad ﷺ.

***Adab* (Courteous Conduct):** A term that can refer to either the possession of a refined nature or the appropriate etiquette of performing a particular act.

***Adhān* (Call to Prayer):** A series of invocations and declarations which is called aloud with the dual purpose of announcing the beginning of a new prayer time and calling believers to congregate for the prayer (*ṣalāh*).

***Ākhirah* (Afterlife):** The life after our resurrection from the graves, which God ﷻ makes perpetual and unending. Determining our destinies in that life is the purpose of this life. In the afterlife, every person ends up in either Paradise (*Jannah*) or Hell (*Jahannam*).

***Alḥamdulillāh* (Praise Belongs to God):** An invocation which is uttered as a means of expressing gratitude to God for bounties. It is a common response when a person is asked how they are doing, etc.

ʿAlī bin Abū Ṭālib: The fourth of the Rightly Guided Caliphs, he was the cousin and son-in-law of Prophet Muhammad ﷺ, married to his daughter Fatima رضي الله عنها. As a young man he was the first, after Lady Khadījah رضي الله عنها, to accept the message of the Prophet. He was among the closest of the Companions (*Ṣaḥābah*) to Prophet Muhammad ﷺ and was known for his piety, sacrifice, and courage on the battlefield.

***Allāh* (God) ﷻ:** The name of the Creator and Sustainer of the universe, Who is beyond our ability to comprehend and Who, by His very nature, alone is worthy of worship. He transcends gender, time, space, and being bound by directions. He created the universe for a purpose, and sent prophets and messengers to teach creation its purpose. He is Independent, and all of creation is dependent upon Him. Because He created us, we are His, and to Him we shall return, for Him to do with us as He wills.

***Allāhu Akbar* (God is Greater):** An invocation that, by means of an incomplete phrase, exclaims God's supremacy over everything. It is a common expression of joy uttered after a momentous event.

Āminah bint Wahb: The mother of Prophet Muhammad ﷺ, who spoke of miracles during her pregnancy and miracles upon the birth of Prophet Muhammad into the world. She passed away when Prophet Muhammad ﷺ was six years old.

***Anṣār* (Helpers):** A classification used to designate those Muslims who lived in Medina and opened their homes and hearts to the incoming Emigrants (*Muhājirūn*). After the Emigrants' arrival, the Prophet ordered that each Emigrant should pair up with a Helper, who would share his wealth and home with his brother in faith.

***ʿAql* (Reason):** The "executive function" of the mind, which can sort through decisions and possibilities and subject the other components of consciousness to its decisions. It interacts with the desires of the ego (*nafs*) and the understandings of the primary nature (*fiṭrah*) in an attempt to reconcile and prioritize them.

***ʿAṣr* (Afternoon Prayer):** One of the five daily prayers, its timeframe starts when an object's shadow is equal to its own length (plus the length of its shadow at high noon) and ends when the disc of the sun touches the western horizon. It consists of four prayer-units (*rakʿahs*), in each of which the Quran is recited silently.

***Āyah* (Verse):** The smallest whole unit of the Quran, of which chapters (*sūrahs*) are composed. Some verses are long passages, others are single sentences, some are phrases, and others still are only letters.

B

***Badr*:** A region nearly halfway between the cities of Mecca and Medina, it was the site of the first major battle of Islam's history. On Friday, the 17th of Ramaḍān, during the second year of the migration of the Prophet, the Muslim army of just over three hundred believers met the Quraysh army, which numbered more than one thousand. Many in Mecca were sure this would be a massacre of the Muslims. The battle was filled with numerous miracles witnessed by the Muslims and the disbelieving polytheists of Mecca. In the end, the Muslims had miraculously defeated the much larger army.

***Barakah* (Blessing):** An important concept, *barakah* is a manifestation of Divine Grace which enhances and increases the bounties of God ﷻ in our lives. Blessing makes us able to do many things in a short amount of time; it makes a small amount of something sufficient for a large group; it makes the money that we receive from God enough for our needs. Certain times, places, and objects contain especially great blessing and are thus a means of accessing this grace to benefit our lives.

Battle of the Trench: An important battle between the polytheists of the Quraysh and the Muslims in Medina, wherein the former created a coalition of allies and led an army of over nine thousand to attack the city of Medina itself. At the passage-way into Medina, the Muslims dug a wide trench that was impassable, surprising the invading coalition. The battle ended when the Prophet's supplication (*duʿā'*) was answered by a great and t windstorm which scattered the invaders, causing them to abandon any hope of taking Medina.

***Bidʿah* (Innovation):** The introduction into the religion of an act or belief that has no basis or foundation in Islamic law (*sharīʿah*). Scholars of Islamic law examine the purpose and result of any newly initiated practices, measuring them against the spirit of the sacred law. Anything that they reject as inconsistent with religious teachings is deemed a blameworthy innovation (*bidʿah*).

***Bismillāh* (In God's Name):** An essential part of a Muslim's life, saying *Bismillāh* is the means by which blessing (*barakah*) can be derived, simply by uttering it at the outset of any action whatsoever. It is common for Muslims to use this phrase when leaving the house, opening a door, starting the car, etc.

Black Stone: A sacred stone which descended from heaven white as milk and was blemished by the sins of men. This heavenly stone is the cornerstone of the Sacred House (*Kaʿbah*) and was kissed by Prophet Muhammad ﷺ. All who visit the Sacred House seek to kiss it and make prayers before it.

Burāq: A heavenly steed which Prophet Muhammad ﷺ rode to Jerusalem on the Night Journey and Ascension. The white riding beast with wings was brought to him in Mecca by Archangel Gabriel (Jibrīl).

D

***Dhikr* (Invocation):** Also called the remembrance of God ﷻ, *dhikr* is an action of the tongue and heart in which the name of God, or His praise, is uttered repeatedly, with the purpose of bringing Him to the forefront of the heart and mind. A transformative practice that spiritually purifies a believer, it is a means to draw nearer to God.

Dimensions of Islam: The three elements that together make up the comprehensive nature of the religion: *īmān* (faith), *islām* (devotion), and *iḥsān* (spiritual purity).

***Du'ā'* (Supplication):** A direct petition to God ﷻ, in any language, by which believers may directly beseech Him for any of their needs, whether worldly or spiritual.

***Dunyā* (Transient World):** The temporal realm of this worldly life, with all of its inherent challenges, difficulties, and tendencies to pull the soul away from awareness of God ﷻ. This term can be also used to refer to indulging in materialism, as opposed to properly using this world as a means to gain God's good pleasure.

F

***Fajr* (Dawn Prayer):** One of the five daily prayers, its timeframe starts when light begins to appear along the eastern horizon. It must be performed before sunrise, when the disc of the sun begins to appear above the horizon. It is composed of two prayer-units (*rak'ahs*), in both of which Quran is recited aloud.

***Farḍ* (Requirement):** An act that God ﷻ has commanded a Muslim must perform. Performing a required act begets reward from God, while neglecting it causes sin to accrue.

***Fātiḥah* (The Opening):** The first chapter in the Quran as it is ordered and arranged (though not the first chapter revealed), it is essentially an affirmation of our commitment to God ﷻ and a prayer for His guidance.

Fāṭimah bint Muḥammad: Also known as Fāṭimah the Resplendent (al-Zahra) ﵂, she was the youngest daughter of Prophet Muhammad ﷺ and was well-known for her intense piety. She married Prophet Muhammad's cousin, the mighty and noble 'Alī bin Abū Ṭālib. They had four children, among them al-Ḥasan and al-Ḥusayn ﵄, the beloved grandchildren of Prophet Muhammad ﷺ. It is primarily through her that, to this day, people can trace their lineage back to Prophet Muhammad.

Filial Piety: A duty ordained upon us by God ﷻ to honor and show righteous behavior towards our parents. It is a right of parents that carries no preconditions and deeply impacts our relationship with God and our ability to receive His divine mercy.

***Fiṭrah* (Primary Nature):** The natural state of the human soul as God سبحانه وتعالى created it. One in this state knows, recognizes, and inclines towards all that is good, beautiful, and pure, and thus innately knows and needs God. Our primary nature also is opposed to everything that is ugly and vile, and senses a void in a life not filled with God. Revitalizing and reconnecting with the primary nature is one of the goals of the path of self-purification.

Five Pillars of Islam: The five foundational devotions that make up *islām*, one of the three dimensions of the religion. They are: to state the Testimony of Faith, to pray the five daily prayers, to fast the month of Ramaḍān, to pay the purifying alms, and, if able, to make pilgrimage to Mecca once in a lifetime.

G

***Ghayb* (Unseen):** A realm of God's creation that is beyond human perception. Belief in its reality is an essential component of complete faith.

***Ghusl* (Ritual Bath):** A ritual purification in which the entire body is washed with pure, unaltered water. This form of purification rectifies the state of major ritual impurity.

H

***Ḥadīth* (Prophetic Narration):** Narrations (*ḥadīths*) are verified accounts of Prophet Muhammad's words, actions, and tacit approvals and disapprovals. Some narrations consist of statements made by the Prophet, while others are accounts of things he did, or things that were done in his presence. Each of these gives an indication of part of his Prophetic Way (*Sunnah*).

***Ḥajj* (Pilgrimage):** The fifth pillar of the dimension of devotional practice (*islām*), the *Ḥajj* is the pilgrimage on which Muslims set out from all over the world to converge at the Sacred House at the Sanctuary in Mecca. It is required (*farḍ*), for every Muslim who is physically and financially capable of doing so, to undertake the pilgrimage at least once in his or her life. It consists of various rituals instituted by the patriarch, Prophet Abraham عليه السلام, performed over a number of days. Upon successful completion, if all is done properly and sincerely, a Muslim emerges as sinless as a newborn child.

***Ḥalāl* (Lawful):** A generic term for the broad category of actions that are not forbidden (*ḥarām*). It implies that an action falls under one of the other four legal rulings (disliked, permissible, commendable, or required). This term is sometimes used as a synonym for the permissible (*mubāḥ*) acts.

Another use of the term refers to meat prepared according to the humane guidelines set by Islamic law for animal slaughter ("*ḥalāl* meat"). Common Muslim parlance will sometimes use the term *dhabīḥah* (Arabic for "slaughtered," sometimes pronounced "*zabihah*") to denote the same concept.

Ḥalīmah as-Saʿdīyyah: The Bedouin wet-nurse who took Prophet Muhammad ﷺ, as a child, into her care and witnessed many of his miracles.

Ḥamza bin ʿAbdal-Muṭṭalib: The paternal uncle and close friend of Prophet Muhammad ﷺ. He was a mighty and fierce warrior who would eventually be martyred on the battlefield during the Battle of Uḥud. He is buried alongside Mount Uḥud. Prophet Muhammad ﷺ used to visit his grave regularly.

Ḥarām **(Forbidden):** Acts that a Muslim is commanded never to do. Such an act accrues sin, while avoiding the act is a duty to God ﷻ that begets His generous reward.

Ḥasad **(Resentful Envy):** A mortal vice in which one wishes to possess another person's particular bounty (worldly or spiritual) from God, and at the same time wishes also that the other person should lose that bounty.

Ḥijāb **(Headscarf):** A simple cloth wrapped around the head, traditionally worn to cover the hair of Muslim women when in the presence of marriageable men.

Hijrah **(Migration):** The migration of the Prophet ﷺ from Mecca to Medina in the year 624 CE, from which the Muslim calendar begins.

Ḥirā' Cave: A cave found on the Mountain of Light, a mountain to the northeast of the Meccan Sanctuary. In this cave, Prophet Muhammad ﷺ retreated from the paganism of Mecca and meditated on the transcendent oneness of God ﷻ for days on end. This is where, one night, the Archangel Gabriel (Jibrīl) ﷷ appeared to him and recited the first verses of the Quran.

I

Iblīs: see *Shayṭān*, Satan.

Ibrāhīm (Abraham): The father of the three monotheistic religions of the world, Prophet Abraham (Ibrāhīm) عليه السلام was given the title "The Intimate Friend of God." He showed resolve when his people violently lashed out in rejection of God's message, attempting to burn him alive. God ﷻ commanded the fire to cool itself for Prophet Abraham, miraculously saving him. Later in his life, God would test the faith of Prophet Abraham again by commanding him to sacrifice his son as a test of his obedience. Prophet Abraham asked his son how he felt, and he replied that his father should do as God had commanded. Then God miraculously provided a lamb, so that Prophet Abraham could sacrifice the lamb in place of his son. Muslims commemorate this occasion of faith and reward every year with the Festival of the Sacrifice (*ʿĪd al-Aḍḥā*).

***ʿĪd al-Aḍḥā* (Festival of Sacrifice):** A major Muslim holiday that is celebrated on the tenth day of the Month of Pilgrimage (*Dhul Ḥijjah*), the twelfth month of the Islamic lunar calendar. Its timing coincides with the performance of the pilgrimage (*ḥajj*) by pilgrims from all over the world. On this day, Muslims perform the Festival Prayer (*Ṣalāt al-ʿĪd*). After the prayer, in commemoration of the faith and perseverance of the Prophet Abraham (*Ibrāhīm*) عليه السلام and his son, it is a prophetic practice (*sunnah*) for Muslims to sacrifice a lamb. The meat of the lamb is usually divided between needy families and loved ones, with some kept for oneself.

***ʿĪd al-Fiṭr* (Festival of Completing the Fast):** A major Muslim holiday, the day after the completion of fasting in Ramaḍān (the first day of the month of Shawwal). This is a day of celebration after a month of devotion to God ﷻ through prayer, reading Quran, giving charity, and more.

***Iḥrām* (State of Inviolability):** A ritual state entered into for performance of the pilgrimage (*ḥajj*), or a lesser pilgrimage (*ʿumrah*), via a conscious intention, a ritual bath (*ghusl*), and, for men, the donning of two white cloths, one covering the loins and the other a shawl over the shoulders.

Iḥsān (Arabic: literally, "to make beautiful or good"): *Iḥsān* is one of the three dimensions of the religion and is concerned with the internal constitution of a believer's heart. It was defined by Prophet Muhammad ﷺ as, "to worship God as though you are seeing Him—and while you see Him not yet, truly He sees you."

***Imām* (Prayer Leader):** A morally accountable male who leads the prayer, standing in front of the congregation, with the other worshippers standing behind him. Those following the prayer leader perform each action after the prayer leader has done so.

Imān (Arabic: "to believe"): *Imān* can refer to faith in general, but it is also the specific term for the dimension of the religion comprised of beliefs that must be affirmed in order for a person's faith to be complete.

Infallibility: An attribute of all of God's prophets, infallibility is God's protection over them which granted them the inability to make mistakes in conveying, obeying, and perfectly embodying God's message. Therefore, sins and acts of immorality are impossible for prophets.

***Injīl* (Gospel):** The divine scripture revealed to Prophet Jesus (ʿĪsā) ﷺ. There is some question as to whether the Gospel is the source of current versions of the New Testament, or if it is a separate set of teachings revealed to Prophet Jesus (ʿĪsā) ﷺ and later recorded by his disciples. The Gospel suffered the fate of distortion by men, the most tragic and significant distortion being the insertion of the fabrication that Prophet Jesus ﷺ was himself divine.

***Inshā'Allāh* (If God Wills):** An exclamation that expresses hope for something to take place in the future while indicating the dependence of everything upon the will of God.

***Iqāmah* (Call to Stand):** A series of invocations and declarations which is called aloud to announce the imminent beginning of the prayer (*ṣalāh*), telling believers to rise and line up for the prayer. The Call to Stand is similar to the Call to Prayer, but it varies in the number of repetitions of the statements, and includes one additional statement.

ʿĪsā (Jesus): A Jewish prophet sent by God ﷻ to the children of Israel. He was born of a miraculous conception to the Blessed Virgin Mary (Maryam), a pious woman of noble descent. His miracles began in infancy, when he spoke from the cradle to defend the honor of his noble mother. They continued throughout his life, all occurring by the leave and permission of God, including the healing of lepers and the blind, bringing the dead back to life, and also the miraculous gift of a feast for him and his followers. When the enemies of Prophet Jesus (ʿĪsā) عليه السلام conspired towards his death, God protected him from crucifixion. God raised him up to the heavens, preventing any harm from befalling him. Later, some propagated false beliefs, attributing divinity to Prophet Jesus (ʿĪsā) عليه السلام as the literal offspring of God Himself, Who is transcendent above having offspring. Others created a trinity of deities to be worshipped, distorting the pure monotheism taught by Prophet Jesus (ʿĪsā) عليه السلام himself. Muslims believe that he is the Messiah whom the children of Israel still await, and that he will return to this world before the end of time to battle and defeat the Antichrist and eventually to die, as is the destiny of all mortal men.

***ʿIshā'* (Night Prayer):** One of the five daily prayers, its timeframe starts when the western horizon is dark and the redness in the sky is no longer seen, and ends with the entry of the time for the *Fajr* (Dawn) Prayer. The *ʿIshā'* prayer is four prayer-units (*rakʿahs*) long. In the first two, Quran is recited aloud in their initial standing positions.

Islām (Arabic: literally, "to surrender," or "to submit"): In one usage, *islām* refers to the voluntary submission of living in accordance with God's will. In this sense, *islām* has existed from the beginning of humanity and has been the message of all of God's prophets. In a second sense, Islām is the proper name of the religion brought by Prophet Muhammad ﷺ in the sixth century CE. Lastly, *islām* is one of the three dimensions of the Muslim religion: to surrender to God through devotional practices, as best represented by the Five Pillars.

***'Isrā' and Miʿrāj* (Night Journey and Ascension):** A seminal historical event in the life of Prophet Muhammad ﷺ, during which he traveled in one night from Mecca to Jerusalem and ascended to God ﷻ. On that night, the Archangel brought Prophet Muhammad ﷺ a white riding beast with wings, named Burāq. Upon this heavenly steed, the Prophet rode alongside the Archangel until they reached Jerusalem, where an assembly of God's prophets awaited him. They gathered in prayer, with the Prophet Muhammad leading, and then Prophet Muhammad ﷺ began a heavenly ascent. As he progressed through the seven heavens, he met some of the prophets he had prayed with. The Prophet ﷺ continued to ascend until he reached what the Quran calls "the Lote Tree of the Farthest Limit," which represents the limit of the knowledge of every knower save God Himself. At this point, in this meeting with the Divine, Prophet Muhammad ﷺ was given the command for his followers to institute the daily prayers. After descending to Jerusalem, the Prophet then returned to Mecca, miraculously in time to pray the dawn prayer.

Isrāfīl (Raphael): The archangel whose charge is to blow the Trumpet to signal the commencement of the Last Day. The first blowing will destroy all of creation; the second will awaken the dead.

ʿIzrā'īl (Azrael): The Archangel of Death, who seizes souls from their host bodies at a time appointed by God ﷻ.

J

***Jahannam* (Hell):** A place in which God ﷻ justly punishes those who reject and rebel against Him and die in such a state, if He so chooses. It is an abode of blazing torment, and its inhabitants suffer immense pain and know no joy.

***Jāhilīyyah* (Era of Ignorance):** The period before Islam in Arabia, which was characterized by cycles of lawless bloodshed, a caste-like system, extreme tribalism, and idolatrous polytheism. In this system, the weak could easily be oppressed, and the mighty could get away with anything. The term is also used to refer to the values of that era, most of which are opposed to the values of Islam.

***Jamāʿah* (Congregation):** Any group of two or more people performing the prayer (*ṣalāh*) together, with one of them designated as the prayer leader (*imām*). A prayer in congregation (*jamāʿah*) brings about a twenty-seven-fold multiplication of the reward of prayer.

***Jannah* (Paradise):** A place with which God ﷻ rewards His servants. Its inhabitants dwell therein forever, with peace, joy, and serenity. They know no pain or suffering, nor any unfulfilled wish.

***Jazāk Allāhu khayran* (May God Reward You with Good):** A prayer taught to us by Prophet Muhammad ﷺ as the best way to thank someone.

Jibrīl (Gabriel): God's most exalted archangel, who is the Angel of Revelation. He was the messenger through whom God ﷻ revealed the Quran to Prophet Muhammad, and he accompanied Prophet Muhammad on the Night

Journey and Ascension. He also, in human form, interacted with Prophet Muhammad ﷺ, and other prophets, in many non-revelatory circumstances.

***Jihād* (Struggle):** A broad term that encompasses two main dimensions: internal (also termed "the greater struggle") and external ("the lesser struggle"). The objective of both is to facilitate the recognition and preservation of truth by the removal of obstacles. The internal struggle is against one's own ego (*nafs*), passions, and weaknesses, and can be thought of as a prerequisite to the external struggle, which is the use of armed force either defensively for self-preservation or offensively to remove oppression.

Jinn*:** A species of free-willed and sapient creatures, created long before humans, whose original materials of composition were air and smokeless fire. The forefather of this species was **Iblīs**, the proper name of the **Devil** (Shayṭān***). The jinn descended from him, but, because they have free will, not all jinn disobeyed God ﷻ and followed Iblīs; some followed the prophets and messengers of God.

***Jumuʿah* (Friday Congregational Prayer):** A special congregational prayer service which takes place at midday on the Muslim holy day, Friday. The service consists of two main parts: a sermon (*khuṭbah*) and the Friday prayer (*ṣalāh*) that takes place at midday. As the name indicates, it is a communal act of worship and cannot be prayed alone.

K

***Kaʿbah* (Sacred House):** A large cubic structure, now draped in black cloth, which was built by Prophet Abraham (Ibrāhīm) and Prophet Ishmael (Ismāʿīl) عليهما السلام in the city of Mecca. It was built as a house of worship of the One God. Visitors to the Meccan Sanctuary perform circling (*ṭawāf*) around the Sacred House (*Kaʿbah*), making seven counter-clockwise circuits while in constant supplication and invocation.

Khadījah bint Khuwaylid: Also known as Khadījah the Great رضي الله عنها, she is a very significant figure in Islamic history. She was the first Muslim, a staunch and loyal supporter of Prophet Muhammad ﷺ, his first and most beloved wife, and the mother of his children. She was a widow and a wealthy merchant who employed Prophet Muhammad ﷺ in his earlier years. A noble and virtuous woman, she believed in the message of Prophet Muhammad ﷺ as soon as she heard of it. She gladly underwent many hardships in support of her husband, including subjecting herself, in solidarity with him, to the boycott of the clan of Banū Hāshim, even though it did not apply to her. She died shortly thereafter in what would be called the Year of Sorrow.

***Khalīfah* (Caliph):** An office which stands in the place of the Prophet as the political leader of the nation (*ummah*) of believers. It is the consensus of the scholars of normative Islam that the first four caliphs, who were the four closest companions of the prophet, represent the four best Muslims after Prophet Muhammad ﷺ. They are, listed in order of rank and rule as caliph: Abū Bakr as-Ṣiddīq, ʿUmar bin al-Khaṭṭāb, ʿUthmān bin ʿAffān, and the cousin and son-in-law of the prophet, ʿAlī bin Abū Ṭālib ؓ. This group is called the **Rightly Guided Caliphs**.

***Khuṭbah* (Sermon):** An essential component of the Friday (*Jumuʿah*) Congregational Prayer, the sermon is a speech delivered by the prayer leader (*imām*) to the congregation, meant to inspire them to grow in conscientiousness (*taqwā*) and piety. It is composed of two parts, and is usually brief, lasting approximately fifteen to thirty minutes. In the sermon, the prayer leader reminds the faithful of their duties to God ﷻ and usually selects a topic of religious life to highlight.

***Kufr* (Disbelief):** As a general concept, disbelief is defined as actively rejecting the revealed signs that indicate God's dominion over us and our obligation to serve Him. It can also have a specific usage, based on context: to espouse heretical beliefs that contradict the most fundamental beliefs of Islam, therefore nullifying one's supposed faith.

L

***Laylat al-Qadr* (Night of Glory):** A night during the month of Ramaḍān on which the reward for devotional acts is greater than that of a thousand months of similar acts in ordinary time. The exact date of the Night of Glory is not known with certainty. The Prophet Muhammad ﷺ taught us that it is a night within the last ten nights, on an odd-numbered date.

Legal Ruling: In Islamic law (*sharīʿah*), the legal status of a particular action that defines the divine consequences, good or bad, of that action. There are five possible rulings, which form a spectrum from virtue to vice: required (*farḍ*), commendable (*mustaḥab*), permissible (*mubāḥ*), disliked (*makrūh*), and forbidden (*ḥarām*).

Liability Minimum: The minimum amount of wealth a person must possess to be subject to the obligation to pay the purifying alms (*zakāh*).

M

***Madhhab* (Legal School):** A historic legal institution that utilizes particular methodologies to guide the juridical process of deriving legal rulings from the sources of law. The set of methodologies, and their consequent legal rulings, is based on the founding scholar's interpretive methodology, as refined and upgraded by many other scholars within the school for centuries afterwards. Each school uses the same primary sources (principally the Quran and the example of the Prophet Muhammad ﷺ) and is equally valid to adhere to. For the most part, the differences are minor and nuanced. Four legal schools (Ḥanafī, Mālikī, Shāfiʿī, and Ḥanbalī) eventually came to dominate Sunni Islam, and for centuries Muslim scholars and laymen alike have learned the rulings of devotional acts according to one of these legal schools.

***Maghrib* (Sunset Prayer):** One of the five daily prayers. Its timeframe starts when the disc of the sun falls completely below the horizon and the eastern horizon grays. The *Maghrib* Prayer should be prayed as soon as its timeframe enters, but one has until the entry of the time for the *ʿIshāʾ* (Night) Prayer. It consists of three prayer-units (*rakʿahs*), in the first two Quran is recited aloud in the initial standing position.

Major Ritual Impurity: A ritual state brought about when a person undergoes any of the causes of major ritual impurity of ritual purity. While in such a state, particular rulings of Islamic law (*sharīʿah*) apply. This state is rectified by performing a ritual bath (*ghusl*).

***Makrūh* (Disliked):** A legal ruling indicating that an act is one that a Muslim is encouraged *not* to do. One is rewarded for avoiding these acts, but they do not constitute sins (although some scholars believe that doing them consistently is forbidden and thus sinful).

Maryam (Lady Mary): A pious woman of noble lineage, she is the virgin-mother of Prophet Jesus (ʿĪsā) ﷺ. She is considered the most pious woman in history and is the object of much reverence and respect in the religion of Islam.

***Masjid* (Mosque):** The Islamic house of worship, also known as the House of God. It is a very simple building: The main part of every mosque is the prayer area, a large carpeted area with no furniture, where believers congregate and pray. At the front of the prayer area, on the side nearest the prayer direction (*qiblah*), it is common to have a prayer niche (a large cove indented into the wall), where the prayer leader (*imām*) stands to lead the congregation. Next to the prayer niche is a structure, usually with steps and a podium, from which the prayer leader delivers the sermon in the Friday (*Jumuʿah*) Congregational Prayer.

Mecca: Founded by the biblical patriarch Prophet Abraham (Ibrāhīm) عليه السلام, Mecca is home to the Sacred House (*Kaʿbah*), which was built for worship of the One Transcendent God. Over time, the city, called Mecca the Ennobled, became overrun by idols and polytheists. Its people, the Quraysh, initially rejected Islam, but eventually accepted it. It is the destination of the Pilgrimage (*Ḥajj*) that every capable Muslim must make once in his or her lifetime.

Medina: Known as the Illuminated City, it was originally called Yathrib. It was the new home for Muslims after Prophet Muhammad's migration (*hijrah*). There he continued to receive revelation and built a community of believers living the message he was sent. It is where Prophet Muhammad ﷺ decided to return, even after gaining control of his hometown of Mecca. He is buried there, in his home, connected to his mosque, the Mosque of the Prophet. A large green dome marks the chamber that holds the blessed grave of the Prophet ﷺ.

Mīkā'īl (Michael): One of God's most exalted archangels, who is associated with providing provision and sustenance to God's creation

Minor Ritual Impurity: A ritual state brought about when a person who has ritual purity undergoes one of the causes of minor ritual impurity of ritual purity. This state is rectified by performing *wuḍū'* (ritual washing).

Miracle: The suspension by God ﷻ of the conventional norms of the world (e.g., the laws of physics) through the medium of a particular person. For prophets, a miracle is a sign of the truthfulness of their claim of being sent by God. "Lesser miracles," performed by people other than the prophets, play no role in verifying the authenticity of a claim to prophethood, because the persons involved, sometimes righteous saints, do not receive revelation from

God (nor do they claim to). Both types of miracle are still, in effect, the same thing: the suspension of conventional norms by God for a particular person.

Morally Accountable: A morally accountable person is one who meets the requirements for being subject to Islamic law (*sharīʿah*), which are: being of sound mind, with the ability to exercise good judgment; being pubescent; and having received the message of God's final guidance for humanity, Islam.

***Mubāḥ* (Permissible):** An act that has a neutral quality with respect to the sacred law (*sharīʿah*). Either doing the act or abandoning it results in neither punishment nor reward. The majority of acts fall under this category, and jurists consider this ruling the default for any act, until some Divine or prophetic guidance indicates otherwise.

***Muṣḥaf* (Hard Copy of the Quran)**: A hard copy of only the text of the Quran itself in the original Arabic. If there is extraneous text such as commentary, even in Arabic, it is not considered a *Muṣḥaf*. Particular conditions of ritual purity must be fulfilled before it is permissible to touch a *Muṣḥaf*.

***Muhājirūn* (Emigrants):** A term used to designate those Muslims who left the persecution of Mecca and moved to Medina to found a community of believers. Distinguished by the sacrifice that they made, they have a special status among the Companions (*Ṣaḥābah*).

Muhammad: Born in Mecca, Arabia, in the 6th century CE, Prophet Muhammad is the last and final messenger of God سبحانه وتعالى to all of humanity; the final seal of prophecy and revelation. His life is a perfect model for believers to follow. At the age of forty, while the Prophet was meditating on God سبحانه وتعالى in a secluded cave, the Archangel Gabriel (Jibrīl) brought him the first of a series of revelations from God. The revelations, which would make up the Quran, would continue for twenty-three years, until shortly before he passed on. He eventually migrated to the city of Medina, where he founded a new community of believers who would live in peace. He lived there for ten years. He passed away at the age of sixty-three and is buried in Medina.

***Munāfiqūn* (Hypocrites):** A group of people in Medina who outwardly embraced Islam—usually for political gain—while secretly disbelieving. These people were insincere in their commitment to the Prophet and the religion, and worked to undermine his mission at pivotal moments.

Munkar and **Nakīr:** The names of the two angels who interrogate a soul in its grave, asking it three questions: "Who is your Lord? What is your religion? What do you say about the messenger that was sent to you?"

Mūsā (Moses): A prophet sent by God ﷻ to save the children of Israel from the slavery and oppression of Pharaoh. Prophet Moses (Mūsā) ﷷ, himself a Jew, was saved from Pharaoh only to be raised by him in his home. God spoke directly to Prophet Moses and sent him to warn Pharaoh against his oppression and disbelief. He sent him with miracles, including a staff that transformed into a serpent, to prove his prophethood to Pharaoh. The arrogant Pharaoh commanded his subjects to continue to worship him and rejected God and the warning of Prophet Moses ﷷ. The children of Israel escaped with the miraculous splitting of the Red Sea. Pharaoh and his men witnessed the miracle, but they drowned in the returning waters as rejecters of God.

***Mustaḥab* (Commendable):** A legal status in Islamic law given to an optional act which is considered a good deed. Performing such an act gains reward from God, but not doing it, although a missed opportunity for serving the Divine, does not incur sin.

N

***Nabī* (Prophet):** A person chosen by God ﷻ to receive revelation from Him and sent to a people, bearing a message that God wants them to follow. Prophets, including those in the subcategory of "messengers", are infallible—protected from error with respect to God's commands, always truthful, and conveying God's message with integrity.

***Nafs* (Ego):** The part of our consciousness with an "animalistic" nature that tends towards fulfillment of desires and is primarily concerned with self-serving passions for food, drink, sex, and the like. It is predisposed to base characteristics such as anger, jealousy, and arrogance. Being primarily concerned with self-satisfaction and stimulation, usually through the bodily senses, it must be suppressed for self-purification.

***Najāsah* (Filth):** A category of substances, defined by Islamic law, which must be removed from a person's attire, prayer area, and body in order to perform the prayer (*ṣalāh*) and certain other devotions.

Nūḥ (Noah): A prophet of God ﷻ who was sent to his people and called them to God's way for a miraculous 950 years. They rejected and ridiculed him and his followers. God commanded him to build an ark to carry away the believers before God sent a storm that would flood and destroy his people. Prophet Noah ﵇ was given the title "The One Rescued by God."

P

People of the Book: A special categorization given to people from two faith traditions—Judaism and Christianity—establishing a special status for them within Islam: The adherents of these religions are granted specific legal rulings not applicable to other non-believers. This status applies even in those religions' current forms, despite their historical alterations, simply because they spring from divine sources.

Proof-text: A text—usually a Quranic verse, prophetic narration (*ḥadīth*), or statement of an authoritative scholar—used as the basis for deriving a legal ruling or religious understanding. It is generally the role of specially trained scholars to derive understandings from proof-texts. Laypeople can also find benefit from knowing the proof-texts for a scholar's reasoning, although non-experts should not attempt to interpret them independently without qualified scholarly guidance.

Purification: This term refers either to the process of removing filth to attain *ritual cleanliness* or to the performance of the ritual washings to attain the status of *ritual purity*. Both modes of purification require the use of pure, unaltered water. Rituals of purification include *wuḍū'* (ritual washing) and the ritual bath (*ghusl*).

Q

***Qadr* (Divine Decree):** The foundational Islamic belief that all matters—both good and evil—are known to God ﷻ and a direct result of His willing them, decreeing them, and having the power and ability to make them so. This means that nothing happens independent of His will, and of course, that nothing can alter the command of God. It is all written: our lifespans, our financial provisions, and our destinations in the next life. This belief does not preclude the role we play in bringing God's decree to fruition, nor our moral accountability in doing so.

***Qalb* (Heart):** The heart is the point where the components of consciousness interact, and thus it is the center of our consciousness. It is the seat of our spiritual experiences, the means by which we connect to and interact with revelation and the Divine, and the portal through which we achieve piety in devotion. The term is sometimes used as a synonym for the soul (*rūḥ*).

***Qiblah* (Prayer Direction):** The direction of the Sacred House (*Kaʿbah*) in Mecca, which a person faces in prayer (*ṣalāh*) from wherever they are in the world.

***Qiyām al-Layl* (Night Vigil Prayers):** Voluntary prayers (*ṣalāh*) that are performed in the last half or third of the night (calculated based on the time from sunset to dawn). It is a time most beloved by God ﷻ, because it is when those burning with the desire to draw nearer to Him are aroused, and when their clarity of heart and mind is greatest.

Quran (or *Qur'ān*): Literally "the often recited," this divine scripture is the last revelation from God ﷻ. Revealed to Prophet Muhammad ﷺ in the Arabic language in the 7th century CE, the Quran is the direct verbatim word of God, which will be protected eternally from distortion by God Himself.

Quraysh: The most prominent tribe of Mecca, they were charged with caring for the pilgrims that came from all over Arabia to visit the Sacred House (*Kaʿbah*). They are the tribe of Prophet Muhammad ﷺ, and as a pagan and idolatrous people, they opposed his message and tortured his followers in the early years of his mission. Even after the migration of the Muslims to Medina, they continued to launch offensives aimed at ending the mission of monotheism in Arabia. Eventually, Prophet Muhammad ﷺ defeated the Quraysh but allowed them to surrender peacefully, with no bloodshed.

R

***Raḍi Allāhu ʿAnhu* (May God Be Pleased with Him):** A prayer uttered after the mention of one of the Companions (*Ṣaḥābah*) of Prophet Muhammad ﷺ.

***Rakʿah* (Prayer-Unit):** The building block of the prayer (*ṣalāh*), a prayer-unit is composed of a specific set of actions, performed in a particular sequence, and repeated multiple times throughout the prayer. A prayer-unit includes four positions: standing, bowing (*rukūʿ*), prostration (*sujūd*), and sitting (*julūs*).

Ramaḍān: The ninth month of the Islamic lunar calendar. As a natural phenomenon, lunar months vary in length, having either twenty-nine or thirty days. Ramaḍān is the month of required fasting (*ṣawm*), which is the fourth pillar of Islam.

Raqīb and **ʿAtīd**: Also titled the Honorable Recorders, they are two angels who sit on our shoulders. Their charge is to record each good and evil act we perform.

Rasūl **(Messenger):** A messenger is a prophet who received a revelation that includes a revealed scripture and a consequent legal system. Messengers possess the same qualities of infallibility as prophets.

Ritual Cleanliness: One of the two types of ritual purity related to devotional acts, it is present when an object or space is devoid of certain substances designated by Islamic law (*sharīʿah*) as filth (*najāsah*).

Riyā' **(Showing Off):** A disease of the heart consisting of performing acts for the purpose of gaining other people's admiration. The worst form of this vice is performing religious and devotional activities in order to gain praise, rather than to please God. For this reason Prophet Muhammad ﷺ called it the minor form of *shirk* (associating partners with God ﷻ).

Rūḥ **(Spirit** or **Soul):** The *rūḥ* is the immaterial essence of a human being. It is what gives life to the body, and its true nature is unknown to man. God states in the Quran: "They ask you, [Prophet], about the Spirit. Say, 'The Spirit is part of my Lord's domain. You have only been given a little knowledge'" (17:85). The term *rūḥ* is also used as a synonym for the heart (*qalb*), which is the focal point of the soul's interaction with God and the other facets of our consciousness.

Rukūʿ **(Bowing):** One of the four main positions of the prayer (*ṣalāh*), the bowing position is comprised of bending at the waist and resting the palms above the knees, to make the back parallel to the ground, to the best of one's ability.

S

Ṣabr (Patience): To have grace in adversity, remaining content with the difficulties God ﷻ has decreed; to persevere in obedience to God, and to silently endure the trials of life, without complaint or resentment.

***Ṣadaqah* (Charity):** A voluntary sharing of wealth with the needy that can take many forms and need not be financial in nature—"even a smile" can be rewarded by God as an act of charity. Because there are no restrictions on the categories of persons to whom voluntary charity can be given, believers may freely give to anyone they deem in need of help.

***Ṣaḥābah* (Companions;** singular: ***Ṣaḥābī*):** A category which refers to those believing Muslims who met the Prophet ﷺ during his lifetime. The direct students of Prophet Muhammad ﷺ, they are considered the best generation of believers overall.

***Saʿī* (Treading):** A ritual of the pilgrimage (*ḥajj*) based on the events of the life of Lady Hagar, it consists in passing seven times between the two hills of Ṣafa and Marwah near the Sacred House (Kaʿbah).

***Ṣalāh al-Ibrāhīmīyyah* (Abrahamic Prayer):** A prayer that is recited in the last sitting of prayer (*ṣalāh*) after the Testimonial Invocation (*at-Tashahhud*).

***Ṣalāh* (Prayer):** A devotional act, structured and formalized, provided to us through the Prophet Muhammad ﷺ. It includes various devotional positions, recitations from the Quran, and invocations of God. The term is used both for the required daily prayers, which occur at specified times defined by the position of the sun with respect to the horizon, and also for voluntary prayers, which are commendable means of drawing nearer to God.

***Salām* (Greeting of Peace):** The traditional Muslim method of greeting one another when we meet or begin a conversation. It consists of the statement *as-Salāmu ʿAlaykum*, which means "May peace be upon you." The response is *wa ʿAlaykum as- Salām*, which means "And peace be upon you, too." The same phrases are used for concluding the encounter or conversation.

***Ṣalawāt* (Blessings Upon the Prophet):** The act of asking God ﷻ to send blessings and salutations upon Prophet Muhammad ﷺ and his noble family

Much divine benefit can be derived from sending blessings upon the Prophet. This act has particular significance and reward on Fridays.

***Ṣalla Allāhu ʿAlayhi wa Sallam* (God Bless and Grant Him Peace):** A prayer which we are commanded to say after any mention of Prophet Muhammad ﷺ. It is a source of immense blessing and reward for the one who says it.

***Ṣawm* (Fasting):** A devotional act in which believers abstain from eating, drinking, and sexual relations from the time when the dark night sky is broken by the first rays of dawn until complete sunset.

***Shafīʿ* (Intercessor):** A very important and central role of Prophet Muhammad on the Day of Judgment. On that day, God ﷻ will grant Prophet Muhammad ﷺ the ability to intercede with Him, petitioning on behalf of his followers until anyone who said and believed in the Testimony of Faith (*Shahādah*) is removed from Hell (*Jahannam*).

***Shahādah* (Testimony of Faith):** A statement, consisting of two testimonies, which, when believed and proclaimed by a person, formally enters him or her into the religion of Islam:

Lā ilāha ill-Āllāh	***Muḥammad rasūl Allāh***
Nothing is worthy of worship except God	Muhammad is the messenger of God

***Sharīʿah* (Sacred or Islamic Law):** A set of codes and principles, based on divine revelation and derived through complex legal reasoning, by which all important matters of Muslim life are guided. It is generally described as having two realms: the devotional, which governs the interaction between humans and the divine, and the social, which governs interaction among humans.

Shayṭān* (Devil):** The forefather of the *jinn*, a free-willed species created from fire, **Iblīs**, the proper name of the **Devil** (Shayṭān***), is the declared enemy of humanity. When God ﷻ created Adam, the forefather of humanity, He commanded those in the divine presence (both angels and jinn) to bow in reverence before God's new creature. All obeyed except Iblīs, who objected to the command, feeling he was superior to Adam based simply on the materials from which he was created. This arrogance and envy led to Iblīs' expulsion from the divine presence, after which he requested God to grant him reprieve of punishment, delaying it to the Last Day. After God granted Iblīs his request, Iblīs vowed to devote himself to leading astray as many of Adam's offspring as he could. The jinn descended from him, but, because of their free will, not all of them disobeyed God and followed Iblīs; some followed the prophets and messengers of God.

***Shirk* (Associating Partners with God):** Any belief that violates the oneness (*tawḥīd*) of God, particularly any belief that sets up deities to be worshipped alongside God, or holds there to be divisions of God. Also under this category is the rejection of God ﷻ altogether (atheism). Orthodox belief holds that to believe anything has power or ability *independent* of God constitutes making partners (*shirk*). It is the one and only unforgivable sin, if one dies without repenting and correcting the erroneous beliefs.

***Shukr* (Gratitude):** A sense of indebted gratitude to God for His countless bounties upon us.

State of Ritual Purity: One of the two types of ritual purity related to devotional acts, it is a metaphysical status that a person can bring about or invalidate, based on particular actions and events.

***Suḥūr* (Pre-Dawn Meal):** An important prophetic practice (*sunnah*) associated with fasting, *suḥūr* consists of eating some food, even if just a small amount, before dawn's light strikes the horizon and the time of the fast enters.

***Sujūd* (Prostration):** One of the four main positions of the prayer (*ṣalāh*), in which a person places the forehead and nose to the ground, palms resting on the ground on either side of the shoulders, with the toes and balls of the feet turned forward, placed on the ground as well.

***Sunnah* (Prophetic Way or Prophetic Practice):** The specific meaning of the term *Sunnah* depends on the context in which it is used. In the context of Islamic law (*sharīʿah*), it refers to a higher grade of commendable (*mustaḥab*) acts—those that were performed by Prophet Muhammad ﷺ regularly. In the broadest sense, *Sunnah* means the Prophetic Way of Prophet Muhammad; it includes the aforementioned category and much more. It may also be used as a synonym for narrations (*ḥadīths*) of Prophet Muhammad ﷺ. Note that some commands contained within the narration literature create rulings that do not carry the legal ruling of a prophetic practice (*sunnah*), but can be required (*farḍ*) or permissible (*mubāḥ*).

ūrah (Chapter): The main division of the Quran, a *sūrah*, or chapter, is a ollection of verses (*āyahs*). The Quran contains a total of 114 chapters of arying length, each with its own title. After the first chapter, "The Opening l-Fātiḥah)," the chapters are basically arranged in order of length, from ngest to shortest.

T

ābiʿī (Follower): A term which refers to the generation of believers that et any of the Companions (*Ṣaḥābah*) of Prophet Muhammad. One generation removed from Prophet Muhammad, they are the second best generaon of believers overall.

albiyah (Response of the Summoned): The mantra of the pilgrimage ajj), it is a declaration of God's oneness and a pilgrim's active response to is call, repeated until the pilgrims reach the Sanctuary of Mecca.

aqwā (Conscientiousness): Sometimes translated as "piety," *Taqwā* (conientiousness) is a spiritual awareness of God's right over you and your uty to Him. It incorporates doing what God commands, avoiding what He as forbidden, embodying the spiritual virtues, and ridding yourself of the iritual vices.

arawīḥ Prayers: A special form of voluntary prayer (*ṣalāh*), the *Tarawīḥ* rayers are congregational ritual prayers that take place every night during amaḍān. Islamic jurists differ regarding the number of prayer-units akʿahs) that should be prayed in Tarawīḥ. Some recommend offering eight rayer units, others twenty, and some even more. Each of these recommenations is based on a different valid legal opinion.

ashahhud (Testimonial Invocation): An invocation that is recited in oth the second and last prayer-units (*rakʿahs*) while in the sitting position.

awāf (Circling): A ritual devotion, instituted by the Prophet Abraham ﷺ, which can be performed only at the Sacred House (*Kaʿbah*). It consists of aking seven counter-clockwise circuits around the black cubic structure hile in a constant state of supplication and invocation of God ﷻ.

awakkul (Reliance Upon God): Putting your trust in God that He will uide your affairs, and that, ultimately, it is He Who is your protector and sustainer. To rely upon God means that, while you strive to do your bes you ultimately place your hope not in your own efforts, but in God. It als includes trusting that whatever outcome results, that is what God, in Hi infinite knowledge, has deemed best for you.

***Tawbah* (Repentance):** The process through which a person may have sin absolved. It includes feeling a sense of remorse for the misdeed, immediatel abandoning the misdeed, resolving in your heart never to return to the ac and rectifying the harm you may have caused to another.

***Tawḥīd* (Oneness of God):** The most fundamental component of a Muslim' belief, *tawḥīd* indicates the reality that there is only one deity, Who is th All-Powerful, the Creator of everything, Who is in complete control of a of His creation. It also implies other beliefs regarding the nature of Go that He has no beginning, can have no end, does not have offspring, an was not brought into existence. He is transcendent above the limitations c His creation, and thus it is inconceivable that the distinction between th created and the Creator can be blurred.

***Tawrāt* (Torah)**: The divine scripture that was revealed to Prophet Mose (Mūsā) ؑ. It contained laws for the Children of Israel and was a source c light and guidance for them, but over time it fell victim to distortion.

U

Uḥud: A sacred mountain which the Prophet called "a mountain that love us," Uḥud was the site of the second major battle of Islam. The Qurays were three thousand in number, and the Muslims were seven hundre Early in the battle, the Muslims were winning and the Quraysh were i retreat, but some of the Muslims disobeyed the instructions of Prophe Muhammad ﷺ, causing their defeat. In this battle many were martyre including the mighty Ḥamza ؓ. Prophet Muhammad was also wounde and was initially rumored to have been killed.

ʿUmar bin al-Khaṭṭāb: The second of the Rightly Guided Caliphs, ʿUmar ؓ was a mighty warrior feared by his people. He initially opposed Islam an set out to kill Prophet Muhammad ﷺ, but on his way to do so, he hear some verses from the Quran which so impressed him that he entered th faith. Known as "the Distinguisher" (between truth and falsehood), he ha a deep and undying commitment to justice and integrity.

***mmah* (Nation of Believers):** A term denoting the entire body of all elieving Muslims, in which each Muslim is the brother or sister in faith f other believers. The Prophet Muhammad ﷺ instilled a unified conscious- ess into the Nation of Believers, instructing us to have mutual concern for ach other's welfare and guidance.

***mrah* (Lesser Pilgrimage):** A devotional ritual performed at the Sanc- ıary in Mecca that begins with entering a state of inviolability (*iḥrām*), ıllowed by performing the circling (*ṭawāf*), then the treading (*saʿī*) between ıe hills Ṣafā and Marwah. The lesser pilgrimage is concluded with either having or trimming the hair to end the state of inviolability.

naltered Water: Water that is colorless, tasteless, and has no smell and ıus can be used in ritual purification. Both types of purification—removing lth (*najāsah*) and attaining a state of ritual purity—are obtained through rocesses requiring unaltered water, due to its purifying quality.

V

oluntary Act: An optional devotional act which helps to bring a believer earer to God. Voluntary acts are not required by God, but the reward for ıch acts is immense, and they make one's surrender more complete.

W

***alī* (Saint or Ally/Friend of God):** A person whose purity of heart and ghteousness of acts has granted him or her a closeness to God which entails ivine protection and fulfilled prayers. Muslim doctrine requires believing ıat this class of people exists, that they can be granted "lesser miracles," nd that we should seek out their supplication (*duʿā'*) on our behalf.

***ird* (Litany):** An arranged series of invocations (*dhikr*) and supplications *luʿā'*) that a person regularly recites. There are many famous litanies ompiled by various scholars and saints. Their regular recitation acts as strengthening regimen for the heart and has a cumulative effect upon ıe heart.

***uḍū'* (Ritual Washing):** A ritual washing of the limbs of the body per- ormed with unaltered water, by which a person can remove the status of ıinor, but not major, ritual impurity.

Y

Yathrib: See *Medina.*

Z

***Zabihah*:** A term in common Muslim parlance that refers to *ḥalāl* mea meat prepared according to the humane guidelines set by Islamic law fo animal slaughter. This is a phonetic variant of the Arabic word "*dhabīḥah* which literally means "slaughtered."

***Zabūr* (Psalms):** The divine scripture that was revealed to Prophet Davi (Dawūd) ﵇.

***Zakāh* (Purifying Alms):** A required (*farḍ*) tax on certain types of wealt and assets to be distributed to the needy. Only those who are above th poverty line, as determined by the liability minimum, are required to pa this tax. The standard rate is two-and-a-half percent, or one-fortieth, of th applicable amount.

***Zakāt al-Fiṭr* (Alms for Completing the Fast):** A gift of charity that ever Muslim must pay before the day of the Festival of Completing the Fast (*Ī al-Fiṭr*). The amount is based on the value of a particular volume of foo (roughly 2 liters, based on measurements used by Prophet Muhammad ﷺ which would constitute a meal for a person of average socioeconomic statu

Zamzam: A blessed well which pours forth sacred water, Zamzam wa discovered by Prophet Ishmael (Ismāʿīl) ﵇ as a baby. In barren Mecca, h became thirsty, and his concerned mother, Lady Hagar, ran between tw hills, looking for any sign of water or help. She did this seven times, until sh heard the bubbling of water and saw that a spring had erupted from beneat the feet of the kicking babe. This well still runs today, and pilgrims drin from its sacred water, from which they seek blessing, healing, and answer to their prayers.

***Zuhd* (Detachment):** A saving virtue which counteracts the ego's tendenc towards material indulgence. A person with detachment uses this world a a means to an other-worldly end, recognizing that material wealth shoul be in our hands, not in our hearts.

***Ẓuhr* (Midday Prayer):** One of the five daily prayers, its timeframe starts when the sun moves past the zenith and ends with the entry of the next prayer time, the *ʿAsr* (Afternoon) prayer. It consists of four prayer-units (*rakʿahs*), in each of which the Quran is recited silently.

ENGLISH-TO-ARABIC GLOSSARY

This is a reverse listing that allows you to look up Arabic terms by their English equivalents.

Abraham: see Ibrāhīm
Abrahamic Prayer: see *Ṣalāh al-Ibrāhīmīyyah*
Afterlife: see *Ākhirah*
Afternoon Prayer: see *ʿAṣr*
Alms for Completing the Fast: see *Zakāt al-Fiṭr*
Associating Partners: see *Shirk*
Blessing: see *Barakah*
Bowing: see *Rukūʿ*
Call to Prayer: see *Adhān*
Call to Stand: see *Iqāmah*
Chapter: see *Sūrah*
Charity: see *Ṣadaqah*
Circling: see *Ṭawāf*
Commendable: see *Mustaḥab*
Companions: see *Ṣaḥābah* Sing. *Ṣaḥābī*
Congregation: see *Jamāʿah*
Conscientiousness: see *Taqwā*
Courteous Conduct: see *Adab*
Dawn Prayer: see *Fajr*
Detachment: see *Zuhd*
Devil: see *Shayṭān*
Disbelief: see *Kufr*
Disliked: see *Makrūh*
Divine Decree: see *Qadr*
Ego: see *Nafs*
Emigrants: see *Muhājirūn*
Era of Ignorance: see *Jāhiliyyah*
Fasting: see *Ṣawm*
Festival of Completing the Fast: see *ʿĪd al-Fiṭr*
Festival of Sacrifice: see *ʿĪd al-Aḍḥā*
Filth: see *Najāsah*
Follower: see *Tābiʿī*
Forbidden: see *Ḥarām*
Friday Congregational Prayer: see *Jumuʿah*
Gabriel: see Jibrīl

God Bless and Grant Him Peace: see *Ṣalla Allāhu ʿAlayhi wa Sallam*
God is Even Greater: see *Allāhu Akbar*
God: see *Allāh*
Gospel: see *Injīl*
Gratitude: see *Shukr*
Greeting of Peace: see *Salām*
Hard Copy of the Quran: see *Muṣḥaf*
Headscarf: see *Ḥijāb*
Heart: see *Qalb*
Hell: see *Jahannam*
Helpers: see *Anṣār*
Hypocrites: see *Munāfiqūn*
If God Wills: see *Inshā'Allāh*
In God's Name: see *Bismillāh*
Innovation: see *Bidʿah*
Intercessor: see *Shafīʿ*
Invocation: see *Dhikr*
Islamic Law: see *Sharīʿah*
Jesus: see ʿĪsā
Lawful: see *Ḥalāl*
Legal School: see *Madhhab*
Lesser Pilgrimage: see *ʿUmrah*
Mary: see *Maryam*
May God Be Pleased with Him: see *Raḍi Allāhu ʿAnhu*
May God Reward You with Good: see *Jazāk Allāhu khayran*
Messenger: see *Rasūl*
Midday Prayer: see *Ẓuhr*
Moses: see *Mūsā*
Mosque: see *Masjid*
Nation: see *Ummah*
Night Journey & Ascension: see *'Isrā & Miʿrāj*
Night of Glory: see *Laylat al-Qadr*
Night Prayer: see *ʿIshā'*
Night Vigil Prayers: see *Qiyām al-Layl*
Noah: see *Nūḥ*
Oneness of God: see *Tawḥīd*
Opening: see *al-Fātiḥah*
Paradise: see *Jannah*
Patience: see *Ṣabr*
Permissible: see *Mubāḥ*

Pilgrimage: see *Ḥajj*
Praise Belongs to God: see *Alḥamdulillāh*
Prayer Direction: see *Qiblah*
Prayer Leader: see *Imām*
Prayer: see *Ṣalāh*
Prayer-Unit: see *Rakʿah*
Pre-Dawn Meal: see *Suḥūr*
Primary Nature: see *Fiṭrah*
Proof-text: see *Dalīl*
Prophet: see *Nabī*
Prophetic Narration: see *Ḥadīth*
Prophetic Way or Prophetic Practice: see *Sunnah*
Prostration: see *Sujūd*
Psalms: see *Zabūr*
Purifying Alms: see *Zakāh*
Reason: see *ʿAql*
Reliance Upon God: see *Tawakkul*
Repentance: see *Tawbah*
Requirement: see *Farḍ*
Resentful Envy: see *Ḥasad*
Response of the Summoned: see *Talbiyah*
Ritual Bath: see *Ghusl*
Ritual washing: see *Wuḍū'*
Sacred House: see *Kaʿbah*
Saint or Ally of God: see *Walī*
Sermon: see *Khuṭbah*
Showing Off: see *Riyā'*
State of Inviobility: see *Iḥrām*
Struggle: see *Jihād*
Sunset Prayer: see *Maghrib*
Supplication: see Duʿā'
Testimonial Invocation: see *Tashahhud*
Testimony of Faith: see *Shahādah*
Torah: see *Tawrāt*
Transient World: see *Dunyā*
Treading: see *Saʿī*
Unseen: see *Ghayb*
Verse: see *Āyah*
Voluntary: see *Nāfilah*

Bibliography

Abd-Allah, Umar Faruq. *Islam and the Cultural Imperative.* Date accessed, March 2010. http://www.nawawi.org/wp-content/uploads/2013/01/Article3.pdf

Abd-Allah, Umar Faruq. *Living Islam with Purpose.* Date accessed, March 2010. http://www.nawawi.org/wp-content/uploads/2013/01/Article6.pdf

Badawi, Mostafa. "The Muhammadan Attributes." *Seasons*, Spring-Summer 2005: 81-95.

al-Bajūrī, Imām Ibrāhīm. *Tuḥfat al-Murīd ʿalā Sharḥ Jawharat al-Tawḥīd.* Dar al-Salam, 2002.

Bin Bayyah, Abdallah and Hamza Yusuf. *Sacred Law in Secular Lands,* vols. 1&2. Sandala, 2009, compact disc.

al-Ghazali, Abu Hamid. *The Duties of Brotherhood in Islam.* Translated by Muhtar Holland. Markfield, Leicestershire, UK: Islamic Foundation, 2010.

al-Ghazali, Abu Hamid. *The Inner Dimensions of Islamic Worship.* Translated by Muhtar Holland. Markfield, Leicestershire, UK: Islamic Foundation, 2013.

al-ʿĪd, Ibn Daqīq. *Sharḥ al-Arbaʿīn al-Nawawīyyah.* al-Maktabat al-Turath al-Islamiyyah, 1998.

Keller, Nuh Ha Mim. *Concept of Bid'a in the Islamic Sharia.* Date accessed, March 2009. http://masud.co.uk/ISLAM/nuh/bida.htm

Lings, Martin. *Muhammad: His Life Based on the Earliest Sources.* Inner Traditions, 2006.

Mayyārah, Sīdī Muḥammad Aḥmad. *Mukhtaṣar al-Durr al-Thamīn wal Mawrid al-Muʿīn.* Tunisia: al-Maktabah al-ʿAtīqah, 2008.

Murad, Abdal-Hakim. *Understanding the Four Madhhabs: The Problem with Anti-Madhhabism.* Date accessed, March 2009. http://masud.co.uk/ISLAM/ahm/newmadhh.htm

Murata, Sachiko and William Chittick. *Vision of Islam.* Paragon House, 2008

al-Qayrawānī, Ibn Abī Zayd. *Risālat Ibn Abī Zayd. al-Qayrawānī.* Dar al-Fadilah, 2005.

Shalabi, Abdul Wadod. *Islam: Religion of Life.* Starlatch Press, 2001.

Von Denffer, Ahmad. *Ulum al Qur'an: An Introduction to the Sciences of the Qur'an.* Markfield, Leicestershire, UK: The Islamic Foundation, 2009.

Yusuf, Hamza and Zaid Shakir. *Agenda to Change Our Condition.* Sandala, 2013

Yusuf, Hamza. *Alchemy of Happiness.* Sandala, 2010, compact disc.

Yusuf, Hamza. *Caesarean Moon Births: Calculations, Moon Sighting, and the Prophetic Way.* Fons Vitae, 2008.

Yusuf, Hamza. "Chess and the Divine Decree." *Seasons*, Spring 2006: 16-17.

Yusuf, Hamza. *The Content of Character: Ethical Sayings of the Prophet Muhammad.* Sandala, 2005.

Yusuf, Hamza. *The Creed of Imam al-Tahawi.* Sandala, 2009.

Yusuf, Hamza. *Foundations of Islam Series.* Meccacentric, 1998, compact disc.
Yusuf, Hamza. *The Helping Guide.* Sandala, 2015 (forthcoming).
Yusuf, Hamza. *Purification of the Heart: Signs, Symptoms and Cures of the Spiritual Diseases of the Heart.* Sandala, 2012.
Yusuf, Hamza. *Refinement of the Hearts.* Sandala, 2010, compact disc.
Yusuf, Hamza. "Who are the Disbelievers?" *Seasons,* Spring 2008: 31-50.
Zakariya, Mohamed. "The Hilye of the Prophet Muhammad." *Seasons,* Autumn-Winter 2003-2004: 13-22.

Index

References to footnotes are indicated by "n" following the page number; if more than one note appears on the page, the note number is specified. Definitions of terms are found in the Glossary, which is not indexed here.

A

N

P

Q

R

S

Y

Z

ABOUT THE AUTHOR

Asad Tarsin has been designing Islamic educational programs and teaching the basics of Islam for more than a decade. After completing his bachelor's degree in Islamic studies at the University of Michigan in Ann Arbor, he continued his study of Islamic theology, sacred law, philosophy and spirituality with some of the country's most prominent Muslim scholars including Shaykh Hamza Yusuf and Dr. Sherman Jackson, among others.

He has served as the curriculum director for the Deen Intensive Foundation for the last ten years and has a particular interest in creating sustainable models of education for new and returning Muslims. He lectures and teaches courses on Islam across the country. *Being Muslim: A Practical Guide* is his first published work. He is an emergency physician by training and lives in California with his wife and three children.